PRAISE

Big Russ and Me

"A wonderful book."

—Tom Brokaw

"Russert is characteristically forthright, unpretentious, respectful, and values-laden."

—*New Yorker*

"An evocative memoir of a happy childhood."

—*People*

"*Big Russ and Me* by Tim Russert, an autobiography full of tough love from the author's father. Here is Buffalo-based anecdotal advice about the value of honesty, loyalty, responsibility and a firm handshake. Throw in a little baseball (it does), and the whole thing is a testament to solid values, hard work and filial devotion."

—*New York Times*

"A profoundly satisfying story of a father and his son."

—*Wall Street Journal*

"Russert writes of his roots with an engaging warmth and humor."

—*USA Today*

"Russert's loving portrait of his dad will inspire you to call home."

—Entertainment Weekly

"The *Angela's Ashes* of Buffalo."

—New York Post

"[H]eartfelt meditations on the importance of work and family."

—Chicago Tribune

"With charming self-deprecation, the ever-smiling Russert . . . depicts a 1950s working-class childhood as simple and good as any that were idealized in 1950s TV shows."

—Los Angeles Times

"There's no high style in *Big Russ & Me*; it's water from the tap of life, part Bible, part Baltimore Catechism, and the rest canny street smarts."

—Boston Globe

Big Russ and Me

FATHER AND SON: LESSONS OF LIFE

Tim Russert

WEINSTEIN BOOKS

Printed in the United States of America.

Cataloging-in-Publication data for this book is available from
the Library of Congress.

ISBN: 978-1-60286-262-3 (print)
ISBN: 978-1-60286-263-0 (e-book)

Published by Weinstein Books
A member of the Perseus Books Group
www.weinsteinbooks.com

Weinstein Books are available at special discounts for bulk purchases in
the U.S. by corporations, institutions and other organizations. For more
information, please contact the Special Markets Department at the
Perseus Books Group, 2300 Chestnut Street, Suite 200,
Philadelphia, PA 19103, call (800) 810-4145, ext. 5000,
or e-mail special.markets@perseusbooks.com.

Originally Published by Miramax Books 2004

First Weinstein Books Edition 2014

10 9 8 7 6 5 4 3 2 1

TO DAD, MOM,
B.A., KATHY, TRISH,
MAUREEN, AND LUKE

CONTENTS

PREFACE

by Luke Orth Russert

SIX YEARS LATER, it happens more often than you'd think. I'll be walking down the street, or sitting in a restaurant, or grabbing a coffee at an airport and somebody will approach me, usually with a frozen smile, their eyes a little moist. With a nervous hesitancy in their voice they'll ask, "You're Tim Russert's son, right?" Almost immediately after I say yes they say, "Gosh, I really loved your dad, he was the best." Usually that's followed by a back slap, a "Go Bills!" or a hug. I can honestly say it never really gets old. I know why I loved my dad; he was my best friend. But now, years after his death, I often wonder why the man who threw around the baseball with me, watched games, made me laugh, and forced me to memorize vocabulary flash cards still resonates so vividly with so many.

Perhaps the answer lies in something that a gentleman in Alliance, Ohio, told me a few years ago. I was on assignment for NBC News, trying to take the pulse of a swing state congressional district. While I introduced myself to voters in the parking lot of a diner, hoping to secure a valuable "man on the street" bite for a TV spot, a man caught my last name. He asked me if I was related to Tim Russert. I said that I was indeed and, in fact, his son. He extended his well-worked hand, gripped mine, looked me straight in the eye and said, "We loved him. He was for us—he cared."

Those last words have stuck with me because they're so simple, yet carry so much weight: he cared. The man was right, my father did care—about his family, his faith, his friends, and perhaps most of all, his country. He viewed his job as an opportunity to serve, to instruct and hold those with so much power to the highest standards. He did not do this for money, personal fame, or professional accolades; he did it because, through faith, he carried the conviction that he must ask the important questions on behalf of the American people. That his voice must rise above the petty politics that so often kill reason in Washington, and provide an outlet for the truth. This unwavering belief in his duty coupled with his broad-shouldered, husky frame and jolly Irish demeanor made my father special. He was the guy with the serious job whom you not only wanted to have a beer with but also share a laugh and a cry.

Perhaps his best quality was that he always "got" people. Whatever their race, age, gender, sexual orientation, or nationality, my dad could relate to anyone. Six years later it's still hard to accept that he's gone, but as he wrote in this book, "To accept faith we have to resign ourselves as mortals to the fact that we are a small part of a grand design." I'd argue that he was a large part of the contemporary American grand design, but he'd humbly tell me I was overstating it and that his own father, "Big Russ," didn't teach me to brag.

As much as this book is about my dad, it also tells the story of the man known affectionately as Big Russ. I never called him that; to me he was always "Grandpa." He didn't speak much, but he didn't have to with me. His genuine kindness and playful manner always made more than enough of an impact. I still hear his Santa Claus–style "he-he-he" laugh when I drive by a Ted's Hot Dogs in Buffalo. He'd say to me, "Lukie, you eat it with extra Weber's mustard."

He was a dutiful man, and if he taught me anything, it was about the importance of doing the job you were tasked to do. One family vacation Fourth of July when I was around sixteen, I couldn't make the family barbecue because I had a double shift at the local public golf course cleaning out carts and picking the driving range. I might have expected Grandpa to be disappointed that I wasn't there, but when I got home later in the day, he couldn't have been prouder. He told me that working when nobody else wants to "shows 'em you're reliable." When I told him I had to take out many loads of garbage, he flashed a huge grin. "Sanitation work. We do that—it's a badge of honor!" Now when I get some crazy assignments like covering Congress on New Year's Eve well into the early morning, I think about Grandpa's words and know that, if nothing else, at least I'm reliable at that moment in time.

Grandpa outlived Dad and passed away at the age of eighty-five. Even as his mind started to slip away, he tried to laugh when he could. When I went to his viewing, I was sad, but I couldn't help but crack a smile. The viewing happened to fall on a Sunday during a Bills home game. Many of his best friends and family paid their respects and then went to watch the game in a room in the back of the funeral home. Now, many might find this offensive, but it's exactly what Big Russ would have wanted. He loved his Bills; he loved watching them with my dad and my late uncle Bill. You could say he literally lived and died with them. Of course, the Bills lost the game that day.

I'M FOREVER THANKFUL that my father wrote *Big Russ and Me*. Not just because it's a wonderful book, but for the more selfish reason that it has given me my father's playbook as I have embarked on my own life. I find myself leafing through it hoping to hear his soothing voice jump off the page and push me in the right direction. Whenever I'm lost, I look over some of the appropriately named chapters for guidance: Respect, Work, Faith, Discipline, Loss, Washington, Politics, Baseball, Food, and Fatherhood—though I'm years away from that last one!

When my father finished *Big Russ and Me* he confided to me that he was nervous about how it would be received. He wondered if folks outside of the Rust Belt could relate to his steel-city parochial Catholic upbringing back when the American promise was fresh and had been boosted by the Allied victory in World War II. He wondered if the lessons he had learned in the 1960s were similar to others who were not quite progressive radicals but also not conservative hardhats. He also admitted that he didn't know if the book-buying public would care about a newsman's upbringing and his take on fatherhood: for years they had turned to him for the news, not a how-to manual.

Well, his doubts were answered when this book became a number-one *New York Times* bestseller. He was proud of that, so much so that he clipped the list out of the newspaper, framed it and put it on his office wall at home. He jokingly referred to it as his "long-desired Super Bowl ring" and was straight-up giddy when *Wisdom of Our Fathers* accomplished the same feat. For a kid from South Buffalo to have a bestselling book—as my Big Russ would say, "What a country!" Through writing he revealed his feelings about the lessons he'd learned from his past and what he thought was his most important job title: dad.

Fatherhood was my dad's passion. A day never went by that I didn't know my father loved me. In fact, the first time I did not speak to my father for more than twenty-four hours was when I went on my first sleepover camping trip in the eighth grade. The Russerts of South Buffalo were many things, but they were not campers. As my dad's friend Mike Barnicle said, "Tim was from a cement sidewalk . . . he rarely saw a river without a paper mill or steel plant next to it."

Dad took me to an army surplus store to get properly outfitted, and you would have thought I was spending a year in the wilderness with Davy Crockett given the amount of gear he "insisted" I needed. When I arrived at the camp site, the guide told me to "drop about thirty pounds" of gear, so gone were the three backup flashlights, the folding cot, and the totally necessary triple-lined camouflage winter parka. (Mind you, the trip was in the humid spring.)

I got along fine camping, but after five days I knew it wasn't necessarily for me. Unlike Dad, I grew up on more than cement, and through my mom's West Coast roots, I inherited a love of the ocean. At the end of the week, when the bus pulled into the school parking lot to drop off dozens of my classmates and me, I heard loud laughs from my best buddies. My pal Paul Grayson screamed, "Luke, look at your dad!" I first saw my mother, standing off to the side with a huge smile, and then there was Dad with a jack-o'-lantern grin, waving an American flag and holding up a sign that read WELCOME HOME BOYS!

Some might find it strange that the well-known host of *Meet the Press* was yelling and waving a flag like a maniac, but that was Dad. He was so excited to see me and his love was so strong that he didn't care that he might look silly greeting me as if I had just been deployed. At first I was a little annoyed at him because I thought his stunt was corny, but he rounded up my friends and shouted, "We're going to Burger King! After a week of rabbit food, supersize for everybody!" You just had to love him. But even then, I didn't fully appreciate his intense love till I left for college. It was hard on both of us because I knew I could no longer just open his door, plop down in a chair and talk, but we adapted, thanks to cell phones. If my future kid ever reads this, we'll be on the unlimited texting plan because I'll be blowing up your phone!

WHILE DAD'S LOVE FOR ME RAN DEEP, he had an affinity for all children. When friends called the house the first question out of his mouth would be, "How's your boy, how's your girl, how'd their soccer team do?" The day my father passed, my colleague Chuck Todd said on NBC that he had never before had a boss who was as interested and as happy talking about other people's children as he was about his own son.

My father was certainly comfortable with his emotions but like my grandpa, he rarely cried openly. I can count on one hand the number of times I saw him in tears, and four of those had to be the Bills Super Bowl losses! But the time I remember most was when I was in second grade. Because I had a booming voice, my Sunday-school teacher decided that I should read the prayer intentions at the children's mass the following Sunday. Dad was thrilled; being a talented public speaker, he always took pride when I excelled at the craft. During that week we practiced my prayers around the kitchen table. One was for "all the children in the world who are sick, sad, tired, suffering or alone." Twenty years later, I remember those words exactly. When I said them out loud, my father choked up and his eyes became wet. He paused, stared at me and said, "Think about that, buddy. Think about it."

He never missed an opportunity to help children. Whether it was working with the Boys & Girls Club or Catholic Education, Dad always said yes. He gave dozens of commencement speeches and in his closing paragraphs, he almost always said:

"Unless we instill in our young the most basic social skills and cultural and moral values . . . we will be a very different society. We must motivate, inspire—yes, insist—our children respect one another . . . 'love thy neighbor as thyself.' . . . No matter what profession you choose, you must try, even in the smallest ways, to improve the quality of life of all the children in our country. When my life is over, there's nothing more I'll be judged on than what kind of father I was." In another commencement speech, he added: "If we are serious about continuing as the world's premier military, and economic and moral force in the world, we have no choice. We need all of our children contributing and prospering."

This is a great country, but when it comes to fatherhood, and two-parent households, he knew we were falling short. One out of three children grows up without their biological father in the home. Statistics show that this means they're more likely to be poor, have a higher chance of being incarcerated or becoming pregnant as a teen, using drugs, dropping out of school, or suffering from behavioral issues. What better way for children to achieve than to have their fathers in their lives? This is an epidemic in 2014, and if my father were still around, he'd shed light on it.

I'm at an age now where many of my friends are getting married and starting their own journey into fatherhood. I'm often asked what sort of lessons my father passed down to me on the topic. Since he died when I was twenty-two, we never really had the official how-to-be-a-dad conversation. Yet I can imagine what he would say based on how he raised me and on the stories his friends have told me.

A colleague of mine at NBC once told me she always asked my father to stick around for an additional taped interview after his *Today* show appearances, which on most days were on at around seven in the morning. Almost every time he would politely tell her, "No, I got to take my kid to school." She admitted that she was often perplexed as to why staying fifteen or twenty minutes longer was such a big deal to him. A few years ago I got an email from her; she told me that as a new mom not only did she totally understand where my dad was coming from, but she would do everything in her power never to miss dropping off her daughter at school, because the time was too precious.

It's true; the greatest gift my father ever gave me was his time. Here was a man who worked seven days a week, rarely slept more than six hours a night, and yet I can never remember a time when he wasn't there for me or didn't make a Herculean effort to be present. Heck, he tried to interview Florida politicians when I had spring-training JV baseball games! I understand that not all fathers can afford to do that. Jobs, commitments, etc. don't always lend themselves to kids being number one all the time. However, I do know that if a father makes an effort to be there, a kid will always notice and always appreciate it because as a kid you feel loved, wanted, and cared about, and you can't ask for more than that.

Another thing my father was big on was conversation. He would inquire about my day over dinner, call me to ask a simple "How ya doing?" Through these conversations we bonded over sports, politics, music, and just simple human interests. Sometimes after watching a Bills game together, I felt like we had solved the world's problems! When I was a young kid, on Fridays after work Dad would sometimes take me to his local watering hole. A few beers for him, and some Coca-Colas for me as a reward if I had behaved during the week. If I hadn't I was stuck with milk. He would usually meet a friend or mom after her exercise class, but sometimes it was just the two of us. He'd give me money for the jukebox and a request: "Springsteen." How do you spell it, I'd ask, and he'd say, "*Spring* like the season and then *s-t-een*; no *ei*, just *een*."

I would play three Beach Boys songs (my favorite) and then

one Bruce song for him. He'd interact with customers in the bar. Many were kind and just wanted to shoot the breeze; others wanted to talk about their political opinions, the Buffalo Bills, or had ideas for how *Meet the Press* could be even better. I noticed that no matter what, Dad would always try to be nice. He told me that came from Grandpa, and the old lesson that "it takes just as long to be mean to somebody as it does to be nice."

Working in TV news I'm exposed to a fair amount of, shall we say, people who take the time to be mean. In fact, people these days seem to relish the art of "trolling" or being perpetually "snarky." I'm not quite sure what that says about us as a society, but I feel as if the days are behind us when someone like my dad stood at a bar and talked to people. Inclusion and communication are important, both in parenting and basic societal understanding. Talk to kids—they'll relish it—and maybe carry on a conversation with a person in front of them so they learn how to do more than just stare at a phone screen.

FATHER'S DAY was my dad's favorite day. For me it's a holiday of mixed emotions: Father's Day will never be the same for me because it usually falls a few days after the anniversary of my dad's death. This book is about the eternal relationship between fathers and sons. I hope this book deepens the love between all fathers and their children.

Loss is hard, and on Father's Day those of us without a dad tend to be in a funk. My friend Bo Blair is a father of three, but he also lost his dad at a young age. He told me once, "God this day sucks, but when you do something your dad loved it feels so much better." I try and go to a baseball game and soak in the joy of the fathers who are there with their kids. Friends will call and check in; my college buddy Mike Greeley makes sure to tell me he's drinking a Rolling Rock in honor of TJR. I do that, too.

Not a day goes by that I don't miss my dad and recall his face from the last time I saw him, but I know he's here. He's in these pages, in these stories, and he's with everyone who believes being a father is the most important job in the world. There are many different walks of life in this country, but fatherhood is the great equalizer. You don't have to be rich to be a good dad. You don't have to have a fancy degree to be a good dad. Or drive a nice car. You just have to care, and that's something we all can do because that's what Tim Russert did—he cared.

May, 2014
Washington, D.C.

INTRODUCTION

ON ELECTION NIGHT 2000, I sat on the NBC set with Tom Brokaw as state after state was projected for either George W. Bush or Al Gore. In trying to make sense of the election results, I started writing, in bold print on the back of a legal pad, the names of the states that were still being contested. As I added new states and crossed out others, and held up my home-made chart to the camera, I could almost see my dad nodding his head and saying, "Now I understand. Now I get it. Keep it simple. Forget those fancy computers."

Jeff Zucker, who was producing our election coverage and who liked my low-tech efforts to explain the latest developments, noticed that the cardboard I was writing on was becoming increasingly messy and difficult to read. So he sent somebody to buy a couple of white dry-erase boards, which would be easier to work with. For the rest of the night, I used those boards to show how close each candidate was to the 270 electoral votes he needed to become our forty-third president.

Over the next few days, NBC News received a lot of positive comments for the way we kept track of an enormously complicated election with what one reviewer described as "homespun comfort." My son, Luke, who was fifteen, said, "Dad, what are you going to do with that board you were using?"

"Actually, there were two of them," I said. "I promised one to the Newseum," the museum of news in Washington, D.C., that had opened in 1997.

"How about the other one?" he asked. "Could I have it?"

"Sure," I said. I was moved that my son wanted this keepsake of his father's work on election night. Just as I was starting to get emotional about the bond between us, Luke said, "Thanks, Dad. You know what this thing is worth on eBay?"

The legal pad that I used on Election Day was an idea that came straight from Dad. As long as I can remember, he has used an 8½-by-11 yellow legal pad to keep track of the household budget. I wouldn't be surprised if he's still using the very same kind he had when I was a boy.

When I was in high school, my older sister Betty Ann's boyfriend, Bill Buckenroth, came to our house to ask Dad for her hand in marriage. Dad was in his usual spot, sitting in the living room with the newspaper.

"Mr. Russert," Bill said, "I want to marry your daughter."

Dad dropped his paper on the floor. "You what?"

"I want to marry your daughter."

"You do? You're still in school! How the hell are you going to support her?" Without waiting for an answer, Dad got up, walked out of the room, and went downstairs to take a shower.

He was gone for at least forty minutes. As he waited for Dad to come back, Bill paced nervously. My sister cried, and my mother tried to comfort her.

Finally, the shower water stopped. Ten minutes later, we heard footsteps on the stairs, car keys jingling, and the sound of a door slamming. Big Russ was gone.

About an hour later, Dad came back, went to the bedroom, pulled a sheet off his legal pad, and brought it into the living room. "Bill," he said, "I want you to show me in black and white how you're going to support her. Keep it simple, so I can understand it. Nothing complicated and nothing phony. Just give me the real numbers." Bill went to the kitchen table and Dad went back to his chair. A few minutes later, they went over the numbers together. Dad must have liked what he saw, because the next thing I knew, he and Bill were driving over to the Legion Hall to celebrate the engagement over a couple of cold ones.

On Election Day 2000, I was doing it Dad's way—first with my legal pad, and then with the two dry-erase boards. As for my sister and Bill, they recently celebrated their thirty-fifth wedding anniversary.

THE OLDER I GET, the smarter my father seems to get. Hardly a day goes by when I don't remember or rely on something that Big Russ taught me. As I began to think about the lessons I learned from him, I started talking to some friends about the lessons they learned from their fathers. Jayce Caulfield's dad,

Thomas, who was known in our neighborhood as Sarge, was superintendent of parks for the City of Buffalo. Sarge used to hire teenage boys to keep them off the streets and to "give them a shot," as he liked to say. If a kid didn't show up to work in the morning, Sarge would drive to his house, go upstairs, and personally drag him out of bed. Now that's tough love.

My friend Dick Eaton used to refer to his father as "the Wallet." (I know what he meant: my son sometimes refers to me as the human ATM.) As they got older, Dick and his brother started calling their father "the Apple," because he was the apple of their eye. Dick's father, Paul F. Eaton, is a small-town lawyer who never thought of himself as being smarter than the big city rainmakers, although he probably is. "He knew," says Dick, "that if he worked harder and prepared more than other lawyers, his chances of success were that much better. That's what he taught us: preparation is everything."

My friend Larry Tierney is a physician in California. His father, who was known as D. T.—for Doc Tierney—was a doctor, too. Doc Tierney taught his son that treatment is the easy part of medicine; the real challenge is getting the diagnosis right. And the key to the right diagnosis, he would say, comes from really listening to the patient. He warned his son against the danger of arrogance. "The minute you think you're any good in this business," he told Larry, "that's when you're going to start harming your patients."

MY DAD AND I SHARE THE SAME NAME, and when I was very young, he was known as Tim and I was Timmy. When I was around ten, people called us Big Tim and Little Tim. In high school, when I shot up to six foot two and no longer qualified as "Little" Tim, I started referring to Dad as Big Russ, as in, "There'll be hell to pay when Big Russ finds out about this," and I've thought of him as Big Russ ever since. Not long ago, I overheard Luke referring to me as "the Big Guy," as in, "It sounds okay, but I have to check with the Big Guy."

Although Dad and I have always been close, our relationship has never been marked by open displays of affection. But that changed a few years ago, when NBC organized a series called "Going Home," in which the network's news anchors and the hosts of its major news programs returned to the communities where they grew up and talked about the values and the cultures that shaped their lives.

On January 1, 1997, I traveled to the American Legion Post 721 in South Buffalo, where Dad had once been the commander. Every New Year's Day, the Legion hosts an open house for its members and their families, and I asked Dad what time I should arrive with the NBC news crew. He said we should come at noon. I asked him what time the festivities started. He said they ran from one o'clock to four.

"Then why should we be there at noon?" I asked.

"Because the food and the drinks are free."

At the Legion Hall, we pushed some tables together and sat with Dad and his buddies. Dad looked into the camera and talked about the men like himself who returned home after World War II. "They wanted community," he said. "They wanted a home. They wanted a good reputation with their kids. What's the old saying? 'Your nose to the grindstone and hope for the best.'"

That expression—it's actually two expressions squeezed to-gether—captures the essence of Dad: endlessly hardworking and eternally optimistic.

The next day, I went down to city hall to visit with Anthony Masiello. Tony's dad, Danny Masiello, used to work on the garbage trucks with my dad. They would dream about their sons having a better life, and I guess their dreams came true. Today, one is the moderator of *Meet the Press*, and the other is the mayor of Buffalo.

We concluded the piece for NBC *Nightly News* by walking down the sidewalk in my old neighborhood. As we walked along, side by side, I spontaneously put my hand around Dad's shoul-der. In closing, I said, "They shaped our destiny. We stand on their shoulders. Tim Russert, NBC News, Buffalo, New York."

When the piece aired two weeks later, I was deluged with let-ters and calls from around the country. People wanted to talk about their dads, and to thank me for acknowledging mine. I heard from men who wished they'd had a chance to share their thoughts and feelings with their fathers while they were still alive. And I realized that my relationship with Big Russ had changed forever.

The following year, 1998, I was invited to address the eightieth annual convention of the New York State chapter of the American Legion, which was held in Buffalo in July. They wanted to give me a journalism award and thank me for using the American Legion as the centerpiece of my "Going Home" segment on NBC. I flew to Buffalo with Luke, who was then twelve. When it came time for the award presentation, I stood at the podium and looked at my dad and my son, who were sitting together in the front row. I said a few words about the importance of the American Legion to our family, and then I spoke about Dad. I described what he had done in the war, and how hard he had worked when he came home.

"I am honored to accept this award," I said, "but I want to dedicate it to someone much more deserving. He never graduated from high school, but he taught his four kids by his example, his hard work, and his basic decency. Today, he celebrates his fiftieth anniversary as an American Legionnaire. It is with enormous pride, the utmost respect, and the deepest love, that I present this award to the past commander of South Buffalo Post 721—my hero, my dad, the *real* Tim Russert."

The convention hall shook with applause, cheers, and tears. Never had I experienced such a powerful reaction from so few words. I knew immediately that the response was not only for Big Russ; it was also an expression of the love and respect the audience felt so deeply for their own fathers.

When I asked Dad to come up and accept the award that the Legion had given me, he burst into tears. I was surprised: in my whole life, I had seen Dad cry on only two occasions—at his mother's funeral in 1967, and at his father's, three years later. But now he was wiping his eyes with the back of his hand—no handkerchief, no tissues, just using that big paw to stop his tears. He looked around the dais and saw all these grizzled war veterans, men very much like himself, men who didn't cry very often. And when they saw Dad crying, they started crying, too.

The seeds for this book began to germinate right there, at the Legion convention. I have learned so much from Big Russ, and I feel so grateful to him, that I wanted to write a book about the two of us, and also about the other important teachers in my life, who have reinforced Dad's lessons and taught me a few new ones. I learned a great deal from Mom, too, who was, and still is, a central force in my life. As my childhood pastor, Father Denis Donovan, loved to say, "The hand that rocks the cradle rules the world." But the father-son relationship is unique, and that's what this book is about.

I hope this book will encourage readers to think about the things they learned from their fathers. Whatever we achieve and whoever we are, we stand on their shoulders.

I.

My Father's War

"It was a lot tougher for the guys who died."

NOT LONG AGO, I took part in an online conversation hosted by the *Washington Post*. As I sat at a computer, people around the country sent in questions about *Meet the Press* and other topics, and I did my best to answer them. Near the end of the hour, somebody asked if there was one individual whom I would especially like to interview. The person who submitted that question was probably expecting me to name an elusive political figure, or perhaps a fascinating character from history, such as Thomas Jefferson, Christopher Columbus, or my first choice, Jesus Christ. But I took the question personally, and answered it immediately and from my heart: more than anyone else, I would like to interview my dad.

Big Russ has never been much of a talker, especially about himself. Part of it is his modesty: talking about himself probably feels like bragging, which he dislikes in other people and goes out of his way to avoid. It's not that he's silent, because Dad is a sociable and friendly guy, and in the right setting, and with people he knows well, you can get him going on any number of topics—politics, baseball, the Buffalo Bills, television, the best kind of hot dogs, and how Canadian beer tastes better when you buy it in Canada. But, like so many men of his generation, he won't tell you much about his life, his thoughts, or his feelings.

When I was a boy, I knew that Dad had been overseas in World War II, and had served in what was then called the Army Air Force. But whenever I asked him about the war, he avoided my questions and tried to change the subject. When I persisted, he would say, "I'm not a hero like those guys in the planes. I stayed on the ground and just did my job."

Every summer, our family used to rent a cottage for a week at Wasaga Beach in Ontario, where Dad, a strong man who loved the water, used to let my sisters and me lie on his back while he swam. One morning, when I was five or six, we were on the beach in our bathing suits when I noticed that Dad had several scars on his back. I had probably seen them before, but this was the first time I really noticed them. When I asked Mom why they were there, she told me that Dad had been injured in a plane crash during the war.

So of course I went over and asked him, "Dad, were you really in a plane crash?"

"Yeah," he said, but the word was barely out of his mouth before he jumped back in the water. Even at that age, I could see that he was running away—or in this case, actually swimming away—from my question.

As the years went on, especially on Memorial Day, when we went to the local cemetery to plant little American flags on the graves of war veterans, I sometimes asked him about the war. Although I desperately wanted to know what had happened, I was careful not to push too hard. It was clear that he didn't want to talk about it, and I imagined that I might feel the same way if something that terrible had happened to me. Every time I asked about the war, he would parcel out another detail or two. One year he said, "Everybody did their job, and I did mine. I was a parachute rigger." Another time, referring to the crash, he said, "It was a foggy day, really bad weather."

When I was in high school, the two of us were in the basement one day when Dad walked over to his desk, opened a drawer, and took out a manila folder. He handed me a yellowed clipping from the October 27, 1944, edition of the *Southport Weekly*, an English newspaper. The headline read, U.S. BOMBER CRASHES IN FLAMES AT AINSDALE, and the article described the crash of a B-24 Liberator at an air base in England. I read it quickly and zeroed in on the key lines: "The plane, which had been circling round as though preparatory to landing...somersaulted into a field, immediately bursting into flames. When the plane crashed it broke up, and some of the airmen were thrown clear."

Dad, I realized, had been one of them.

"This is amazing," I said.

He looked at me and said, "It was a lot tougher for the guys who died." Then he took back the clipping and put it away without another word. The conversation was over.

A year or two later, he told me about the Polish kid from Chicago who had saved his life when their plane went down. Dad has no memory of this, but he learned later that when the plane hit the ground, he and several other men had been thrown clear. Dad, who was badly hurt and evidently in shock, had climbed to his feet. With his clothing engulfed in flames, he had started stumbling back toward the burning wreckage. Bullets from the plane's machine guns were bursting in all directions, but Dad was dazed and oblivious to the danger. Billy Suchocki, a friend of Dad's and a fellow passenger on the flight, whose clothes were also on fire, was being helped by two British railway men who had run to the scene of the crash. As they rolled Billy on the ground to suffocate the flames, he pointed to Dad and yelled, "Help him! Help him!" The railway men ran to Dad and pulled him out of further danger.

One Christmas, when I was home from college, I looked up Billy Suchocki's phone number in Chicago. I wanted Dad to be in touch with the man who had rescued him, and I knew he would never make that call on his own. With Dad's permission, I dialed the number and put the two old army buddies on the phone. I heard only Dad's end of the conversation, which was brief and unemotional. They wished each other a Merry Christmas and talked briefly about Red, the dog who went overseas with them, and who returned home with Dad after the war.

After the call, which seemed so casual in view of what had happened, I said, "Dad, this guy saved your *life*, and you're joking about a *dog*? Why didn't you thank him for rescuing you?"

Dad looked at me thoughtfully and said, "He knows, and I know." Then he lowered his head. Enough had been said.

Later on, Dad told me a few more details about his experiences during the war, but I still hesitated to ask him about the crash. Years later, when my friend Tom Brokaw published *The Greatest Generation Speaks*, a follow-up to *The Greatest Generation*, the story of that brave and selfless generation of Americans who came of age during the Great Depression and then went off to fight for freedom and democracy in the Second World War, Dad opened up a little more. Brokaw had been kind enough to mention Dad in the book—which was a little ironic, given its title—and Dad was pleased to be acknowledged. He told me that the army experience had been good for him, that it had helped him become more disciplined and had taught him in a dramatic fashion that everyone has a role to play.

There was so much more I wanted to know about Dad's experiences during the war, but I have always respected his wish not to talk about it. Eventually, I realized that I could learn some of the details from other people, including Billy Suchocki and several other veterans from the 446th Bombardment Group, which Dad had been part of, and from a book about the 446th by Ed Castens, one of its members. Then, in early 2003, I received a letter out of the blue from Ron Tompkins, a resident of Bermuda whose older brother, Alva, had died in the crash that had almost killed Dad and Billy Suchocki. Mr. Tompkins, the seventh in a family of eight children, had been five when his eldest brother had been killed, and had spent much of his adult life investigating the accident. He had made two pilgrimages to the airfield where the plane went down and was in touch with several of the survivors. He sent me a packet of information that made it clear that this terrible event, which killed ten men and left ten others badly injured, could easily have been avoided. But before I had a chance to meet him, his son Christopher wrote to tell me that Ron Tompkins had died.

DAD HAD ENLISTED in November 1942, at the age of nineteen. "All my friends had joined," he told me, "so there was nobody really left in the neighborhood." Was he being modest, or was his decision to enlist really that casual? After being poked, prodded, and questioned at the induction center, he was sent off, by train, of course, to a training camp in Fresno, California, where he learned how to march, how to salute, and above all, how to be patient. Like millions of other recruits, he soon learned that the army's unofficial slogan was "Hurry up and wait."

Hoping to become a pilot, he volunteered for the Army Air Force, where he was disappointed to learn that his eyesight wasn't good enough for him to fly. It must be a family trait. When I was three, I had to wear an eye patch as a way of strengthening my weak eye. The first time Dad saw me with it, he shook his head and said, "I guess you've got my eyes—and not just the color."

After basic training, Dad spent several weeks at Chanute Field in Illinois, where he took a course in parachute rigging—packing and inspecting parachutes that the air crews wore on every mission while hoping never to need them. Parachutes in those days were made of silk, which is both light and strong, and men who used them to escape from a damaged plane became members of an unofficial society known as the Caterpillar Club, not only because silk is made from the cocoons of caterpillars, but also because the transformed creature emerges from the cocoon with the ability to fly. It used to be that apprentice parachute riggers were not certified until they actually "jumped their chutes"— that is, jumped out of a plane with a parachute that they themselves had inspected, repaired, and packed, but that requirement was dropped in 1941 to save time. There was a war to fight, and the Americans were needed overseas as soon as possible.

Dad passed through bases in Utah and Arizona before being sent to Lowry Field in Colorado, where the 446th Bombardment Group was activated on April 1, 1943. At Lowry, Dad and some of his pals met up with Red, a big red chow with a black tongue. Red was not a friendly dog, but the men were fond of him and were determined to bring him overseas. They had little hope, however, of smuggling a large dog on the long train ride to New York, and even less of sneaking him onto the ship that would transport them to England.

Somehow, they persuaded a bombardier on one of the flight crews to take Red over on a B-24. It wasn't easy: at first, when the pilot tried to get to his seat, Red wouldn't let him into the cockpit. When Red finally relented and the pilot settled in, Red settled in right behind him. On one of their many stops en route, Red noticed a long line of bags in front of a building; perhaps inspired by the challenge, he proceeded to pee on every single one. Despite his outrageous behavior, or maybe because of it, the crew continued to bring him along. When they landed in Dakar and a Senegalese soldier tried to stab Red with a bayonet, the crew intervened to spare his life. During a stopover in Marrakesh, Morocco, they took Red with them to the movies, where he curled up in a plush chair that they later learned was reserved for the mayor; when the movie ended, Red left his calling card in the mayor's seat. When the flight crew arrived at their home base in England, Red was reunited with the parachute group. But Red wasn't the only dog that made the trip from Lowry Field; a female named Whitey on one of the other bombers delivered a litter of pups en route. It was widely believed that Red had something to do with this development, but Red wasn't talking.

Dad and his fellow soldiers in the ground unit took a slower route to England. In October 1943, they traveled by train from Denver to Camp Shanks, New York, their last stop before going overseas. It was a long, tedious trip, as their train was often sidetracked to allow much-needed military equipment to make its way to port cities on both coasts. They were moving through western New York when Dad looked out the window and realized that the train was passing through his own neighborhood in South Buffalo. He yelled out to some waving onlookers, "Tell Frank Russert that his son Tim is on this train, and we're going overseas!" The message got delivered to his parents.

Camp Shanks was on the Hudson River, just north of Manhattan, where they would soon board a ship for England. From this point on the men were not allowed to make phone calls or send letters. The precise arrival and departure dates of troop ships was a closely guarded secret, giving rise to the famous expression from that era, "Loose lips sink ships."

From Camp Shanks they were taken by truck to excursion boats that ferried them south to Pier 90, where they boarded the famous *Queen Mary*. It was Winston Churchill who had proposed using the enormous luxury liner to transport troops across the ocean. Gen. George C. Marshall, the American chief of staff, hadn't wanted to risk putting thousands of men on a single ship with too few lifeboats, but Churchill prevailed. As Dad and his unit prepared to board, they watched as huge supplies of food—

good food, the kind they hadn't seen in quite a while—were loaded onto the ship. *At least we'll eat well*, Dad thought. "But once we sailed," he told me, "the rations they gave us were so meager we couldn't believe it." Shortly before they reached their destination, Dad spotted a group of English crew members having dinner. "They were eating like kings," he said. Knowing how Big Russ feels about food, I'm surprised that he didn't organize a mutiny.

As the men of the 446th Bombardment Group boarded the ship, a band played and Red Cross volunteers passed out coffee and doughnuts. Soon they were moving past the Statue of Liberty and into the ocean.

The ship, repainted camouflage grey, and known as the Grey Ghost, was able because of her great speed to evade German submarines and torpedoes. As long as she was moving fast, the troops on board were relatively safe, and for that reason she was under strict orders not to stop for any reason. On one crossing, the *Queen Mary* sailed past a group of lifeboats with men aboard, but kept moving at top speed. The Americans were under strict orders to make sure that no light could be seen emanating from the ship. One night, someone in Dad's group brushed up against a curtain, accidentally exposing a flicker of light. "The whole group of us spent the night in the slammer," Dad said.

During normal times, the *Queen Mary* carried eleven hundred passengers, plus a sizable crew. When Dad's group made the crossing there were more than fourteen thousand men on board, which was not unusual during the war. Berths were everywhere—stacked six high in lounges, function rooms, and even in empty swimming pools. The men slept in shifts. They were fed twice a day, also in shifts, and were given only a few minutes to eat. To ease congestion, all pedestrian traffic on board was one way: to move forward you walked on the starboard side; to move back you used the port side. All passengers had to wear life jackets in case they were attacked. There was no smoking, and even chewing gum was forbidden because it was hard to remove from the decks. The weather was rotten and many of the men were seasick. When I think about the crossing, I can't imagine how men of my own generation would have fared on board.

As the ship approached its destination, but long before it reached land, British ships and planes came out to protect the men from possible attack by German U-boats and planes. (Hitler had offered a huge cash reward and an Iron Cross to the captain or pilot who could sink the *Queen Mary*, but the ship made eighty-six crossings without once being attacked.) On November 3 they docked at Greenock, in the Firth of Clyde, not far from Glasgow, Scotland. Trucks carried the men to trains, and trains took them to Flixton, their new home, in England. Station 125, as it was known, was one of many air bases on the eastern coast, not far from the English Channel and two miles from the sleepy village of Bungay.

When they arrived in England, the great majority of these men had never before set foot outside the United States, although a few, like Dad, had been to Canada. They were given a publication from the War Department that reminded them, among other things, that they were guests of Great Britain, and that England and America were allies. It sounds obvious today, but if you lived in South Buffalo in the 1940s, it was a reminder worth hearing. "If you come from an Irish-American family," the men were told, "you may think of the English as persecutors of the Irish, or you may think of them as an enemy Redcoat who fought against us in the American Revolution and the War of 1812." If that's what you think, they were told, think again; this wasn't the time to bring up old grievances. The pamphlet went on to explain that the British were more restrained and private than Americans, and that it would be a mistake to interpret their reserve as hostility. "Don't be a show-off," the visitors were told. They were also advised to keep in mind that Britain had been at war since 1939, and that the Americans had come from a country where food was still plentiful and the lights were still burning.

The men of the 446th were part of the Eighth Air Force, whose mission was to fly over Germany and bomb a variety of industrial and military targets. Every morning, weather permitting—and often in bad weather, too, including snowstorms—planes from each base took off for missions over Germany. When they lined up on the runway, taking off at thirty-second intervals, the entire base shook. The men used to say that when the Eighth Air Force took off, so much weight went into the air that all of England rose six inches. After the bombers crossed the channel, their targets included ports, bridges, chemical plants, U-boat installations, aircraft factories, oil refineries, and virtually every other part of the Nazi war effort. Casualties were very high: the 446th lost fifty-eight planes in combat and another twenty-eight in other mishaps. Often, the men came back and reported that the flak was so thick you could walk on it. Returning planes were often full of holes and carried men who had been injured during the mission. When they landed after a bombing run, everyone on board was offered a shot of whiskey.

Even takeoffs were dangerous: the B-24s were so heavy with bombs and fuel that the slightest mistake could cause a crash and kill the entire crew.

Parachutes were inspected after every mission and repacked whenever it was necessary. Because they were made of silk, they were susceptible to damage from mold and fungus. They could also be damaged on board, where they might be exposed to fuel or hydraulic oil. As a parachute rigger, Dad was responsible for inspecting and repacking the chutes, and for fitting the harness to the crewman. This had to be done carefully, because a badly fitting harness could cause real pain in a man's nether regions.

Each of the ten men on a B-24 was given a parachute shortly before takeoff, and they had all heard the old joke, "If it doesn't work, bring it back and we'll give you a new one." In fact, the parachutes did work; the tragedy was that many men never got to use them. If your plane was hit, it could be hard, or even impossible, to get out. If the plane started falling, the crew would be pushed to the ceiling. Pilots did their best to keep the aircraft steady enough so the men could jump, but if your plane had lost a wing, you were done for.

If you jumped, almost anything could happen. When your parachute opened, you might drift gently down to earth. You could also pass out from the lack of oxygen. You could come down hard into a tree, or you could hit the ground with so much force that you were knocked unconscious. On your way down, you could be shot at by soldiers or civilians on the ground. Or you might be using a parachute that, for some reason, failed to open. If your plane was hit, your immediate survival depended on men like Dad, who had packed your chute. Your life was in their hands.

If and when you landed safely behind enemy lines, your first task was to gather up your parachute and hide it. Your second task was to avoid being captured. Along with a parachute, each member of the ten-man flight crew was issued a first-aid kit that was supposed to contain morphine and Benzedrine (but often didn't), along with maps, foreign currency, a compass, and a "Mae West"—an inflatable life jacket worn around the neck. Some men who used their parachutes were rescued. Others became prisoners of war. Still others were killed by farmers or townspeople as soon as they landed.

When you talk to the men who flew in these planes, or you read about the harsh and freezing conditions they endured, even on missions that returned safely, it's easy to understand why a mechanic, a cook, a driver, an ordnance man or a parachute rigger might be reluctant to talk about his experiences. "In my job I wasn't in danger," Dad told me. "German bombers would fly over, but they didn't bomb our base when I was there." For a while, a lone German plane flew over the base every night to bomb the runway; the men called its pilot Bedcheck Charlie, but he wasn't considered much of a threat. When they went into London, however, Dad and his friends saw buzz bombs— jet-propelled armaments that the Germans sent over the Channel in swarms. They made a buzzing noise until, at a predetermined time, the engine shut off and the bomb fell to earth.

How did all this affect Dad? On the base, the ground crews and the air crews lived in separate quarters, and some of the flyers referred to ground crews—especially the officers—as paddle feet or pencil pushers. These were not terms of endearment. And what was it like for the ground crew when a plane failed to return? Or, in Dad's case, did the plane crash at Ainsdale make these other questions irrelevant? Billy Suchocki told me that when Dad was in the army, he was popular, happy, and full of good humor. He was that way after the war, too, but I find it hard to believe that the crash didn't affect him or change him in some fundamental way.

And what was life like at the air base? One thing is clear: everyone complained about the food, especially the powdered eggs, which were served from enormous cast-iron vats. There was no butter, just orange marmalade. The men had plenty of meat, at least in theory, but most of it was Spam, or imitations of Spam, which was baked, breaded, or fried until the Americans were sick of it in any form. Once, on a visit to London, Dad and his friends went into a restaurant and ordered Welsh rarebit— which is often pronounced *rabbit*—in the hope of finally enjoying a good meal. They expected rabbit, and were deeply disappointed when the waitress brought them a concoction made mostly of melted cheese. Another disappointment for Dad, and for many other young Americans, was that the excellent English beer was always served warm. Dad gave up beer altogether, which for him was a sacrifice; during the war, he made do with scotch and soda. When he came home he switched back, because, as he put it, "I couldn't afford scotch on a beer budget."

Because the bombing missions over Germany were so dangerous and so stressful, about halfway through their tours, flight crews were given a week of rest and recuperation at various rest homes, sometimes known as flak shacks, that were operated by the Red Cross. Here the men could relax out of uniform and were free to ride horses or play golf or tennis. The food was good, too, with bacon and fresh eggs for breakfast and steak and ice cream on the dinner menu. The Palace Hotel in Southport was the largest of the Eighth Air Force's rest homes, and on the morning of October 25, 1944, a B-24 left Flixton to take some of the men for a well-deserved vacation on the other side of the country. Several others on board had completed their missions and were on their way home. There were a couple of other passengers as well. "They asked if anyone wanted to go," Billy Suchocki said. "Your dad and I went along for the ride."

The plane took off in mid-morning. Just before 1 P.M., the pilot, Donald Cheffer, circled the landing field at Birkdale and began his third and final approach. "Cheffer was told not to land," Lloyd Furthmyer, a survivor, remembered. "The visibility would have made any sane man not land. There was a field twenty miles away where the conditions were good, but he was blockheaded and determined to land."

Another survivor, named Bert Dice, recalled that he heard copilot Alva Tompkins shouting to Cheffer, "You're too low, you're too low!" Cheffer responded, "Shut up!" and banked sharply to the right—so sharply that the wing hit the ground and the plane flipped over. According to an eyewitness on the ground, "One of the wings went straight up in the air, and the next moment the plane was a mass of flames." Cheffer, Tompkins, and five others were killed instantly. Three more men died the next day.

The moment the plane went down, three railway men who

were working nearby ran to the wreckage and carried several of the passengers away from the crash site. One of them was Billy Suchocki. Another was Dad. Billy has never forgotten what he saw: "I can close my eyes any time of the day, and I still see your dad stumbling back toward that burning plane."

Dad remembers the first two approaches, but not the crash itself. The next thing he knew, he was waking up in the hospital with bad burns and a broken jaw. The nurses brought him steak, but he couldn't eat a thing because his jaw was wired. Later, during his long recuperation, he became friendly with a young nurse named Margaret, and when his condition improved, they went out for a walk together. When he came back, one of his hospital buddies told me with a wry smile, the rubber bands on his jaw were all broken. So I guess Big Russ really was a young man once.

THERE IS NO QUESTION that Cheffer took an unnecessary risk when he insisted on trying to land the plane in bad weather. They had taken off with eight hours of fuel on board, which was more than enough to return to Bungay if a safe landing at Ainsdale or another nearby field was impossible, so he was certainly prepared for that contingency.

It's tempting to focus on the pilot, but there were heroes in this story as well. Dad told me that the British doctors and nurses were extraordinarily kind and attentive, and I feel grateful, too, to Billy Suchocki and the railroad men who put themselves at risk to save several of the passengers. I don't know what went on in their minds, but they chose to love their brothers, and I'm thankful they did. Dad's father had started out as a train man, so a train man brought him into this world, and other train men, on another part of the planet, kept him alive in it.

Thanks to Ron Tompkins, and to some of the survivors of that accident, I have learned everything I could about that day, and I have relived that awful flight in my mind. When Billy Suchocki described what had happened, I closed my eyes and tried to imagine the roaring fireball of a crashed plane and the badly injured young man who was going to become my father staggering toward his death. Only because his army buddy and two total strangers stopped him, do I have the honor of having Big Russ as my dad.

THE PLANE CRASH took place about a month before Dad's twenty-first birthday. What was he thinking and feeling in that hospital bed? Was he angry at the pilot? (I am, but he probably wasn't.) Was he feeling sorry for himself? (I doubt that, too.) Did he blame himself for going along on that flight? (Possibly.) Did he wonder why he was spared when ten other men died? (That seems more likely, but I don't really know.) No matter what he was going through, it was an awful lot for a young man away from home to absorb, especially in a society where you didn't discuss your feelings. But he did say this: "I was thankful, because I knew my experience could have been a lot worse. Some of my friends suffered like hell." Didn't he realize that he, too, had suffered like hell? Even after that terrible accident he retained his innate optimism.

Dad's bravery and his stoicism are in such stark contrast to the scenes we see played out every day in newspapers and on television, where people can't wait to describe their pain and their agony in front of an audience. Dad wants no part of that. Despite everything he went through, he considers himself fortunate. After all, he came back from the war when many men did not. He spent the war thinking about terrifying scenarios, doing what he could to try to save the lives of men who were forced to bail out of a falling plane over enemy territory. He prepared parachutes for men in the worst of circumstances, but he never had to use one himself. Instead of feeling sorry for himself, Dad felt blessed and grateful that he was able to make a contribution.

It wasn't just Dad, of course; it was a whole generation that embarked on a mission they had never even imagined, much less prepared for. When duty called, they answered immediately. They performed bravely and well, and if they complained, they did so with humor. Learning about Dad's experience in the war has made me more aware of the many men, and women, too, who sacrificed and did their part to defeat the German and Japanese armies. They didn't talk about it; they just did it.

"When I look back on it now," Dad told me not long ago, "it was worth giving up three years of my life rather than be ruled by someone like Hitler." If that scenario sounds improbable half a century later, it's only because our side won the war. It's easy to forget that Germany and Japan were mighty adversaries, and that when World War II began, America was almost totally unprepared for combat. Had events occurred in a slightly different way, we would be living today in a vastly different world.

It wasn't until 1980, when I was thirty, that I really began to understand how Dad's generation had affected the course of history. I was working in Washington when I was offered a fellowship to visit Europe for five weeks. I wasn't sure I could spare the time, but my boss encouraged me and finally insisted that I go. I had never been overseas, and except for Dad during the war and my ancestors who were born there, nobody in my family had ever been to Europe. When I arrived in Germany, I decided to visit Dachau, the site of the notorious concentration camp, which is not far from Munich. As much as I had learned about World War II, and about the Holocaust, nothing prepared me for what I saw and felt at Dachau. The remnants of the camp were still there, including the barracks, the gas chambers, and the ovens where the bodies were burned.

Suddenly, another visitor, a short, older man, came running up to me. He threw himself at my knees, grabbed my ankles, and started sobbing. Then he stood up and started talking to me in Polish, of which I understood not a word, except for "American," over and over again. I nodded yes. Then a woman came over and began to translate. This man was a Jew who had been a prisoner at Dachau when it was liberated by the Americans. He had come back to visit for the first time in thirty-five years, and when he saw me, looking like an American, he was overcome with grief and gratitude. Over and over he kept saying, "Thank you, America. Thank you, America." He was crying, I was crying, and so were the other tourists who had gathered around us. He led me to a marker where one of the buildings had been, and he motioned for me to take his picture there.

It was hard to believe what had actually happened at Dachau, and being there did not make it any easier. But my encounter with this survivor, the embrace of this man who was liberated and saved from certain death, touched me to my core. I thought of Dad, and of all the other young Americans who went overseas in World War II to save the world from the tyrannical Nazi regime. When I returned to Munich, I went straight to the post office, and for the first time in my life, I placed an overseas call. I wanted to tell Dad what I had just experienced. And I wanted to thank him for going to war.

2.

South Buffalo

"People are people, and if they like you,
they'll give you the benefit of the doubt."

WHEN THE MEN OF BIG RUSS'S GENERATION who were fortunate enough to survive the war returned home, they embarked on a second mission—starting families of their own and working to provide for the comfort and education of their children. In doing so, they created a social phenomenon that was new in America: a thriving middle class, where people were able to own their own homes and give their children opportunities that they themselves could only dream of. This second effort lacked the drama of war, but it transformed our nation.

I grew up in South Buffalo, a warm and tightly knit neighborhood where most people were Irish Catholics and everyone seemed to know one another—and one another's relatives. (How many South Buffalonians does it take to change a lightbulb? I don't know, exactly, but my neighbor's cousin's girlfriend's priest knows a guy who will help you out.) If somebody's mom or dad wasn't out on the front porch on a summer evening, maybe they were sick, and a neighbor would bring over some soup, or even a meal. Big Russ had his own remedy. Gulp a hot toddy—whiskey, water, honey, and lemon—sleep for ten hours, and sweat it out. When our mother, Betty, had pneumonia, Mrs. Baryza brought over a broth with the horrible name of blood soup, from an old Polish recipe that was said to include the blood of a duck. We couldn't imagine eating such a thing, but it seemed to help Mom. On Easter Sunday, after church, Joan and Stanley Baryza would have us over for a traditional (and bloodless) Polish breakfast with delicious homemade bread and pastries.

If your family went away for a couple of days, you didn't have to ask your neighbors to keep an eye on your house; people looked out for one another as a matter of course. Although the houses on Woodside Avenue were crowded together and many had no driveway, neighbors got along remarkably well. Nobody locked their doors or worried about crime. The neighborhood was unusually stable: many of the families who lived in South Buffalo when I was growing up are still there today, often in the same house, a generation or two later.

When we weren't in school, and the weather was even close to nice, we played outside with the other kids on our block. If nobody was outside, all you had to do was show up on some-body's porch and sing out his name: "Oh Mike-y. Can Mikey come out and play?" There were always kids to play with. The Cammaranos had nine children, and Mr. and Mrs. Barnes had thirteen. The Geary family had five children, including Paul, who was a little older than I, and who once hit me in the head (by accident) with a lamp cord, which required a trip to the emergency room. His father, Huck Geary, a security guard at the Ford stamping plant in Woodlawn, had played baseball for the Buffalo Bisons in the International League before I was born and spent a couple of years with the Pittsburgh Pirates. I recently heard from Joanne Geary, Paul's sister, who told me that Paul had served in Vietnam, where he had been shot twice, that he never fully recovered, and died of hepatitis in 1999. He was awarded two Purple Hearts and at least two other medals, and when he returned to South Buffalo from Vietnam, he opened his house to young men in the neighborhood who were down on their luck.

THERE WERE FOUR KIDS IN OUR FAMILY: Betty Ann (who is known as B.A.), me, Kathleen, and Patricia, which made us one of the smaller households on the street. The neighborhood children were carefree and happy, although, of course, not every kid was good all the time. We didn't realize how well protected we were, or that a powerful but invisible neighborhood watch system was always in effect. If you misbehaved or did something dumb or dangerous, one of the other parents didn't hesitate to step in. If an adult reprimanded you, you paid attention. I can still hear Mrs. O'Mara say, "Come on, now, Timmy, you can't be doing that," as I tried to turn her clothesline into a tripwire. I can also remember Mr. Maloney confiscating my arsenal of water balloons. But to this day, I don't know which of the neighborhood snitches told my parents that I was the one who had taken a piece of yellow chalk and had written a four-letter word, beginning with S, in large print on the street, for which I paid a terrible penalty: I had my mouth washed out with soap.

IT WAS A WONDERFUL WAY TO GROW UP, full of innocence and fun. Of course we sometimes argued, and arguments had a way of turning into fights. When a kid on our block beat me up, Dad said, "You've got to draw the line here." He instructed my sister B.A. to push the bully over while I knelt behind him. Dad promised that if we fought him together, he would never bother us again—and he didn't. Parents in our neighborhood warned their children that if we didn't behave, we'd end up with coal in our Christmas stockings, and our local bad boy, Mickey Griffin, actually did. He picked on other kids, broke an occasional window, and once killed a worm by holding it under a magnifying glass on a sunny day. When they were teenagers, some of Mickey's friends built a wooden fort in one of the backyards, where they went to smoke cigarettes and sneak looks at *Playboy*, which was a pretty racy thing to do back then.

For a couple of years our days were filled with endless games of hide-and-seek and relievio—a version of capture the flag where players were continually being put into a makeshift jail in somebody's driveway, and then freed in a series of daring raids by their high-spirited teammates. One or two summers were marked by contests to see how long you could stay on a pogo stick without falling off. I would get flushed and dizzy trying to keep up with my older sister, which was a hopeless task because B.A. was the undisputed pogo stick champion of Woodside Avenue. Even when she was hit by a bicycle and her leg was in a cast, she insisted on climbing back on. I admired her bravado, but B.A. had gone too far. It was one of the few times I ever heard Mom raise her voice.

In 1958, when hula hoops came along, B.A. could keep hers going forever. As much as I tried, this was one toy I could never master. One of the great delights of my childhood was watching Dad trying to wrestle a hula hoop. He'd come home from work exhausted, only to find two or three hoops cluttering up the hallway. He'd try to fold them or stack them, but the hula hoops refused to cooperate. Ultimately, all he could do was throw them, which he did. "Get these damn things out of here!" he'd tell us. And then, mellowing, "What are they, anyway?" as we dissolved in laughter. One day Dad stunned us by trying to use a hula hoop, but it was an immediate mismatch. The score, after one round, was hula hoop 1, Dad 0, and that's how it stood. But you should have heard us laughing!

My generation was blessed with some other wonderful low-tech toys as well, including the Slinky, Etch-A-Sketch, and Silly Putty. Like most of the boys on our street, I collected baseball cards, which we bought at Ullenbruch's, the corner store that stocked the basic necessities of life: candy, cards, milk, and bread, pretty much in that order. Baseball cards were five for a nickel, and came with a thin slab of pink bubble gum, which was often stale and sometimes left a grainy residue on the nearest card. We carried our cards in our pockets and treated them roughly: we flipped them, shot them against schoolyard walls (the closest card to the wall won the others), and best of all, wedged them between the spokes in our bicycles to make what we told ourselves was the sound of a motorcycle, never for a moment imagining the preposterous possibility that a few of those cards would eventually be worth considerably more than the bikes they were enhancing.

There was an art to buying baseball cards, or so we believed. When the storekeeper reached for a pack, we asked if we could pick our own, which involved reaching deep into the box, down to where the good ones were hiding. (Every kid knew there was a system, and we all believed that it was only a matter of time before one of us figured it out.) Before leaving the store I'd rip the pack open to see if I had picked up any good ones, which in Buffalo meant anyone who played for the Yankees, plus a handful of stars from other teams. Mickey Mantle was the card of choice, but I loved Yogi Berra, and the word on the street was that Timmy Russert might let you have a Willie Mays, a Hank Aaron, or even a Mantle if you dangled a Yogi in his direction. After glancing at the cards, I'd take out the gum and stick it in my pocket, where it would eventually melt and turn my pockets pink. Sometimes I'd go over to Liberty Shoe Store to pick up another shoe box, which were perfect for storing cards. I arranged mine by team, but kept a few favorites in a plastic case under my bed.

It almost goes without saying that when I was in college, my mother threw out my entire collection without bothering to check with me. If 99 percent of American mothers hadn't done that, older baseball cards would be worthless today. But Dan Orth, my wife's brother, was fortunate enough to keep his cards, and Dan had a really good collection. In 1998, when we were about to trade in our Toyota station wagon, Dan said he'd love to buy it. "I don't want any money," I told him, "but if you're willing to part with your baseball cards, we can probably make a deal." Dan ended up with a fine old Camry, and I once again have a baseball card collection. In fact, Dan's cards were so good that I had to kick in some money as well.

Like so many boys, I intended to become a professional athlete, and spent long hours training for my future job. We had a basketball hoop attached to our garage, but Mom didn't want us to trample on her peonies, and P. J. Griffin's driveway, two doors away, had more room. We played half-court games for hours, two on two, or three on three, with a lot of elbows thrown and many bloody noses. When we got tired of running we'd play Pig, a shorter version of Horse, where you had to make the same shot the other guy had made, or Around the World, where you kept shooting at the basket from farther and farther away until you missed, at which point the next guy started shooting. The interesting element here was that if you missed your shot, you had the option of trying it again. But there was a catch: if you missed the second one, you had to go back to the beginning and start over. We stayed out on the court as late as our mothers would let us, while our sisters were busy with hopscotch, roller skating, and jump rope.

We climbed trees and sometimes jumped garages, leaping from one to another when our parents weren't watching. In the winter, when the water froze in the makeshift skating rink in the Gearys' backyard, we'd build goals out of snow and play hockey with our boots on. In the fall we played touch football on the street or tackle in the park. Baseball required a playing field, and sometimes we'd walk over to one of the diamonds in nearby Cazenovia Park. Often, though, we settled for games of Home

Run Derby on the street or in somebody's backyard, using tennis balls or a whiffle ball. We came up with elaborate rules as to what, exactly, constituted a home run, and whether hitting the roof of Paul Montgomery's house should count as a grand slam. We probably spent as much time arguing as we did playing.

Occasionally we were dumb enough to play on the street with a real baseball. When I broke a window in Mr. Riemen's garage, I ran home and told Mom, who said I should tell Dad. Dad said, "Look, the first thing you have to do is go over there and tell him you did it. You'll also have to pay for it out of your own money." I wasn't happy about that last part, but it was still preferable to admitting the truth to Mr. Riemen. But I knew Dad was right, and with some trepidation, because Mr. Riemen was not one of our warm and fuzzy neighbors, I knocked on his door and confessed. He hadn't noticed it yet, and he came out with me to have a look.

"What happens now?" he asked.

"We'll get it fixed and I'll pay for it out of my paper route earnings," I said.

"And when will that be?"

"As soon as I can, sir." Shortly after I left his house, I went back and knocked again.

"What is it now?"

"Mr. Riemen, can I have my ball back?"

"Only after you fix the window." This was a man who knew how to close a deal.

That afternoon, Dad bought a pane of glass and fixed the window while I watched. Then he sent me home to get a broom and a dust pan. When we had cleaned up all the broken glass,

Dad told me to bring him a shoe box. "Never put glass in a paper bag," he said, "because the guys could cut themselves." ("The guys," of course, were garbagemen, and Dad had undoubtedly learned this the hard way from his job on the garbage truck.) I watched as he carefully put the pieces of broken glass into the cardboard box, covered the glass with crumpled newspaper, and then taped the lid shut with masking tape. I learned how to dispose of broken glass, but the real lesson I learned that day was about accountability. If you break somebody's window, it's not enough to fix it. You have to be man enough to go to that person and tell him, to his face, what you have done.

Our neighborhood was filled with men like Dad who came from modest backgrounds, went to high school, though they didn't necessarily graduate, went off to war in 1942 or '43, came home again, got married, and found jobs as policemen, firemen, or steelworkers. In what little free time they had, they mostly stayed inside or sat on the porch. But I still remember the day our neighbor Chuck Eberhardt told us he had seen a rat in the garbage behind his house. He put out a couple of traps, but they failed to catch the culprit, and the idea of calling in an exterminator was unthinkable in our self-sufficient neighborhood. Chuck came out one evening, bare-chested, holding a rifle with a scope. "I'm gonna get that bastard," he announced to all of us. Dad came out, too, with a cigar in his mouth. "Everybody in front," he ordered. Before Chuck got down to business, Dad made sure that all the kids on our block were present and accounted for.

Next to the garbage, Chuck had put out a piece of cheese the size of a hubcap, big enough to feed every rat in Erie County. He took his rifle, went up to the attic, and opened the window. There was a long silence, followed by two loud shots. "Stay here," Dad commanded, as he walked across Chuck's lawn and down the driveway. "He got him!" Dad called excitedly. Soon Chuck came out with his rifle, triumphantly holding the tail of a rat that looked to be the size of a small rabbit. The neighbor-hood exploded with joy, as if a powerful enemy had been brought to its knees. Dad took a cigar from his shirt pocket and handed it to the rifleman. "Nice shot, Chuck," he said. It was a great childhood moment, and an impressive demonstration of the power of our fathers.

Although we loved our fathers, there was a distance between us and a recognition that they inhabited a very different universe than we did. It was not just that they were usually working, although that was part of it. It was that our fathers and mothers were adults, and we were kids, during a time when grown-ups and children lived in separate worlds and were exposed to very different things. (A small example: in the 1950s we never saw a bad word in print or heard an off-color remark on the radio or on television.) Nobody I knew ever called grown-ups, even close family friends, by their first names, and the grown-ups never suggested that we should. To this day, when I go back to Buffalo and I run into one of our old neighbors, I still address them as "Mr. Griffin" or "Mrs. Geary."

Shaking hands with adults was very important, at least for boys, and it was something I practiced with Dad until it became second nature. Dad insisted on a firm handshake, and he worked with me until I developed one. "When you meet somebody," he would say, "you want to make them feel that you're proud and happy to know them. So don't put a wet fish in their hand. Give that hand a good shake, snap your wrist, and look them in the eye. People are people, and if they like you, they'll give you the benefit of the doubt. Treat them the way you'd like to be treated."

A good handshake seems so basic, but it's a useful lesson to learn and an easy one to overlook because it sounds so obvious. But a good handshake doesn't always come naturally, and it's one of those skills that kids don't necessarily master unless their parents make a point of teaching it. These things were so ingrained in me that I passed them along to my son, Luke, almost without thinking. When he was four or five, I heard myself echoing Dad's words as we practiced what to do when he met an adult for the first time—or the twentieth. I'd say, "Come here, buddy, and let's shake hands," and I undoubtedly used the phrase "wet fish" as part of the lesson. Dad also taught me to say "sir" and "ma'am" to adults, and I made sure Luke learned that, too. It's all about making a good impression and showing respect to other people.

When Luke was a junior in high school and we went to visit a few colleges, one of the deans took me aside and said, "That is one impressive young man you have there." I was happy to hear this, of course, and I silently hoped he would elaborate, which he did. "Your boy shook my hand," the dean continued. "He looked me in the eye and engaged me in conversation." That's all it took! And from the way the dean said it, I could tell this wasn't something he saw every day. I was proud of Luke, but even more, I was grateful to Dad.

Both parents impressed upon us the importance of good

manners. If, at the dinner table, you said, "Pass the potatoes," Mom or Dad would say, "Excuse me?" until you added the magic word. If somebody gave you a gift or did you a favor, you were expected to thank them in writing. Later on, when I worked for Sen. Daniel Patrick Moynihan, I noticed that he always took the trouble to send a note of thanks to the volunteers who drove him around and the police officers who escorted him to an event. It's a basic rule of politics, and of life, too: people like to be asked, and they especially like to be thanked.

FOR MY SISTERS AND ME, and all of our friends, the high-light of the summer was our annual trip to the amusement park at Crystal Beach, Ontario, which was just over the Peace Bridge that linked the United States and Canada. Niagara Falls was even closer, but for us, at least, it wasn't much of a draw. It was certainly something to see, but once we had seen it, even from the Canadian side, which was a lot nicer, we felt no great desire to return. Oscar Wilde once said, more or less, that Niagara Falls would be far more impressive if the water flowed the other way. "Every American bride is taken there," he noted, "and the sight must be one of the earliest, if not the keenest, disappoint-ments of American married life." We were too young to know what he meant, but we agreed with the general sentiment: Niagara Falls was strictly for visitors and tourists. As kids, one of our favorite jokes was this little dialogue:

"But Mom, I don't want to see Niagara Falls."

"Shut up and get back in the barrel."

Crystal Beach, however, was one of the *real* wonders of this world. It was our Coney Island. In late June, when school let out, you would take your report card to Loblaws, the local supermarket, where they'd give you a certain number of free ride tickets for every A. (One of the nice things about Crystal Beach was that there was no general admission fee. You paid only for the rides you went on.) A boat called *The Canadiana* sailed to Crystal Beach from Buffalo every day, but we always drove.

The amusement park included the Wild Mouse, a fun house, a hall of mirrors, and various other attractions, including my own favorite, the bumper cars. But the real point of going to Crystal Beach was to ride the Comet, a classic, wooden, death-defying roller coaster where a boy got to show what he was made of. The Wild Mouse was scary, no question about it, and because its cars had no wheels in front, it gave you the sensation of going off the track. At certain moments on the Wild Mouse, you felt as if you were hanging over thin air, with nothing between you and the ground. But there was something transcendent about the Comet. Riding it was like staring death in the face, and surviving. In fact, people are still riding it today. When the amusement park at Crystal Beach closed in 1989, the Comet was taken apart and reassembled five years later in Lake George, New York.

On my very first ride on the Comet, I sat next to Dad. My hands and my jaws were tightly clenched, but I was able to sneak a look at him, and I thought I detected fear. When it was over he clapped me on the back and said, "So?"

"That was great."

"Nothing like the Cyclone."

As impressive and intimidating as the Comet was, our parents and other adults used to talk reverentially about its legendary predecessor, the Cyclone, which everybody agreed had been even more exciting and much more frightening, but which closed down in 1946, before my friends and I were born. We were pleased to know, however, that parts of the Cyclone had been used to make the Comet. In 1927, on the Cyclone's first day of operation, a crowd estimated at seventy-five thousand broke down a fence just to get a look at it. The Cyclone, which was said to be the most terrifying roller coaster ride in the Western world, began with a steep drop that left riders convinced that they were about to plunge into Lake Erie. In a brilliant piece of marketing, a uniformed nurse was on duty at all times, ostensibly to treat riders who passed out—and some did. I can't vouch for this story, but Grandpa Russert told me that when he first took Grandma to Crystal Beach, he told her the Cyclone was a sightseeing ride, and that "when you get to the top, you're supposed to stand." According to Grandpa, that ride almost ended their courtship, which, I realized later, would have had some rather serious implications for me.

The beach itself, which was next to the amusement park, was beautiful and clean, with pure white sand. You could walk out into the water forever and still not be in over your head. (For the most part, Canadian beaches were nicer and cleaner than their counterparts on our side of the border.) Dad's brother, Uncle Fran, used to rent a cottage at Crystal Beach, and we always drove over to visit him and his family. Nutritional rules were suspended at Crystal Beach, and no visit was complete without a cinnamon sucker, an enormous lollipop that seemed to exist only there. We gorged ourselves on french fries, which we ate Canadian-style, with vinegar, and washed them down with loganberry, a longtime Buffalo favorite juice drink.

As long as we were in Canada, Dad used the occasion to buy firecrackers, which were not available in New York State. In Ontario, by contrast, they seemed to be sold on every street corner. When we drove back from Crystal Beach, I'd be sitting on boxes of smuggled fireworks, but during all that time it never occurred to me that we were breaking the law.

The Fourth of July was a big event on our block, as Dad put on a show with his Canadian contraband. "Everybody back," he'd shout, before lighting the various fireworks with his cigar. The show included ladyfingers (tiny firecrackers that went off in a series and sounded like a machine gun); Roman candles, which shot colored balls into the air; pinwheels, which Dad nailed to a tree before lighting; and of course, sparklers, which were safe enough to hold in your hand. Today, I'm sure, there are TV commercials with more dazzle than Dad's fireworks, but a little flash went a long way in the 1950s, and our neighbors would sit on their porches, drink beer, and applaud.

DAD'S HOME AWAY FROM HOME was the American Legion Post, which was so central to our lives that it was almost like a second church. Dad was a commander at the Legion in 1960–61, and he'd represent Post 721 at various meetings. The commander runs the post and makes sure the bills are paid, and one of his perks was free bar privileges. When Dad was commander, I was proud for two reasons: First, he was elected the same year as President Kennedy. Second, the sign near the bar read, Timothy

J. Russert, Commander. It was the first time I had ever seen my name on a sign.

On Memorial Day at the Legion, the veterans would line up outside and shoot their rifles into the air, and we would scurry around and pick up the empty shells. Fathers and their children would get into their station wagons and drive to Holy Cross Cemetery, where we'd visit graves of veterans going all the way back to the War of 1812. We brought along hundreds of tiny American flags, and we would fan out all over the cemetery, planting flags in the ground next to the headstones. A large tent was erected, and a memorial Mass was said. The visit to the cemetery was a major and meaningful event in our lives, and it made a real impression on me when we honored these men, many of whom had made the ultimate sacrifice for their country before they were able to be fathers. I was always aware that if events had happened just a little differently, Dad would have been lying in one of those graves instead of visiting them with me.

Mostly, though, we went to the Legion for happy occasions, such as Christmas parties, family picnics, and corned beef and cabbage dinners after the parade on St. Patrick's Day. We often went on Sunday afternoons as well. Dad had a lot of friends at the Legion, which was the focal point of his social life, and he enjoyed chatting with his pals over a couple of beers. The Legion was fun for kids, too. The men were always nice to us, and they made a point of watching their language when we were around. We'd have popcorn and a soft drink, and there was an enormous pretzel jar at the bar that you could reach into and help yourself. There was also a coin-operated pool table, and somebody would always flip us a quarter so we could play a game or two.

Today, when I visit the Legion with Dad, memories of my childhood come rushing back. The place has a timeless feel, and the last time I checked, in the spring of 2003, along with the Stones, Bette Midler, Genesis, and the artist formerly known as Prince, the jukebox at Legion Post 721 offered up songs by Dean Martin, Frank Sinatra, Judy Garland, Bing Crosby, the Mills Brothers, and believe it or not, Al Jolson. There's a sign on the wall that looks like it's been there forever: "What a club this would be if every member would try to do only half of what they expect other members to do."

The men at the Legion came from all walks of life: Bart Danahy was a lawyer, Matthew Burke was our family doctor, Charlie McMahon was an undertaker, and Pat Griffin, who lived on our street, was a fireman. There were two men in particular whom we always saw there, who were especially kind to children. They were both bachelors who lived at home with their parents, which wasn't all that unusual in South Buffalo. Gene Hughes had a big, Jay Leno–ish jaw and worked at Merchants Mutual Insurance. At Legion parties, he always distributed Howdy Doody ice cream bars from a big white freezer. Whenever we saw him, Dad would say, "It's Mr. Hughes," and I would greet him with, "Hi, Howdy Doody."

Dad: "It's *Mister*."

Me: "Sorry. Hi, Mister Howdy Doody."

Dad: "No, Mr. *Hughes*."

Whereupon Mr. Hughes would laugh and say, "Howdy Doody's just fine."

Gene Hughes, who had been a military policeman in Alaska, was the third of five brothers who had all served in World War II at the same time. Men at the Legion knew this and respected it, and they told us how there came to be a law that prevented a group of brothers from serving in the same unit. It was passed after the well-known tragedy of the Sullivans, five brothers from Iowa who had enlisted in the Navy after their friend was killed at Pearl Harbor. When the Sullivan brothers insisted on serving together, they were assigned to the USS *Juneau*. In early 1943, when the ship was lost at sea, a black sedan pulled up at the Sullivans' house in Waterloo, Iowa, and three uniformed men got out. This could only mean bad news.

"Which one?" asked the boys' father.

"I'm sorry," said the commander. "All five."

When I was growing up in the 1950s, World War II was still very much in people's consciousness. That was especially true at the Legion, where you had the impression from conversations about the war that it had ended just a couple of months ago.

The other great character at the Legion was John Collins, a man so colorful he had two different nicknames. He was the oldest of eight children, and when he was young, a distant relative came to visit the family. Rather than learn all the children's names, the visitor gave the boys new ones: Jack became Twee, Dennis was Twy, Francis was Twoo, Vince was Twiddle-Dee, and John was known as Twum.

At the Legion, however, Twum Collins, whose face was the color of a bright and painful sunburn, was known as Shinyface. Mr. Collins always claimed that his face looked that way because he scrubbed it so hard, but everybody assumed it was the booze, and he didn't deny it. "Tim," he would tell my dad, "if you have a little too much to drink some night, I've found that half a pint of ice cream the next morning is the best cure for the hot coppers." He was obviously speaking from experience, but sometimes the cure is as bad as the disease. Shinyface died from heart disease and diabetes at the age of fifty-two.

Shinyface Collins was a memorable man, but not because of his name. Colorful nicknames abounded in South Buffalo, and included such monikers as Fuzzy Malloy, Googoo Mahoney, Diapers Riordan, Weepers Kavanaugh, Rubbernose Boland, Ice O'Grady, Pig Iron Sullivan, Spongy Quinn, Bow Wow Flanigan, Finky Conners, Big Eye O'Brien, Pork Chops Ring, Weiners Conners, Hippo McGrath, Cherrynose Kurowski, Gasman Furlong, Snowcrop Smeeding, Potatoes McGowan, Dirtyshirt McGee, Bunny Ears Slattery, and brothers Duck and Drake Downey, Hydrant Head and Bug Head Smith and Larson and Arson Finnegan.

Like his father before him, Shinyface Collins worked on the New York Central Railroad, where he was a baggage clerk. He was a big, friendly man who lived with his parents and claimed he never got married because, out of Christian charity, "I could never condemn a person I loved to a life of horror as my wife." Every December he dressed up as Santa Claus and gave out candy canes while we sat on his lap and told him what we wanted for Christmas. When I was little, I had no idea it was him, but by the age of nine or ten I began to notice that Santa's laugh sounded very familiar. He also smelled of beer, but that didn't exactly set him apart at the Legion. Shinyface's sister,

Patsy Collins, was a Religious Sister of Mercy nun who later became principal of Holy Family School. A few years ago, she invited me back to reminisce about my time there, and when I walked in I was greeted by a big blowup of five-year-old Timmy Russert in kindergarten, and all my old report cards.

Shinyface was best known for his dramatic and memorable recitation of the classic poem, "Casey at the Bat." He knew it by heart, all thirteen stanzas, and when somebody called out, "Shiny, do Casey!" you knew you were in for a treat. He'd grab a broom or a mop, whatever was handy, and he'd hold it like a bat. As the poem went on, you found yourself being swept up in the story:

> Then, while the writhing pitcher ground the ball into his hip,
> Defiance flashed in Casey's eye, a sneer curled Casey's lip.

Shinyface would *become* that pitcher, staring in at Mighty Casey. He'd go into his windup with a big leg kick, and when he threw that imaginary ball, you could almost see it speeding toward the batter. The first pitch was a strike. So was the second one, although the fans disagreed:

> "Fraud!" cried the maddened thousands, and the echo answered, "Fraud!"

When Shinyface called out that first "Fraud!" which echoed through the room like a rifle shot, some of the men slumped at the bar would be jolted out of their seats. No matter how many times you had heard it before, the volume of that word still startled you. And although you already knew how the story would end, Shinyface would draw you in all over again when he began the last stanza. His voice would slow down a little, but there was some hope remaining as he continued,

> *And somewhere men are laughing, and somewhere hearts are light.*
> *But there is no joy in Mudville—mighty Casey has struck out.*

And then came the crusher,

> *Oh, somewhere in this favored land the sun is shining bright.*
> *The band is playing somewhere, and somewhere children shout.*

We often asked Shinyface to recite the poem, and would have begged him, if necessary, but he didn't need much persuading. It was a great childhood moment, but our fathers seemed to enjoy it even more than we did. Maybe that was because these veterans had all known disappointment and loss, and Casey's story rang true to them. Or maybe it was because, as sports fans in Buffalo, they had learned not to expect happy endings. These men were not lovers of poetry, but this poem obviously touched them. Part of it, of course, was the brilliant recitation by one of their pals. Another part may have been, as Big Russ once put it, "it gets better by the glass."

3.

Respect

"If you embarrass yourself, you embarrass all of us."

I CAN'T EXPLAIN HOW IT HAPPENED, exactly, but our parents had certain expectations of us, and we met them—most of the time, anyway—without question or complaint. After supper, nobody had to remind us to do our homework; it was part of our daily routine and we just did it. Mostly it was book work, with plenty of math problems and other exercises, and a fair amount of memorizing, especially of poems.

We didn't have as much homework as kids do now, and I certainly don't recall having to construct dioramas or other projects that require adult intervention, a visit to a lumber yard, or a degree in mechanical engineering. This may sound hard to believe, but when my sisters and I were in school, homework was something that children did all by themselves.

We did ours around the kitchen table, not only because we liked being near Mom, but also because there was no room for desks in our bedrooms. My three sisters shared a room. As the only boy in the family, I was one of the few kids in our neighborhood with a room of his own. It was small, but it was all mine. We'd start our homework before Dad left for his night job, and sat there obediently like good little students. We could smell what Mom was baking, and we knew that when we finished our work, we were entitled to a piece of cake or pie, or, on a really good day, a brownie with ice cream. Our goal was to trade our pencil for a fork.

There was plenty of competition in school, and peer pressure to do well. The honor roll was posted for everyone to see. But if you received good grades, and I generally did, you were careful not to brag about it. "Don't get too big for your britches," Dad would say, and "Don't get a swelled head." Mom would remind us that "pride goeth before a fall." Doing well in school was expected, and was not seen as a special achievement. It was part of a broader understanding that if you worked hard and played by the rules, things would generally work out. Self-esteem wasn't something you started out with; it was a feeling that you earned through hard work.

Although Mom was much more involved in our school lives than Dad, when we received our report cards, both parents would sign them. It's a small thing, but I noticed it, and I was aware that most of my friends had only one parent sign. My sisters and I did our best to succeed in school, and at least part of our motivation was the desire not to disappoint Mom and Dad. We knew how hard they worked—Dad with his two jobs, and Mom, who was always helping us or making improvements to our home. In our own way, we wanted to measure up to the standard they set.

When our homework was done, we were free to read, play, or watch TV. One of my early favorites was *Howdy Doody*, which actually started in Buffalo, and included Clarabell (played by Bob Keeshan, who later became Captain Kangaroo), Princess Summerfall Winterspring, and the inimitable Phineas T. Bluster. At four and a half, if I remember correctly, I watched the first episodes of *Davy Crockett*, which were shown on a new program called *The Wonderful World of Disney*. I had a Davy Crockett coonskin cap, a Davy Crockett fringed jacket, a toy musket, and a Davy Crockett record that I played on a wind-up record player ("Born on a mountaintop in Tennessee..."). Davy Crockett's motto was, "Be sure you're right, then go ahead," which still strikes me as pretty good advice. It's funny how things come back to you. Not too long ago I received a magnum of wine from the Fess Parker Winery with a tiny coonskin cap on top, and a note from Parker, the actor who played Davy Crockett and a regular *Meet the Press* viewer, reminding me of Crockett's motto—as if I could possibly forget it.

My sisters and I watched the *Mickey Mouse Club* while wearing our Mouseketeer ears, and I would perform the theme song for them, complete with Donald Duck's voice. Another favorite was *Leave It to Beaver*, which was especially meaningful to me because when the show began, Beaver and I were both seven years old. Beaver's brother, Wally, had a best friend named Eddie Haskell, a sycophant who would say obnoxious things like, "A most gracious good afternoon, Mrs. Cleaver. I was just giving some advice to young Theodore." My sisters and I were taught to be polite, but we understood that there was such a thing as going too far. When our parents met one of our friends for the first time, and the kid was excessively polite, we would mutter, "Don't Eddie Haskell me."

When we watched *Lassie* and *Rin Tin Tin*, I was amazed by these heroic dogs, who were such a contrast to our own Mugsy, a boxer who was so big that I used to put on my cowboy hat and ride him. We finally had to get rid of Mugsy, not because he didn't like people, but because he liked them too much. When the doorbell rang, he'd start running from the kitchen, timing his leap so that by the time you walked in the door, he would literally knock you over.

I loved watching *Perry Mason* with Dad, and I think we saw just about every episode. Big Russ had an uncanny ability to figure out who did it, and I was so impressed with Perry Mason's mental abilities that I wanted to be a defense attorney when I grew up. Once, when Dad and I were watching the Harlem Globetrotters on television, Dad said, "The Washington Generals are like Hamilton Burger. They never get to win." Hamilton Burger was the prosecutor on *Perry Mason*, and although I knew it instinctively, this was the first time I realized that both shows involved a setup. Today, in the news business, people still talk about a "Perry Mason moment"—an unexpected question whose answer reveals a great deal.

We watched *Gunsmoke*, which held a special appeal because the red-haired Amanda Blake, who played Miss Kitty, had gone to the same high school as Dad. Every time she came on, Dad would say, "You know where she went to school?" And we'd all answer in chorus, "South Park!" Another graduate of South Park was the Milwaukee Braves' pitcher, Warren Spahn, who won more games than any other left-handed pitcher in history. Mom and B.A.

were huge fans of *I Love Lucy*, and whenever Lucy came on, Dad would call, "Where's she from?" And the Russert chorus would answer, "Jamestown!" It wasn't Buffalo, but it was close enough.

I have a dim memory of sitting with my parents and watching a Sunday morning show called *Meet the Press*. I remember Nixon being interviewed, and Kennedy, and even Fidel Castro. It would be nice to think that as a young child I sat on Dad's lap, watching *Meet the Press* and thinking, *Someday I'd like to have that job*. A defense lawyer? Definitely. A fighter at the Alamo? Certainly. A great baseball player? By all means. The host of *Meet the Press*? It never occurred to me.

Everything, including television, had its time and place. Then came bath time, after which we went to bed on time with no arguments. When Dad was home we kissed him and Mom good night, and at least one of them would remind us to say our prayers. That was the final requirement of the day, and kneeling was optional. When we were very young, Mom would say it for us: "Now I lay me down to sleep, I pray the Lord my soul to keep."

Mornings in our house were just as orderly as evenings. We never slept late on weekends, not even as teenagers. It had never been an option, so we didn't miss it. Maybe it's learned behavior, but I've never had a problem waking up early, and I'm fortunate enough to be able to get my brain in gear without caffeine. When I was a boy, all Mom had to do was go to the bottom of the stairs and whisper my name, and I'd be up and ready to go. Dad was a little less subtle: he'd flip the lights on and off, giving me a low-tech light show while saying, "Come on, let's go."

On Sunday mornings we got up for church, and on Saturday

I had chores, such as helping Dad wash the car, weed the lawn and, all too often, shovel the snow with his old, heavy coal shovel. Dad was a stickler about doing things right, and he resealed the driveway every two or three years. If I didn't shovel it completely, the remaining snow might turn to ice and damage the asphalt. Shoveling all that snow could take hours. Eddie Glinski, a big Polish steelworker who lived across the street, came over one time to show Dad a bright red homemade snowblowing contraption—snow *pushing* would be more accurate—that made a great deal of noise with all of its cranking and spitting, and even moved a little snow. "Tim!" he shouted over the noise of the motor. "You've got to get yourself a snowblower!"

Dad put his arm around me and said, "Eddie, I've got the best snowblower right here." I wasn't sure whether to be proud or embarrassed. In any case, Dad wasn't a big fan of household gadgets or shortcuts; he believed in doing things the old-fashioned way. To get rid of weeds, for example, you got down on your hands and knees and yanked them out. He was the last person on the block to have a rotary dial phone.

Dad knew the value of money, and he did his best to teach it to his children. When one of us asked for a quarter or two, he didn't just hand it over. "The car windows are dirty," he might say, and you went outside with old newspapers and vinegar. "And no streaks!"

Even today, my sisters claim that I tried to pawn off some of my chores on them, but I'm sure I never did anything like that. From time to time, though, I tried to talk my way out of a task, which was always a losing proposition. "You're spending more time coming up with excuses than it would take to finish the job," Dad would say, and although that wasn't really true, he had a way of making it *sound* true. "If you had started doing it when I asked you, you'd be finished by now."

I don't want to give the wrong impression, however. Although we had chores to do and lived in a disciplined environment, we also had far more free time than kids do today. We spent hours playing pickup games on the street or at the park, and nobody arranged playdates. If you wanted to play, you just went outside. There were always kids around.

Dad was a peaceful man, but there were limits to his patience. He never went looking for trouble, but when trouble showed up, he responded. Once, when he was sitting on the porch and a young driver roared down the street in his hot rod, Dad ran out after him, yelling, "Slow down, you bastard!" He was concerned about the safety of neighborhood children, and when the driver returned for a victory lap, Dad went to get his legal pad. The next time he heard that car zooming down our street, he managed to get the first two letters of the license plate. "Come out here," he called to me. "You've got better eyes than I do." It took him a day or two to get all the digits, but as soon as he did, he called the police to complain about the driver. Some people would have left it at that, but Dad believed in finishing what he started. He called again a couple of days later to find out what, if anything, the police had done about the hot rodder. "We caught him speeding," the officer told him. Dad was pleased. He got his man.

He loved me, of course, but every once in a while I did or said something that made him angry. Sometimes, when I didn't do my chores or misbehaved in some other way, he would issue what I later learned was the standard South Buffalo threat: "You'd better watch it," he'd say, "or you're going to Father Baker's."

Father Baker, who died in 1936 and is now being considered for sainthood, had long been one of Buffalo's most prominent and beloved citizens. More than half a century after his death, people still speak about him with admiration and even reverence. A veteran of the Civil War, Henry Nelson Baker became a priest in 1876, and spent the next sixty years setting up and operating a huge charitable network that eventually included an orphanage, a grammar school, an industrial high school, an infants' home, a home for unwed mothers, and a maternity hospital. When he died, the *Buffalo Times* estimated that Father Baker had provided fifty *million* meals to the poor. The paper also called him the city's most influential man of the twentieth century.

Sometimes our family drove to Father Baker's church, Our Lady of Victory Basilica, in nearby Lackawanna. We didn't worship there regularly, but it was exciting to go to the basilica for Mass. On special days we'd also visit the Buffalo and Erie County Botanical Gardens across the street, with its beautiful flowers and plants. (The building that houses tropical plants had to be rebuilt two or three times because of acid rain from the nearby Bethlehem Steel plant.) Then we'd go to a restaurant for lunch, which wasn't something we normally did. Lunch always ended the same way: Big Russ would declare, "Good meal," and would request the check by asking the waitress, "What's the damage?"

Our Lady of Victory Basilica is enormous, with a soaring copper-topped dome and twin bell towers that are visible for miles. The interior is breathtaking, with close to two hundred stained-glass windows and something like two thousand pictures of angels. (Father Baker decided to place an angel in every possible sight line.) I didn't see a bigger church until high school, when, on my first trip to New York City, I visited St. Patrick's Cathedral. But the grandeur of the basilica did not obscure Father Baker's legacy, that the primary mission of the priest was to care for the poor, the orphan, the unwed mother, and others in need. His church was the physical symbol of a great man with an enormous heart.

When Dad threatened to take me to Father Baker's, he was referring to the orphanage, which was still operating when I was growing up. Every year, on our way to the annual Christmas party at the Legion, a number of families, including ours, would stop at Father Baker's to pick up one or two of the kids who lived there, who would join us for the games and the presents. On two or three occasions, the cutest little boy named Mike came with us, and after the 1959 Christmas party, when it was time to drive Mike back to the orphanage, I begged my parents to adopt him so I could finally have a brother. I don't know about Dad, but Mom told me later that she actually considered it. If she hadn't been pregnant at the time with my youngest sister, Trish, it might have happened. I still think about little Mike, and I wonder what became of him.

Once, when I didn't clean up my room after repeated warnings, and Dad tripped over one of my toys and took a hard fall, he said, "That's it. You're going to Father Baker's." He put me in the back of the station wagon and started driving down Woodside Avenue. I was terrified, and I banged on the window. "Please, I promise, I'll do whatever you want!" Dad soon pulled

over and said, "Listen, you know I love you, but you've got to listen to your mom and to me." After all these years, it's still one of
the most vivid memories of my childhood.

Of course I was too young to realize that Dad had no intention of actually taking me to Father Baker's. Nor did I know
that most of my friends had heard the very same threat. Mom
told me later that when she was a kid, growing up on a farm outside of Buffalo, *her* dad, in a fit of anger, once said to her mother,
"Get her clothes packed. We're taking her to Father Baker's."

Mom's dad, who of course never acted on his warning, was a
great character. For eighteen years, Grandpa Seeley owned a
tavern in South Buffalo called Seeley's Grill, where he taught me
to draw a draft beer with a perfect collar when I was three. He
was a showman who could rotate his wrist in a complete circle
while holding a full glass without spilling a drop, and he could
kick out a lightbulb in the ceiling from a standing position.
Although neither event has yet made it into the Olympics,
Grandpa Seeley took great pride in his unusual talents. He lived
to be eighty-two, and family lore has it that he never went to a
doctor or a dentist.

ON WEEKDAY MORNINGS when we came downstairs for
breakfast, the first voice we'd hear would be that of Clint
Buehlman, who had the early shift on WBEN, 930 on the AM
radio dial. Buehlman, who liked to refer to himself as "yours
truly, Buehly," and "your AM emcee, C.B.," was the undisputed
king of Buffalo broadcasters. He worked at the same station
from 1943 until 1977, and before that, he spent twelve years at

WGR. Mom and Dad had known Clint Buehlman's voice much longer than they had known each other, and they trusted him completely. We loved it when Clint announced the outdoor temperature "according to Arthur," whose full name, he sometimes reminded his listeners, was Arthur Mometer. A rainy day, to Clint Buehlman, was a "crash boomer" or a "gully washer." But Clint's real role in our lives was to give us the most important news bulletins in a child's life: the announcement of school closing during snowstorms. Because South Buffalo sat right on Lake Erie, our neighborhood was even more vulnerable to snow than the rest of the city. It didn't happen often, but the words we longed to hear were, "All Diocese of Buffalo Catholic schools are closed," or its equally satisfying variant, "The following parish schools are closed today: St. Teresa's, closed. St. Thomas Aquinas, closed. Holy Family, closed." The list went on, but as soon as Holy Family was mentioned, we were dancing with joy.

Radio ruled. We had a television, of course, but nobody in the 1950s, or at least nobody we knew, had a TV in the kitchen or watched in the morning. Our companion was radio, and I still remember some of the advertising jingles:

Shop and save at Sattler's
Nine-nine-eight Broadway... In Buffa-a-lo-o.

Or,

One little, two little, three little Indians,
Let's relax with the Iroquois Indians.

Iroquois was a beer, and Buffalo was a great beer town. Kids drank soda, but we never called it soda, only "pop." My sisters and I liked a citrus-flavored brand called Squirt, which was a little like Fresca, only better. Every time the Squirt commercial played on television and they showed the Squirt mascot, a little blond boy with rosy cheeks and an engaging smile, Dad would smile back at him and say, "There you are!"

My friends and I collected bottle caps, and there seem to have been many more brands of soda in those days than we have now. Sometimes we'd hit bottle caps with a baseball bat, which was fun until Dad decided it was time to cut the lawn, at which point I'd have to pick them all up. Sometimes, to earn a little money, we'd collect empty pop bottles and bring them to the store, where they'd pay us two cents for each one.

At one point, one of the radio stations ran a promotion for Vernors ginger ale, or, as they referred to it on WKBW, the city's most powerful station the signal of which could be heard hundreds of miles away, "Vernors *va-va-va-voom* Ginger Ale." If they called your house and you answered with "va-va-va-voom," you'd win a prize. For a while, my sister B.A. and I dove for the phone every time it rang, just in case. Dad hated it when one of his workers was calling in and we answered that way. "Look," he'd say, "would ya knock off the 'va-voom' and just answer the phone?"

When I was very young we had a party line—a telephone shared by two households—which probably sounds like more fun than it actually was. When the other family was using it, you had to wait until they were finished. When we graduated to a private line it seemed like a luxury, but as Dad reminded us, "that doesn't mean you can stay on it all day." Our phone number, back when everybody's number had only six digits (and

postal codes had only two), was TR-3561. TR stood for Trian-
gle, but when I was very young and Dad taught me our phone
number, he insisted that it stood for Tim Russert, the name we
shared.

Dad taught us early on that our name was important. He'd
say, "All I'm asking—wait, I'm not asking, I'm *telling* you—is,
Don't do anything to embarrass our family name. If you embarrass yourself, you embarrass all of us. We all make mistakes, but
if you go out there and do something you *know* you shouldn't be
doing, that's a tough one."

He didn't like gossip. If one of us talked about somebody
else's troubles, Dad would say, "Mind your own business. Let
them deal with their own problems." He would also say, "What
you hear at this table stays at this table." I don't recall hearing
any secrets at home, and to this day I'm not sure exactly what
Dad had in mind. I think he was expressing his deep sense of
privacy. Although my own life has been much more public, as a
father I sometimes hear myself telling Luke, "What you hear in
this house stays in this house." What, exactly, am I referring to?
That Luke is going to run over to ABC with one of my scoops?

My early childhood included two clearly memorable moments.
When I was five, I stupidly climbed up on four empty milk bottles, and all five of us tumbled over, leaving me with a badly cut
lip. Mom was wrapping my mouth in a towel just as Jimmy
Young, our milkman from the Sterling Amherst Dairy,
appeared at the door with four fresh bottles. "I can't stop the
bleeding," she told him. Jimmy carried me into the milk truck,
chipped a piece of ice off the big block in the back, and handed it

to Mom, who held it to my mouth. We sped off to Mercy Hospital, where a doctor put in a couple of stitches.

I had another minor mishap that winter when I jumped off the side of our front porch into a deep snowbank and couldn't climb out. "Mom! Mom!" I called, but Mom was inside and couldn't hear me. I started crying. Then I heard someone at the mailbox. It was Jerry Maher, our mailman. "Jerry! Jerry!"

"Who's that? Where are you?"

"It's Timmy. I'm over here!"

Jerry took the leather strap from his mailbag, tossed me one end, and told me to take off my gloves and hold on tight. I remember not wanting to take them off, but he insisted, and he pulled me out. I was sobbing uncontrollably. Even after I was safe inside, I kept crying about my gloves.

The first big test in my childhood was getting to school. When I was a boy, grown-ups loved to tell us how tough life had been when they were our age, and their testimonies of the various hardships they endured invariably included an enormously long and arduous walk to school. "Yes sir, it was eleventy thousand miles, and it was uphill, both ways. It took us two weeks to get to school in the morning, and another two to get home— and that's when the weather was *nice.*"

Our eyes would glaze over when we heard these stories, and yet I feel compelled, for some reason, to describe my own walk to school. Holy Family was at most a mile from our house, but that was quite a distance when I was in kindergarten or first grade, and it seemed a lot longer during those cold Buffalo winters. No matter how bad the weather, we always walked. My parents shared one car, which Dad drove to his jobs, but that wasn't the reason. In those days, at least in our neighborhood, nobody drove their kids to school; it just wasn't done. Our daily walk was twice as long because Holy Family School had no lunch room, so we were all sent home for lunch. None of the mothers we knew worked outside the home, and they all had lunch waiting on the table when we walked in. We ate quickly, because twenty minutes after we came home it was time to return to school.

Four miles of walking a day does not constitute cruel and unusual punishment, but in the early grades it was quite a challenge. It meant that when you were five, six, or seven years old, you had accomplished something real and tangible each morning by the simple act of getting yourself to school. I can't prove it, but I believe these walks made us tougher and better prepared for some of life's hardships. More than once, when facing a problem or a difficult challenge later on, I found strength from telling myself, This is nothing compared to walking to school backward, against the wind, at the age of six in a howling Buffalo snowstorm. Looking back on it, I have a little more empathy for all those adults who used to describe their arduous walks to school. These things stay with you, and maybe they weren't bragging or complaining so much as affirming an important childhood experience.

When I started kindergarten at the age of five, B.A., who was seven, walked to school with me, down Woodside Avenue and then right on South Park. Can you imagine that today, allowing a seven-year-old and a five-year-old to walk a mile to school? But in the mid 1950s, nobody in our neighborhood, or the rest of the country, for that matter, worried much about crime or kidnapping. Even the poorest, grittiest neighborhoods were reasonably safe.

As we walked to school, real life was unfolding right in front of us. Four times a day we'd walk past the little general store Ullenbruch's, a delicatessen, Vince's Barber Shop, Belvidere Cleaners (although I don't remember anyone in our family ever going there), Mike's Sub Shop, a five and dime, a pool hall, and a drugstore. We also passed by two or three bars, or gin mills, as they were known in Buffalo, and often, as early as lunchtime, we'd see a patron or two who had already enjoyed a couple of drinks too many. There was the local branch of the public library, where I was constantly taking out sports biographies (mostly of baseball players like Willie Mays, Babe Ruth, and Jackie Robinson) and Hardy Boys mysteries with their plastic library covers, making sure, always, to return the books on time to avoid the fine of one cent per day, which seems ludicrous today, but was real money when a penny could buy you a piece of candy. As it happened, the library was directly across from the police station, and occasionally we'd see the full spectrum of life in a single glance: on one side of the street, a suspect was being brought in for questioning while on the other, a library patron, the epitome of civic virtue, was walking out with a stack of books, presumably to continue his education.

Holy Family stood at the intersection of two busy streets, South Park and Tifft. We had to cross them both to get to school, and we did that with the help of a crossing guard, a lady we knew as Hazel, who wore a hat and white gloves and carried a whistle. We were taught early on to respect and obey Hazel as if she were one of the nuns, but that wasn't hard because she was very kind to us. She was also very strict. "I don't want to see any feet on the street," she would say. "Young man, your toes are part of your feet." Any child who dared to disobey Hazel would hear about it from the principal, Sister Gaudencia, who would tell your parents, which meant that you'd find yourself in trouble from three different directions. "You be nice to that woman," Dad would tell us, "because she's got a tough job."

I can still picture Hazel, with her horned-rimmed glasses, her frizzy hair, and the official-looking crossing-guard badge on the sleeve of her dark blue, long-sleeved shirt. On our way to school in the morning, when we caught a glimpse of Hazel we relaxed a little, knowing that we had just about completed our trek. She would greet us individually and gather us together, and then move a whole cluster of kids across South Park, and wait with us over there until she took us across Tifft Street. By this time, two or three dozen more children would have gathered on the other side, and were waiting for Hazel to return for them.

While working on this book I was surprised by how vividly I remembered Hazel, and how grateful I still am to her. So, with the help of some friends back home, I decided to find out a little more about our crossing guard. She was born Hazel Reeves in West Pittston, Pennsylvania, a few miles southwest of Scranton, in 1902, and was married to Joe Tighe, a brakeman for the Lehigh Valley Railroad. In her late sixties she converted to Catholicism, which came as a complete surprise to her family, although her husband was Catholic. She died in 1994 at the age of ninety-one, having lived through most of the twentieth century. "She loved you kids," her daughter Betty told me, but we already knew that. You could feel it.

Hazel Tighe worked outside Holy Family School for eighteen years, until 1970, when she retired. She became a crossing guard when Janet, the younger of her two daughters, was a sophomore at South Park High School. Ironically, soon after Hazel took the job, Janet was hit by a car while crossing South Park Avenue. She wasn't badly hurt, but Hazel saw the accident as a sign that she ought to continue in her new work, which now seemed even more important.

Some people, without ever realizing it, spend their whole lives preparing for a single moment. One day in 1967, Hazel spotted an out-of-control truck heading toward her corner and her kids. Without hesitating, she pushed thirty-five children back to the church grounds so quickly that nobody was hurt. After this incident, she was given an award by the Automobile Club of Buffalo. It was a nice gesture, but it seems so inadequate: how do you thank somebody for saving the lives of children? Hazel did so dramatically on that occasion, but she kept children out of harm's way four times a day for all those years.

Hazel was always there. She wore badge 473, and in her steady, reliable way, she made our world a little safer. Most people don't even notice crossing guards, or pay much attention to them. Until recently, I didn't, either.

4.

Work

"He lived his life by the grace of daily obligations."

A<small>LL THROUGH MY CHILDHOOD</small>, and well beyond it, Big Russ held down two demanding jobs. But as hard as he labored and as long as he toiled, we never heard a single complaint about his heavy workload or the sacrifice he was making. He didn't talk about it; he just got it done. And if he had had to take a third job to support his wife and four kids, he would have done that, too. He could never understand why people filed for bankruptcy, or why some families remained on welfare for a generation or more. A temporary setback was one thing—"Hey, it happens"—but welfare as a way of life? Incomprehensible.

Like so many members of the strong, silent generation of men who grew up during the Great Depression and went off to war, he had learned long ago that life was hard and nothing was handed to you. In fact, Dad considered it a sign of success, and even a blessing, that he was able to hold down two jobs. He could remember a time when a man considered himself fortunate to have even one.

In South Buffalo, having two jobs was not unusual. When I was growing up in the 1950s and '60s, most of my friends' fathers had a "second front," as we called it. The cop down the street worked nights as a security guard. My Uncle Sonny, a fireman, was also a maintenance man at Mercy Hospital. Another fireman who lived on our block ran a small insurance business on the side. Jack Horrigan, a sportswriter for the *Buffalo Evening News*, supplemented his income by writing under other names for various magazines. Tucker Reddington, the head football coach at St. Joseph's Collegiate Institute, owned a funeral home. Francis Reedy drove a school bus during the day and a city bus at night. Many of the men who worked at Bethlehem Steel in Lackawanna, or the Ford stamping factory, where parts of cars were put together before they were sent to the final assembly plant, either worked overtime whenever they could or did painting, plumbing, or handyman work on weekends. The primary obligation of a husband and a father was to provide for his family, and if that meant working two jobs, that was what you did.

Dad's main job was with the Sanitation Department. He could have made more money at the steel plant, or doing construction work, but his father, who had also worked for the city, had encouraged his two sons, Francis and Timothy, to apply for civil service jobs, rather than higher paying work in industry, because the public sector offered security. That advice suited Dad fine: he believed that slow and steady wins the race. "One day the heyday will be over," he would say, and that certainly proved true in Buffalo during the 1970s, when the economy tanked and thousands of people in private industry were laid off. By working for the city, Dad was choosing payday over heyday.

He started out as a lifter on the back of a garbage truck, and gradually worked his way up to driver. Later, when he took a test to become foreman, his high score earned him a promotion and a raise. A foreman was responsible for supervising and checking up on the various crews in a neighborhood, and for making sure there were enough men each day to complete the job. When I was young, I often woke up at 5:45 A.M. to the sound of Dad on the telephone: "What do you mean you can't come to work? Roy, you can't be doing this. You gotta give me some *notice*! How the hell am I going to find a man—yeah, I know you don't feel well. Listen, I don't feel so hot myself. Do me a favor, will you, Roy? Next time you're sick, could you call me the night before so I can get a man who wants to work? This is brutal!" Slam went the phone.

Maybe Roy really was sick. Or maybe it was snowing too hard, or he had stayed out a little too late the night before. Either way, Dad had a problem that had to be solved, because if even one truck was a man short, it was awful for everyone. He had a list of substitutes—day hires, they were called, and he'd start calling around, waking these men up and trying to cajole them into work. "Come on, Jerry, I really need you to come in." It often took some persuading to pry Jerry out of his warm bed on a cold winter morning when he hadn't been expecting to get up early.

A few years after he became a foreman, Dad took the test to become a superintendent, which meant he would oversee several of the foremen. He did well on the test, and by law, the

Commissioner of the Streets Department had to appoint as superintendent someone who had finished in the top three places. We were excited about this, because Dad might get a big promotion, and the superintendent job came with a car and, of course, a raise. One day, three strangers appeared at our house, which was very unusual, because the only people who ever came to our door were friends, neighbors, or family. "You kids go outside," Dad said, and of course we obeyed. After about twenty minutes, the men got back in their car and drove away. When I asked Dad about the visitors, he said, "Oh, they're just some guys I know from work."

Years later, we were talking about his work and I said, "Dad, whatever happened to that superintendent job?"

"It just didn't work out."

"What happened?"

As I suspected, there was more to the story than I knew, and the three visitors had something to do with it. "They wanted me to sign off the superintendent list," he said. "If they could get the guys with the highest scores to sign off, they could appoint the candidate they wanted, who didn't do so well on the test."

"What did you tell them?" I asked.

"I said no," he answered.

"And what did they say?"

"They weren't happy. They said that if I changed my mind, they would make it worthwhile."

"What does that mean?" I asked. Like some politicians I have interviewed, Dad doesn't volunteer much information. You have to ask.

"They offered to sweeten the deal."

"What did you tell them?"

"I told them I couldn't do it. I know what I could have done with the money, but I also knew what that money would do to me. I told them I didn't want any part of it."

"Do you remember how you said it?"

"I said, 'You've got the wrong guy.' They said, 'Why don't you think about it?' I said, 'I've thought about it. I'll see you later.'"

"Were you tempted to take the money?"

"Like I said, it wasn't the right thing to do. And how could I tell you kids to do the right thing if I ever did something like that?"

That story means the world to me. At the time, Dad was sending two or three kids to parochial school, paying the mortgage, and working two jobs, but he held his ground. Others didn't do the right thing, and Dad didn't get the promotion, but he kept his honor.

DAD LEFT FOR WORK AT DAWN, and when his shift was over, he went over to his second job, where he drove a delivery truck for the *Buffalo Evening News*. Later, when the Sanitation Department made him foreman of the downtown district, he started working nights because trash collection was too disruptive to be done while stores and businesses were still open. This new schedule was fine with him, because now he could drive full-time for the *News*. He'd come home from his day job around 5:30 and eat a quick supper. Then he'd sprawl out diagonally across the bed for a short nap before heading out for the night shift. We had to be quiet during his nap, and stay off the telephone when he was home in case one of the workers was trying to reach him.

Dad didn't have much time off, but when he wasn't working for pay, he was working around the house—changing the storm windows, cutting the grass, resealing the driveway, or taking care of his car. There was a public golf course at the end of our street, but Dad never went there. "Some of my friends picked up golf," he once said to me, "but I never had the time." There may have been a note of regret in that comment, but it was far from a complaint.

Dad talked as little about his work as he did about the war, so for years I didn't know much about either of his jobs. A couple of years ago, an old friend from South Buffalo told me that when he was a boy, he resented the fact that his father, who worked at the steel plant, used to spend every Friday night getting drunk in a bar. My friend served as an infantry squad leader during some of the bloodiest fighting of the Vietnam War, and when his tour was over, he took a summer job in the same factory where his father had worked all those years. "It was awful," he told me. "I lasted exactly three days, and my respect for my father went up exponentially. He went into that awful place every day, and worked overtime to support his family. All was forgiven. Vietnam was depressing, but the steel plant was worse."

I had some idea of what he was talking about. I had always known that Dad worked hard, but I didn't really appreciate what he went through every day until I did it myself. When I was in college, I spent just about every school vacation doing exactly what Dad had done, and was still doing—working on garbage trucks and delivering bundles of newspapers for the

Buffalo Evening News. Every morning I lifted heavy garbage cans, just as Dad had done when he was starting out. It was good, tough, honest work, and I knew it would be hard. But I hadn't expected it would be *that* hard.

The lifter is the man who picks up the cans and empties them into the packer, or compacting truck, where a sweeping bar comes over the top and pushes the trash into the interior of the vehicle, where it is compacted. Each packer carried three men—a driver and two lifters. But sometimes one of the packers broke down and we had to use the old-fashioned fantail truck, which was nothing more than a dump truck piled high with trash. On a packer, the lifter emptied the cans into an opening about three feet off the ground. But on the older trucks, the lifters—and there were always two of us—had to hold full cans of garbage above our heads and pass them to the shaker, who emptied the cans, built the load, and covered the growing pile with canvas so the garbage wouldn't fall into the street. For obvious reasons, the job of lifter was always awarded to the youngest, most inexperienced member of the team. That would be me. And if an old fantail truck had to be pressed into service, you can guess where the college boys were sent.

There was no overtime on this job: you worked until you finished your route, and if, for some reason, your route took longer than usual, that was your problem. Sometimes, especially on Friday, when everyone wanted to finish early, the driver would get out of the cab and give you a hand. On the other side of the ledger, you might be teamed up with Walter "Take a Leak" Scott, who insisted on stopping for a bathroom break every ten minutes. It took me a week or so to realize that he was really going off to take another nip.

When Dad had started out as a lifter, compacting trucks hadn't come in yet. He must have lifted heavy cans above his head every day for years. In his day, incidentally, residents of Buffalo had full garbage service: Before the garbage truck came to your house, a team of rollers would bring your trash cans out to the front. After the truck had taken the trash, the rollers came back and returned the empty cans.

The routes I worked on were full of two-family houses, so there were as many as ten or twelve garbage cans for each one. In winter, on dark, freezing mornings, we had to work our way around high snowdrifts and dangerous patches of ice. Christmas week was especially hard, with all that extra packaging from gifts and all those empty bottles. (This was long before recycling.) Summer presented a different set of challenges, such as picking up trash from a couple of raw clam stands. Take my word for it: there is *nothing* quite like the stench of two-day-old clam shells on a hot, humid day in August. That's an aroma that lingers on your clothes, and in your memory.

Barbara Ehrenreich has written that there is really no such thing as unskilled labor. One of the first lessons I learned on the garbage detail was the proper way of removing a lid from a metal can. It's not complicated, but you had to make sure to pull the lid back toward your chin, using it as a shield to protect your throat in case a rat jumped out at you. Rats were part of the landscape, and we saw them every day. Sometimes I rode shotgun when we drove a load of trash to the dump, which looked like a scene from a horror movie with packs of rats swarming over the garbage.

I soon understood why Dad was so meticulous when it came to throwing things out. He always put the kitchen grease in a coffee can and let it settle and harden, because he knew what it felt like to pick up a bag and have the bottom fall out. He also knew—and I learned the hard way—that some people threw their garbage right into the can, without even bagging it. When they did that, we'd have to smell it, and wear it, for the rest of the day. Others, especially in the Polish neighborhoods, wrapped their garbage so neatly and carefully that you almost expected them to put a ribbon on it. As soon as we picked up their trash, they'd be out there with a hose, rinsing out the empty cans.

Well before I had any hands-on experience, Dad had taught me how to wrap garbage. Part of it was his passion for doing things correctly. "Do it right the first time," Big Russ would say, "and you won't have to do it again." He was also being considerate. If you got into the habit of thinking about the other guy, including the person who picked up your trash, and you realized that you were just one household out of many stops along his route, you could make life a little easier for this father, this uncle, this brother, or this son. To this day I put our garbage out with real care and attention, because I remember what it's like to pick it up.

After a day of lifting garbage cans, my arms and shoulders would be aching, and I still have a problem with my toe from the time I dropped a heavy can on it. But it wasn't all pain and suffering. One summer I was teamed up with a shaker named Willie, a black man with a wonderful sense of humor who liked to sing on the job. Willie loved pizza, and we were sharing one for lunch one day when a well-dressed woman happened to walk by. "My, oh my," said Willie, in a voice just loud enough to be overheard. "Here's a pizza pie that doesn't look more than a day or two old." It worked: the woman yelled at us for eating garbage. But Willie hadn't counted on the possibility that she might call City Hall to report us. When the foreman came by to check on us, we explained that, No, we hadn't been eating any garbage, and where would that poor lady ever get *that* idea? When I told Dad about it, he said that in his day they'd take an apple, polish it, and pretend they had found it in the garbage. "Work is tough," he'd say, "but there's no law against having a good laugh."

Friday was payday. I had to move on to my second job, but most of the crew would repair to a tavern for lunch and stay there for hours. Once, when I joined them for a sandwich, I watched as one man cashed his paycheck at the bar. The bartender gave him half the money in an envelope, which the customer put in his back pocket "for the little woman." The other half stayed with the bartender, and I realized that this man was planning to drink his way through half a paycheck's worth of booze. Dad loved to have a couple of cold ones, but he would never even think of doing something like that. Now I was grateful not only for all that he did for us, but also for the things he didn't do.

"Now I got you this job," Dad reminded me, "so don't embarrass me, okay?" He was never embarrassed about being a garbage man, and even when his title was Foreman of the Streets Division, everybody knew what that meant. Because he was proud of his work, I was proud of him for doing it. He took pride in a job well done, and he wanted to be sure that I measured up. I knew that, of course; I took the job seriously and worked hard. I was aware that Dad had called in a favor or two to get me this job, and he didn't want to hear any complaints about me from his buddies, or even worse, his bosses. One time, my foreman on the garbage route saw Dad on the street and called out to him.

"Hey Tim!"

"Yeah?"

"He's a good kid."

Big Russ took the cigar out of his mouth and said, "Thanks, Whitey. That means a lot."

Dad never mentioned this exchange, but he didn't have to— I witnessed it, and I felt like I had won a medal. There's nothing worse than disappointing your parents, and nothing better than making them proud. Here and there I had pleased him in other ways, mostly at school, in church, or on the playground, but this was different. This was his world, and I had done my job—his job, actually—with some degree of competence.

The money was good and I'm glad I did it, but I had no desire to continue lifting garbage cans. Today, when I see Dad with arthritis in his joints, I picture him hanging off the back of a truck and lifting all those loads. On my last day on the job, I told Phil, the driver, that I was finished. "I'm out of here," I proclaimed. "I've got my college degree, and I'm hoping to go to law school."

"Yeah, they all say that. You'll be back."

"No, Phil, I'm telling you, this is it." With a flourish, I took off my headband, my boots and my gloves, threw them into the packer, and pushed down the blade. Then I got into my car and started putting on my sneakers.

"What did you do?" Phil called to me.

"Everything is in the truck. It's over, pal."

"You'll be back," he said again. Phil, who fancied himself a singer, proceeded to serenade me with an old Peggy Lee song, "Is That All There Is?" Many years later, when I was living in New York, I read in the paper that Peggy Lee was performing in a Sunday matinee. My wife, Maureen, and I went to see her, and when she sang "Is That All There Is?" I was grinning from ear to ear. Phil turned out to be wrong about my coming back, although there were a couple of times along the way when I feared he might be right.

But I don't regret my time on the trucks, and I couldn't have put myself through college without a good summer job. Despite the smells, the cold, the heat, and my aching arms, being a garbage-man was an invaluable experience. After that, no job has ever seemed too difficult.

I learned a few things, too. That there is no substitute for getting up in the morning, reporting to work on time, and putting in an honest day's work for an honest day's pay. That everybody has a job to do and a contribution to make, and that no matter how small that job may seem in the larger scheme of things, if it's worth doing at all, it's worth doing well. That the person who litters, or doesn't bother to wrap his trash, or doesn't show up to work, makes life a little harder for everyone else. I learned, too, that having a certain job at one point in your life doesn't mean you'll be doing it forever. But most of all, I learned how hard Big Russ had worked to support us.

Now that I'm a father, I sometimes wonder how my son will learn the importance of a good work ethic. He's not likely to learn it by working on a garbage truck, but plenty of people have learned that same lesson in other ways. One way or another, if I'm not able to teach him that lesson, or to direct him to a place where he can learn it, it will be a loss for both of us—for him as a son, and for me as a father.

IN 1978, when Dad turned fifty-five, he was eligible to retire from his city job. Now that his kids were grown, he thought that his newspaper job, together with his pension, might bring in enough income to live on. Even so, he kept debating whether or not to leave the Sanitation Department. I knew that this wasn't just about money, but I encouraged him to "retire," although that's an odd word to use for somebody who would still be working full-time. To bolster my argument, I sat down with him to go over the numbers.

"And then I have to figure out what to do with those sick days," he said.

"What do you mean?" I asked.

"My sick days. I never took 'em."

I was stunned. Although in all my years at home I had never seen him miss a day of work, I had never thought of it in terms of sick days.

"Dad, everybody takes sick days."

"Well, I didn't, and now I've got two hundred of them."

"Two *hundred*? Why didn't you take them?"

"Because I wasn't sick."

"Dad, those days are yours. They're made available to you."

"They're made available if you're sick. If you take a sick day and you're not really sick, what kind of luck are you gonna have?" He seemed to be saying that if you faked an illness, you would be punished by being zapped with something far worse.

"But there must have been times when you *were* sick."

"Sure, but if I took off from the morning job, and then I felt better and went to the afternoon job, how would that look? Besides, I didn't want to miss out on double pay. When I was sick, I worked it off and rode it out."

I went with him to city hall to work out his retirement package, which included partial compensation for all the sick days he never took. I shouldn't have been surprised, but I was. I've worked in government and the media all my life, and I've come to know many fine and hardworking people. But I can only imagine how much this country could achieve if everyone had Dad's work ethic.

Which brings me to Cal Ripken, Jr. On September 7, 1995, I took Luke, who was ten, to a baseball game at Camden Yards in Baltimore. Even though you know most baseball records will be broken, you could never know exactly when, for example, Roger Clemens would record his three hundredth win or Mark McGwire would hit his seventieth home run. But on September 7, 1995, everybody knew that unless the game was rained out, Cal Ripken, Jr., was going to break Lou Gehrig's "Iron Man" record just by showing up and playing in his 2,131st consecutive game. This wasn't about something glitzy, like home runs, although Ripken did hit one out of the park that night (which was pretty impressive, given the amount of attention he was getting), just as he had done the night before, when he tied Gehrig's record. I explained to my son that Cal Ripken's record was different from all other records because this one was about loyalty, dedication, discipline, diligence, and persistence.

This one was about getting up every day and going to work, even when you didn't feel like it. There were no high fives that night, no fancy strutting, no commercial sponsorships, or tabloid hype. This was a different kind of achievement. It wasn't about accomplishments, although Ripken had accumulated plenty of those. This was about one man playing baseball for the city he grew up in. Cal Ripken's achievement was a tribute to everyone who gets up every day and does their job. I brought Luke to the game because Cal Ripken had set a wonderful example: work hard and play by the rules.

When the game became official after four and a half innings, Luke and I and thousands of other fans stood and cheered and applauded for Cal Ripken and the old-fashioned values he embodied. I told Luke that night, and I meant it with all my heart, that Cal Ripken had done for baseball what my dad had done for our family.

Not long ago, an old family friend called to tell me that she had been reading *Father Melancholy's Daughter*, a novel by Gail Godwin, where she came across a line that struck her as a wonderful description of Big Russ: "He lived his life by the grace of daily obligations."

5.

Faith

"It was meant to be."

RELIGION WAS EVERYWHERE IN OUR LIVES—not just in church or in school, but at home, too. There were crosses above our beds, and every evening, when we sat down to supper, one of us said grace: "Bless us, O Lord, and these Thy gifts, which we are about to receive through Thy bounty, through Christ our Lord, Amen." We had a statue of the Virgin Mary in our backyard and another, smaller one on top of the china cabinet. During the month of May, Mary's month, we'd light a candle every day, and Mom would bring in flowers from the garden. And like many Catholic households in South Buffalo, we had a picture of Jesus that portrayed His Sacred Heart.

When something in our house was misplaced, the car keys, perhaps, or even the grocery money, Mom would appeal to St. Anthony of Padua, the patron saint of lost objects:

Dear St. Anthony, please come around.
Something is lost and cannot be found.

According to Mom, these invocations always worked. Beyond that, both of our parents would say that certain events were "a sign from God," and Dad would often tell us that something was "meant to be."

Eating meat on Fridays was unthinkable; it was considered a sin. Because Jesus died on a Friday, we honored His death by abstaining from this particular pleasure. Giving up meat was a sacrifice, part of what used to be known in the Catholic Church as mortification. When the no meat on Fridays rule was abandoned in the 1960s as a result of the Second Vatican Council, it came as a huge shock to my generation of Catholics. We had grown up thinking of this prohibition as a firm commandment from God, rather than a church law, devised by men, that might conceivably be overturned. The comedian George Carlin, who grew up Catholic, used to have fun with this: "It's not even a sin anymore to eat meat on Friday," he'd say. "But I'll bet you there are still some guys in hell doing time on a meat rap.... How'd you like to do eternity for a beef jerky?"

At the beginning of Lent, the forty days before Easter, our family would gather around the dinner table and announce to one another what we intended to give up. Dad would always say, "You know, sometimes it's better to do something special than to give something up," but we just smiled and assumed he was looking for an easy way out. Betty Ann would abstain from chocolate, Kathy would give up ice cream, and Trish would forgo cinnamon candy. I usually did without my beloved licorice or pretzels. As far as I remember, the penance always involved some kind of food, but then, in our family, giving up food really was a sacrifice.

On Ash Wednesday, at the beginning of Lent, our entire class would walk next door to the church, where the priest would dip his thumb in ashes and mark the sign of the cross on our foreheads while intoning the ancient line, "Remember, man, thou art dust, and to dust thou shalt return." It was always a jolt when I heard these somber words. Each year, for this brief moment, I had to confront the idea of mortality, which was otherwise the last thing on the mind of a healthy, growing boy.

From time to time my parents would bring me with them to a wake, where the custom was to have an open casket. When my paternal grandparents died, I watched as Dad reached into the coffin and tearfully squeezed their hands in a final gesture of farewell. At the funeral the coffin would be sealed, and that required a different kind of faith as we sent the deceased on his or her way to their eternal rest. Sometimes I would accompany my parents to their parents' graves, where we would offer a prayer and leave flowers.

Religion was serious business. The priests and the nuns impressed upon us the idea that Christmas meant more than toys, and that Easter went beyond candy. It was fine to enjoy ourselves on these special days, but we were always made aware of the deeper meaning behind them. There were constant reminders that life was bigger than you were, and that you were obligated to be a good person in this life, even as you tried to be aware of the next one.

In church on Good Friday, we'd reenact the stations of the

cross, symbolically retracing the steps of Christ as he walked to his death. (I remember, in seventh grade, kneeling in church from noon until three as a form of sacrifice. It wasn't easy.) On Easter Sunday we'd go to church in new outfits, and Dad would buy corsages for Mom and my sisters, who wore splendid hats, their Easter bonnets, just like in the song.

In second grade, the big event of the school year was our first Holy Communion, which also marked the first time we went to confession. In a scene that would be repeated every week during the school year, we entered the confessional individually to talk to the priest, whose face was hidden by a screen. You couldn't see him and he couldn't see you, but some of us worried that he might recognize our voices, so we spoke softly and more slowly than usual. We always prepared for confession by thinking of various sins we might have committed, such as being mean to your sister or the always available wildcard sin of "impure thoughts." Some second graders, I learned later, were scared witless at their first confession, and it wasn't uncommon for children to wet their pants. I guess that's not surprising, because the nuns taught us that during confession, the priest is the same as Jesus, and that Jesus was forgiving us through the priest. Of *course* we were nervous!

After we confessed our sins, such as they were at that age, the priest would ask us to recite the Act of Contrition, which began, "O my God, I am heartily sorry for having offended Thee," and ended with our resolving, with God's help, "to sin no more and avoid the near occasion of sin." The priest then informed us, in Latin, that our sins were forgiven, and told us our penance: a certain number of Our Father's and Hail Mary's, which we then recited privately as we kneeled in one of the pews. Sin was a frightening idea, especially in the 1950s, when priests and nuns spoke openly about the fires of hell. And yet for all the drama and fear in these teachings, we didn't see this as "religious" life. We saw it as life.

By this time we had mastered the Baltimore Catechism, a simple recitation, in question-and-answer form, of the essentials of our faith:

> Who made the world? God made the world.
> Who is God? God is the Creator of heaven and earth, and of all things.
> What is man? Man is a creature composed of body and soul, and made to the image and likeness of God.

There were twelve of these questions and answers, ending with the Apostles' Creed, which we had to memorize.

In those days, which turned out to be the final years of the pre–Vatican II era, religion was taught dogmatically: the nuns did the talking, and we did the listening. If you asked a question, as often as not the answer was, "We don't know. It's a mystery." We learned some big words pertaining to God, such as "omnipresent" and "omniscient," and the biggest one of all, "transubstantiation," and did our best to remember what they meant. Some of the other terms we learned, including "limbo"—the place where unbaptized babies went—are no longer in use. In school we brought in our pennies, including the money we didn't spend on candy during Lent, to help save "pagan babies"—an astonishing phrase by today's standards that sounded perfectly normal to us. The money was used to "adopt" infants in far-off lands, who were given nutritious meals and, not incidentally, a Catholic baptism. In return, our class would receive a picture of the child we had "saved."

Our first Communion was celebrated with a special Mass on a Saturday, and Holy Family Church was filled with family and friends. The boys wore white suits, and the girls wore white dresses with veils and white shoes. (In our family, as in most others in our neighborhood, these once-in-a-lifetime outfits were handed down from one child to the next.) Mass was followed by a party at home, where we were given a special gift. Mine was a brand-new bicycle, a big one with an adjustable seat, the first bike I ever had that wasn't pre-owned, as the car dealers like to say. It came in a box, and Dad assembled it and taught me how to ride. My bike served me well for five years, until, in seventh grade, coming home from a wedding where I had served as an altar boy, I plowed into the side of a car. I survived with a few scrapes and bruises, but the bike was demolished.

Being an altar boy was regarded as an honor, and it made you feel special. The hardest part was learning the prayers in Latin and pronouncing them clearly, as the priests demanded, being careful not to slur the words. There were also bells to be rung, candles to be lit, and Bibles to be opened to the correct reading. And we were the ones who held the wine cruets while the priest blessed them.

Part of your responsibility was to be punctual, which wasn't easy when you were serving the 6:30 morning Mass in the dead of winter. The early shift often included stopping first at the rectory to wake up Father Louis Gonter, the assistant pastor, who was known affectionately as Lantern Louie because he stayed up late and had to be shaken back to life each morning. It all seemed so natural then, but when I look back on it, I'm struck by how much responsibility we had. We weren't even in high school yet, but age-old traditions with great meaning depended on our showing up on time and doing the job exactly right.

There was a brotherhood among the altar boys, and we used to share stories of which priest liked the bigger serving of wine. There was also mischief, or at least talk of mischief. If you had a friend who was receiving the host, you might take the paten, the little golden plate, and accidentally hit him in the throat. Most of the joking centered on the wine, and some of the boys were known to have raided the priests' supply closet—but I'll never tell.

At funerals, to underscore the solemnity of the occasion, the altar boys wore black cassocks, rather than the red ones we normally wore. For me, the funerals of nuns were especially moving. The nuns we knew at school were teachers and disciplinarians, and we rarely saw them as sisters to one another. But when they came together as a congregation and walked slowly down the aisle with their hands folded perfectly, genuflecting in unison, you could see and even feel their holiness. You could hear it as well: from the altar, their voices sounded like an angelic choir, and as they sang the hymns, I saw the nuns in a new and different light. They were no longer instructing us or scolding us. We, their students, were not even in the picture. They were coming together to celebrate the life of one of their own, an elderly sister who had retired and was still living in the convent. I served at only two such funerals, but I'll never forget them.

ANOTHER EVENT IN SECOND GRADE had big ramifications for us, although you didn't have to attend Catholic school to be affected by it. On October 4, 1957, with no advance warning, the Soviet Union launched *Sputnik*, the first spacecraft to orbit the earth. My father, and our teachers, too, explained that the Russians had sent up a small, man-made moon to go around the earth, which didn't help very much because what was the point of *that*? There was no context for such an event, and no precedent in human history, and the adults in our lives were shocked by the news. Until this moment, which brought us a new word, "satellite," we had thought of our country as invulnerable and the Soviets as technologically inferior. Now, suddenly, they had surpassed us in space, which meant that they might have the capacity to defeat us militarily as well. Overnight, Americans began asking themselves why we were lagging so far behind the Russians in science and technology, and what the United States ought to do about it.

Sputnik heightened the idea that we were engaged in a conflict between two diametrically opposed ways of life. This was a battle in which even we, as schoolchildren, had a role to play. Our job was to study, and study *hard*, to enable our country to keep up with an advanced enemy. No longer were we competing only with one another. As schoolchildren, we had been deputized.

The space race that began in 1957 heated up in 1961, when a Soviet astronaut named Yury Gagarin became the first person to orbit the earth. America caught up in 1962, when John Glenn circled the earth not once, but three times. I was in sixth grade by then, and our class watched Glenn's voyage on television.

When his capsule landed safely in the ocean and started bob-
bing in the water, we erupted in cheers.

Today, with the Soviet Union no longer around, it's hard to
recapture the extent to which Americans experienced the space
race as part of the arms race. We were aware of living in a new
and more dangerous age, but Catholics experienced a religious
dimension to the Cold War that made the conflict even more
frightening. This was a struggle between the right to live in
freedom, with the opportunity to worship and believe in God,
and a system that insisted that you couldn't accept *any* God, that
the state itself was your God. People who denied God were not
likely to show any mercy to believers, and we had heard about
the cruel punishments that were meted out to religious people,
not only Catholics, in the Soviet Union and Communist China.
One of the nuns who taught us pointed to her habit and joked,
"If the Russians ever attack, I'm going to tell them that this is
my Halloween costume."

Even as children, we were aware that the Soviet leader, Nikita
Khrushchev, had said, "We will bury you." Sophisticated people
insisted that he didn't mean it literally, but we weren't so sure.
We also knew that in 1959, Khrushchev had told Vice President
Richard Nixon, "Your grandchildren will live under Commu-
nism." When he said that, Dad shook his head and said, "No sir.
No sirree. No sir." I don't think we were aware that Vice President Nixon had responded by telling Khrushchev, "No, your
children will live in Freedom." Nixon was more right than he
ever imagined: forty years later, in July 1999, Khrushchev's son
Sergei became an American citizen.

In the fall of 1960, when Khrushchev, the crude and angry peasant, took off his shoe at the United Nations and banged it on the table, Big Russ took note. "Look at the way he's acting, like a thug. That's what we'd be living under." Dad had given three years of his life to fight the Nazis, and he believed the Soviets were just as bad. At the height of the Cold War, people were genuinely frightened. On the radio and television, starting in 1963, we'd hear what was initially a chilling announcement, "This is a test of the Emergency Broadcasting System." In time we grew used to it, but for the first year or two, it was a frightening reminder that a nuclear war was possible.

But we believed that the Russian people wanted peace, and we knew that their country had a strong religious tradition. It was their leadership, the dictators, whom we opposed. As if to drive this point home, at the conclusion of Sunday Mass the priest would turn around and face the congregation. Spreading his hands, he would say, "Savior of the world—"

And the congregation would answer as one, "Save Russia."

6.

Food

"You gotta eat."

I N SEPTEMBER 1979, with the economy in bad shape and getting even worse, President Jimmy Carter's staff was worried about his prospects for reelection. Above all, White House aides were afraid that Senator Ted Kennedy would challenge the president in the primaries. Their fears were realized on November 7, when Kennedy entered the race.

All of this is by way of explaining why Hamilton Jordan was calling me in late September 1979. Jordan was the president's chief of staff, and I had a similar title in Senator Moynihan's office. "I'm calling about the Pope's visit to Washington," Jordan said. Pope John Paul II was coming to the United States, and his trip was scheduled to conclude on October 6 with a visit to Washington, where he would visit the White House and celebrate Mass on the National Mall. This was the first time a pope had ever come to Washington, and people were truly excited.

"Would you like to come and see him on the White House Lawn?" Jordan asked.

It wasn't a difficult question. Long ago, Dad had taught me that when opportunity knocked, you had to be ready to open the door. Or, as he put it, "If people want to be nice to you, let them."

But Hamilton Jordan wasn't calling to be nice. He was calling because my boss was a well-known Irish-Catholic politician with strong support among mainstream Democrats. More to the point, Senator Moynihan had close ties to the Kennedys. If the Carter people could keep Moynihan in their tent, or at least discourage him from endorsing Senator Kennedy, that would be enormously helpful to the president's reelection effort. Of course, none of this was mentioned during my brief conversation with Hamilton Jordan. Adhering to an old Washington ritual, where much remains unsaid, both of us pretended that he just happened to feel like doing me a favor.

I told him I'd love to see the Pope, and that I would appreciate three tickets. I knew immediately that I would invite Big Russ to fly down from Buffalo, and I figured it wouldn't be hard to make use of that extra seat.

As soon as Dad agreed to come, I invited his old friend, Father Edwin Dill, who lived in the Washington area. The two of them had worked together years ago, when I was a baby, unloading hundred-pound sacks of potatoes from boxcars at the A&P warehouse in Buffalo and repacking them into smaller bags. (Amazing. The Irish flee to America because of the potato famine, and what do they do when they get here? Unpack potatoes!) It was a summer job: Dad spent mornings on the garbage trucks and worked at the grocery warehouse from three in the afternoon until eleven at night. It was hard work, with plenty of heavy lifting, but it paid $1.75 an hour, which was good money back then.

Father Dill was a college student at the time, but he and Dad became friendly and had stayed in touch for years, although it had been a while since they had seen each other. Without telling Dad, I asked Father Dill to join us for lunch at the Old Ebbitt Grill on Fifteenth Street, just a block from the White House. Dad was stunned but delighted to see his old friend, and when lunch was over the three of us strolled over to the White House to see the Pope.

It was a perfect fall afternoon, with warm sunshine and blue skies. About three thousand people, including members of the Supreme Court, Congress, and the Cabinet, had gathered on the North Lawn to greet the Holy Father. It was a colorful scene, with the priests and cardinals in their robes, and hundreds of Polish Americans from places like Buffalo, Cleveland, Chicago, Pittsburgh, Milwaukee, and Detroit—cities with large Polish populations in states with significant primaries—who were excited to honor the first Polish pope in history. As the Holy Father walked up and down the aisles, greeting members of the crowd, Dad ran over and reached out for a quick grasp of the papal hand. Then he came back and said, "Now I'm going to the other side." This time he hit the jackpot: Dad and the Pope shook hands firmly, with Dad putting his left hand on top of the Pope's. The Pope was smiling, and the security guards were looking at Dad as if to say, "Would you tell that guy to please release the Pope?" Father Edwin was busy snapping pictures.

It was a festive and memorable day. As we were leaving, I turned to Dad and said, "Wasn't that something?"

He was beaming. "It sure was," he said. "I can't believe I met the Pope, but that's not all. Did you see who was sitting right across from me?"

The crowd had been filled with familiar faces, and I had spotted Red Sox slugger Carl Yastrzemski, Supreme Court Justice Arthur Goldberg, and many other Washington VIPs. But I had no idea whom Dad was referring to.

"Who do you mean?" I asked.

"Colonel Sanders!" he said, with real enthusiasm.

Now I'm not saying that Dad was as excited to see the colonel as he was to meet the Pope, but the white-haired chicken man was clearly in the race. Colonel Sanders meant a lot to Dad, although he's not normally a fan of fast food. When I was a boy, and one of the first McDonald's opened near our house, my sisters and I were dying to go. But Dad dismissed McDonald's as "junk food" long before the expression was popular. Kentucky Fried Chicken, however, was another matter entirely.

Over the years, when I've mentioned to friends how important food was in my family, and especially to Dad, I've noticed that Jews and Italians don't find this at all surprising. But by the standards of our Irish-Catholic neighborhood, Big Russ was a serious and dedicated eater. As long as I can remember, his favorite expression has been, "You gotta eat!"

Like most families in the 1950s, we had supper together every night. From time to time, Dad would look around at his family and proclaim with satisfaction, "Say what you want, we eat well." I always wondered what he meant by the phrase, "Say what you want." Did he imagine that people were saying, "Those Russerts don't have very much"? Or did he mean, "I'm not able to provide you with everything you might want, but at least there's food on the table"? For Dad, and for many men of his generation, being a father meant, above all, being a provider. And being a provider meant making sure his children had three basic necessities: a house to live in, a school to go to, and food on the table.

Food came first. When Dad drove a newspaper truck all those years, he preferred the rural areas because he knew some of the farmers and most of the farm stands. In the summer and fall he'd come home at night with large quantities of apples, straw-berries, peaches, cherries, corn, and beans, all fresh and inex-pensive, and a treat, too, in the days when you couldn't always find good fresh produce in the supermarket. He loved fresh tomatoes with salt and pepper, and so did I; we had so many around the house that I ate them like apples. Dad brought home far more than we could possibly use, and he was continually pressing fruit and vegetables on friends, relatives, and neighbors.

Sometimes, on a Sunday, we'd go for a drive in the country. When it was time for lunch, we never went to a restaurant. Dad would find a deli, where we'd buy bologna, bread, and mustard, and make our own sandwiches. It was cheaper that way—and better, too. But if we passed a fried chicken joint, especially one of the colonel's, all bets were off.

On Fridays, when Catholics didn't eat meat, we often went to the Legion post, or a restaurant like Hoak's or a takeout place like Trautwein's for the Friday fish fry. In those days, just about every establishment in town served fried fish on Fridays; in South Buffalo, the Friday night fish fry was almost as solid a tra-dition as Sunday Mass. My sisters and I loved the fish fry at the

Legion, because they served big pitchers of draft birch beer, a
Buffalo specialty that's a lot like root beer. "All right," Dad would
say, giving us permission to indulge. "Tonight's the night to rot
your teeth."

Another Buffalo favorite, and certainly one of Dad's, is beef
on weck, which is like a roast beef sandwich, only better. Slices
of juicy, tender roast beef are dipped in gravy, smothered in
fresh horseradish, and served on a "kummelweck"—a hard crusty
roll embedded with caraway seeds and kosher salt. Dad's right:
there's nothing better. Unlike the city's better-known specialty,
those now-ubiquitous Buffalo chicken wings, or simply "wings,"
as we call them, beef on weck has not migrated to other regions
of the country, perhaps because the rolls are so difficult to bake.

At my sister B.A.'s wedding, the ceremony was followed by a
dinner reception in a catering hall, where the bride's father
couldn't wait to explain the intricacies of the buffet: "You go
through the line, you get your salads, your soup, your vegetables,
and then at the end, there, you've got the steam table with a
rump of roast beef. I'm telling you, it's beautiful." As pleased as
Dad was that his daughter was getting married, he was almost as
proud of the roast beef at the end of the table. "Have another
slab," he'd say. "Everything you could want to eat or drink." The
man was born to run a restaurant.

The comedian Jackie Mason, one of Dad's favorite entertainers, used to do a routine where he compared Jewish and
Gentile styles of eating. At one point he discussed what dieters
refer to as portion control: "If you go to a Gentile home and they
give you a piece of cake," he'd say dismissively, "to a Jew it would

be a cookie!" We knew what he meant. Whenever I was invited to a friend's house for dinner, I always came home famished.

"I thought you ate over there!"

"They gave me one pork chop and a little scoop of potatoes."

"Betty, would you please feed the boy?"

Mom fed us very well, although at the time I didn't appreciate how far she managed to stretch a limited food budget. Supper was always a three-course meal: soup or salad, a hot main course, and dessert. We loved soup, especially chicken noodle soup, which we called Jewish penicillin. Mom would cook whatever was on sale that week, and served us pork chops, liver and bacon, ham and cabbage, meat loaf, hamburgers, chicken, and all kinds of soups and stews. When Mom had a little more money to spend, she'd buy roast beef or shrimp. On Friday we'd have creamed codfish, tuna and peas on toast, or macaroni and cheese. Whatever it was, we were expected to finish it all: "Don't leave the table until you can see your face in the plate," our grandparents used to say, although in my case the plate wasn't always wide enough to reflect the entire image. Mom loved to bake, and she served up some great desserts, including lemon, apple, and cherry pie. To this day, she always bakes a cherry pie when I come back to Buffalo.

On your birthday, you had the right to request any meal you liked, but no matter how much we begged, even then McDonald's was out of the question. Sometimes we asked for pizza, which was still a novelty in those days. Once, in high school, I dared to request steak, and hoped I wasn't pushing my luck. Dad picked up some good ones and cooked them outside on our new gas grill. My parents bought one of the first gas grills when the gas company offered them for just five dollars a month for a year. The company installed it and connected it to the gas line in our house. Dad loved that grill, and sometimes, on Sunday evening, he'd cook dinner outside, even in the winter.

On Father's Day, Dad would host a big cookout for several families. The two of us would drive to the Broadway Market on the East Side, which wasn't a store but a huge ethnic food market, a collection of vendors under one roof, including some wonderful butcher shops with sawdust on the floor that offered up some of Buffalo's best food, which is saying a lot.

The variety of food at the Broadway Market was astonishing, and constituted a vegetarian's worst nightmare. The display cases showed, among other offerings, pork neck bone, smoked pork neck bone, jellied tongue, Polish bacon, slab bacon, double smoked hunter bacon, German-style wieners, Italian sausage, pork roll sausage, hot or mild beef sausage, barley sausage, beer sausage, something called "smoked butt," which I'd rather not know about, chopped ham, smoked hocks, turkey gizzards, smoked turkey parts, chicken feet, chicken liver, chicken fat, fresh oxtails, and ribs of every type. Just before Easter, people of Polish descent came in to buy butter lambs—butter in the shape of a sacrificial lamb, to which they affixed a red ribbon to symbolize the blood of Christ.

We kept it simple. Dad would buy sausages and fresh hot dogs—but only certain brands were acceptable, all locally made and strung together like the wieners in old cartoons: Malecki, Sahlen, Redlinski, Szelengowski (known as Shellies), and Wardynski. "Don't give me that bologna!" went their radio jingle. "I want Wardynski's!" It didn't rhyme, but it sounded just right.

When Dad put the hot dogs on the grill, he'd cut each one three times with "paper cuts" so the flavor would burst through.

Hot dogs are a serious food in Buffalo, especially "charred" hot dogs. In my day, just about every neighborhood had a hot dog stand, usually with a real charcoal fire that stayed lit all day. Even today, the Galleria, the city's biggest shopping mall, has an indoor charcoal hot dog stand, with huge ducts and fans to deal with the smoke. It opens at 11 A.M., and by noon the line stretches around the corner.

Before leaving the Broadway Market, we'd pick up a bottle of Weber's Horseradish Mustard (made in Buffalo!), relish, hamburgers, macaroni salad, potato salad (hey, you gotta eat!), and corn on the cob, which Mom boiled in the kitchen and we layered with plenty of butter and salt. On the way home we'd stop at the Quality Bakery for freshly baked hot dog rolls; the bland supermarket version was simply unacceptable. And no Father's Day cookout was complete without a real keg of beer for the grown-ups. The keg, wrapped in an old plastic tablecloth, was wedged into a big washbucket packed with ice. That was another of Dad's rules: if you served beer, it had to be cold—ice cold.

Although Dad appreciates good food, he doesn't like to get too fancy about it. In the fall of 1992, I brought him with me to Los Angeles, where I was going to make an appearance on the *Tonight Show* with Jay Leno. "And tonight, Jay's guests are—Cindy Crawford! [wild applause] Gloria Estefan! [wild applause] Kevin Spacey! [wild applause] And from NBC's *Meet the Press*, Tim Russert! [tepid, polite applause]."

In the Green Room before I went on, Dad spotted Cindy Crawford. "Good-looking girl," he said. "What's her name?" He had just seen one of the most beautiful and recognizable women in the world, but Dad wasn't kidding. When Jay Leno came in to say hello, Dad leaned over to him and said, "Good-looking girl, isn't she?"

"Yeah," said Leno, "we found her on the street."

After the taping, my NBC colleague Maria Shriver took us to dinner at Spago, on the Sunset Strip in West Hollywood, which was one of the city's trendiest restaurants. After we were seated, a waiter came over and asked, "Would you like still water or sparkling?"

"What the hell is he talking about?" said Dad.

"Do you want water?" I asked him.

"Sure, I'll have a glass of water."

"We have bottled water, sir."

"Bottled water? What the hell is that? Welcome to California!"

Spago's menu was so complicated that you almost needed a dictionary to get through it. After studying it for a while, Dad turned to me and said, "Can you translate this?"

"Dad, why don't you tell me what you'd like?"

He pointed to a man in the kitchen who was preparing little personal pizzas. "I'd like a couple of those—only bigger—with pepperoni and mushrooms."

"And to drink?"

"Beer."

"Sir, we have Anchor Steam, Peak's Pure Red—"

"How about Genesee?" he said, naming a Buffalo favorite that used to be advertised with the slogan, "Pure hemlock water makes the difference!" (Hemlock water? When I was in fifth grade, I wondered about that. Didn't the Genesee people know that hemlock had killed Socrates? Somebody must have, because that slogan disappeared during the 1960s. What they meant was that Genesee beer was made from the pristine waters of Lake Hemlock, which is south of Rochester.)

"No, sir, we don't carry that brand."

"Labatt's?"

"I'm afraid not."

"What kind do you have?"

"Would you like a dark beer or a light beer?"

"I just want a beer!"

"Do you have Budweiser?" I asked the waiter.

"Sure."

Big Russ got his Bud, and Maria ordered a bottle of white wine, which arrived in a bucket of ice. That ice bucket looked pretty good to Dad. "Listen," he told the waiter, "why don't you bring me a couple more Buds and stick 'em right here, in the ice?"

Maria burst out laughing. "Mr. Russert," she said, "I love you, I really do."

"Yeah? Why?"

"Because you know who you are. But I'll tell you something. If I had known that all you really wanted was beer and a pizza, I would have given you a six-pack and taken you to Chuck E. Cheese."

THESE DAYS, Dad spends his winters in Florida. He likes to drive down, but a couple of years ago he had back surgery, and I urged him to fly.

"I don't want to fly," he told me. "You know, it's probably faster to drive."

"What?!"

"Really. The flight is at nine, which means I have to get up at four and be at the airport at five. By the time you take off your shoes, and you take off your belt, and you take off your pants —"

"Dad —"

"Then they ask for your ID, and you get on the plane, and then they make everybody get *off* the plane. I see it all the time on the news."

"Dad —"

"By the time they're ready for takeoff, I'm already passing the Georgia border, if I'm driving."

Eventually, the only way I could get him not to make that long drive was by chartering a plane to take him to Florida.

About half an hour after he was scheduled to land, I called him in Florida.

"Dad?"

"Yeah, I just walked in."

"How was the flight?"

"Let me tell you, that was the best pineapple I ever had! And you know those muffins where you can't even find the blueberries? Well on *these* muffins, they were hanging off 'em like fruit on a tree!" He had just taken his first noncommercial flight since the war, and all he wanted to talk about was the food.

When I turned fifty-three, Dad called early in the morning to wish me a happy birthday.

"What are you gonna eat?" he wanted to know.

"Dad, I don't know, it's eight in the morning."

"I know, but you've gotta have a good birthday meal."

I assured him I would, and I kept my promise. Dinner consisted of salad, pasta, steak, and birthday cake, washed down with a couple of cold ones. Like the man says, you gotta eat.

7.

Baseball

"You do everything you can, and then just a little more."

BASEBALL. If there's a more beautiful word in the English language, I have yet to hear it. I love the game for any number of reasons, but one of them, certainly, is that baseball has served as such a powerful link between Dad and me, and later, between me and my son.

I grew up with the proud knowledge that Uncle Fran, Dad's older brother, had played left field for a team known as the Burke Brothers. Sponsored by a local menswear store, the Burke Brothers had represented Legion Post 721—*our* Legion post—in American Legion junior baseball. Although the members of that team now had sons and daughters of their own, in South Buffalo the Burke Brothers were still a household name. Back in 1929, this group of high school students had won the Erie County championship, and then the New York State championship. The Burkes kept on winning, and went all the way to the American Legion national championship. They won that, too. You could look it up.

Every time Dad and I went to the Legion, we'd stop and admire the display case, which contained a photograph of Uncle Fran and his teammates, a baseball signed by all the players (which was positioned so you could see Fran Russert's autograph), and a trophy that read "Junior World Champions." The last time I checked, these items were still there, almost seventy-five years later. Sometimes, one of the Legion men would come up to me and say, "Your uncle was a great left fielder. What a player!" The Burke Brothers' success was so real to these people that they sometimes forgot they were talking to a boy who hadn't even been born yet when the team won the title. Dad referred to it often as well, and it wasn't until years later that I realized that he was only six years old when his big brother's team went all the way.

Uncle Fran was a police detective who carried a badge and a gun, even when he came to visit us after church on Sunday. (He always assured us that the gun wasn't loaded.) He was already a glamorous figure to me, but when I started going to the Legion with Dad and seeing that picture of him in his baseball uniform, he became even more heroic. Sometimes, when he came to our house, I used to close my eyes and picture him as a young left fielder. This was a new and startling idea, that an adult I knew had once been a child, just like me.

They were just a group of teenagers playing amateur ball, but baseball was king in Buffalo, and championship teams were rare. (I guess some things don't change.) To this day, no other Buffalo team has won the American Legion championship. It

was true then, and it's still true today: when a Buffalo team suc-
ceeds, it means the world to us. A newspaper headline before
the championship game captured a city's dreams: ALL BUFFALO
WAITS AND HOPES THESE BOYS LEAD BURKES TO VICTORY.

Uncle Fran liked to tell me that when he played for the
Burke Brothers during their championship season, he met Babe
Ruth, who autographed a baseball for him. I was fascinated by
that story: my father's brother had met Babe Ruth! Naturally, I
longed to see the baseball that would confirm this wonderful
tale, but whenever I asked Uncle Fran to show it to me, he
always put me off. I began to wonder whether it actually existed,
and I asked Dad, "Did Uncle Fran really meet Babe Ruth, or is
he teasing me?"

"Uncle Frank is a great teaser," Dad replied, "but he's family.
He's my brother, and he loves you like a son. If he tells you
something, it's true."

Uncle Fran is no longer alive, but his son Mike told me how
his father ended up with that baseball. In Chicago, during one
of the games leading up to the championship, Francis Russert
had hit the game-winning home run. That evening, there was a
knock on the door of his hotel room: "Hey kid," somebody told
him, "the man across the hall wants to say hello." When Uncle
Fran knocked on the door, it was opened by none other than
Walter Johnson, the great pitcher for the Washington Senators.
"Come on in, young man," said Johnson, pointing to an open
door. "My roomie here has been having a little trouble hitting
home runs. He'd like to know how you can hit a baseball that
far." Uncle Fran walked into the connecting room, and there,
sitting on the bed, was Babe Ruth. Both players autographed a

baseball for the young visitor, and so did the promoter who had arranged their barnstorming tour. I wish I knew more about that encounter, and what it felt like for Uncle Fran to meet the most famous man in America. But I can imagine it, and that will have to do.

My cousin Mike still has his father's uniform and his bat. He also has that signed baseball, which he keeps in his bedroom. He, too, had grown up hearing about Babe Ruth's autograph, but his father didn't show it to Mike until he was a teenager. In the spring of 1996, when Mike's son Cullen was graduating from high school in Cambridge, New York, I was invited to give the commencement address. When I went to Mike's house, I asked to see the ball, and Mike went upstairs to get it. He was gone for a long time, and once again I wondered if somebody was putting me on, but he came back with the autographed ball in his hand. After all those years, this was the first time I had ever seen it.

When I was six or seven, and I asked my father for a base-ball glove, he gave me one of Uncle Fran's—one of those lumpy, shapeless, old-fashioned mitts without any lacing, the kind you see in old photographs. But I wanted a *real* glove, preferably a Rawlings or a Spalding. On my next birthday, Dad brought me a new glove, but it didn't have a brand name that I recognized, and it was yellow, rather than orange-brown. I didn't hide my disappointment, and to this day I regret it. Dad bought me a gift that he could afford, and I wish I had shown more apprecia-tion for it.

Sometimes Dad would take me into the backyard or the driveway to play catch. "Remember," he'd say, "Uncle Fran's the ballplayer." Maybe so, but I loved playing catch with my dad. When we played in the driveway and I couldn't handle his throw, the ball would roll into the street, and I'd have to retrieve it—carefully, of course. "Knock it down," Big Russ would say. "Get in front of it. If you can't catch the ball, try to block it. Don't let it get behind you." It was good advice, and not just about baseball.

I couldn't wait to play in a real game, and eventually I got my chance. In fifth and sixth grade I played on teams sponsored by the Police Athletic League. Our games were played in one of the many fields in Cazenovia Park, the recreational center of our neighborhood, and a large, beautiful space that had been designed by the great nineteenth-century landscape architect, Frederick Law Olmsted. I had more desire than talent, but I played second base well enough, and I loved to imagine that someday, after Bobby Richardson retired, I would play that position for the Yankees. It could definitely happen, I told myself. For one thing, I was the nephew of Fran Russert. For another, the great Warren Spahn came from our neighborhood, and he had grown up playing ball right here in Caz Park.

Once in a while, at Legion post picnics, the fathers would play softball against the sons, and we'd howl with laughter as our dads took the field. These guys were our *fathers*. How could they possibly play baseball? They weren't all that adept defensively, but when they started swinging the bat and hoisting balls into the trees beyond center field, the laughter soon faded.

Dad was rarely able to see me play, but my own work schedule has allowed me to see just about every one of my son's games, both in Little League and in high school. A couple of years ago I brought Dad to an exhibition game in Port Charlotte, Florida, where Luke's junior varsity team was matched up against one of the local high schools. What a wonderful feeling it was, sitting with my dad and watching baseball in the Florida sunshine. What made it even sweeter was that a kid named Luke Russert was playing first base for St. Albans. Late in the game, with the go-ahead run on second, Luke got a hit, and Dad became so excited that he stood up, caught his foot on something, and toppled over. Fortunately, he wasn't hurt. As I picked him up, dusted him off, and retrieved his glasses, he waved off my concern. He had only one question: "Was he safe?" Yes, I told him, the runner had scored. I have never seen Big Russ so excited. "Lukey," he called out, "way to go!" Luke must have enjoyed that moment, but I was beaming.

SOMETIMES DAD AND I went over to Caz Park to watch the talented young men who played for the Simon Pures, the premier amateur team in our neighborhood. They were named for, and originally sponsored by, one of Buffalo's many breweries, but when the brewery closed down—and Simon Pure was the last to go—the team somehow survived. The Simon Pures, the Ramblers, and a handful of other teams belonged to the city's Municipal Baseball League, and when they played on warm summer evenings, several thousand people showed up to watch them, looking down on a beautiful diamond from the side of a green grassy hill.

Sometimes we went to Offermann Stadium, where the Buffalo Bisons played against other teams in the International League—

just one step, but a big one, below the majors. Opening Day in Buffalo was practically a civic holiday. Marching bands converged on the old ball park, and many offices closed at noon so workers could go to the game. It's hard to believe, but seventh and eighth graders in South Buffalo's Catholic schools were excused from class early that day and allowed to attend the game, as long as we brought a note from home. I went with my friends, accompanied by one of their dads, usually a fireman or a cop whose schedule allowed him an occasional day off in the middle of the week. I imagine that girls were allowed to go too, but as far as I know, they never did. They stayed in school that day, early baseball widows, in some cases, who were getting a foretaste of hard times to come.

The real thrill of Offermann Stadium was going with Dad to a night game and staying up late to watch baseball under the lights. Offermann, which had been in use since 1924, was an old, crumbling, wooden ballpark with a seating capacity of just fourteen thousand, but to me it seemed like a palace. The stadium had been built in a residential area, and the people who lived on Woodlawn Avenue used to watch the games from their rooftops and second-floor windows. The district around the stadium was known as the Fruit Belt, because the streets had names like Peach, Orange, Grape, and Lemon. It was a rough neighborhood, but in those days it wasn't considered dangerous to go there. Dad would park the car on the lawn of a nearby house and pay the owner. "It's a package deal," Big Russ liked to say. "You get parking and they protect your tires." Each house would accommodate two cars on the lawn, and sometimes three. "Park it over there and leave the keys," we'd be told, but Dad didn't care for that arrangement. If he couldn't keep his keys, we'd find another spot.

We always bought our peanuts in advance to save money, but once we entered the stadium gates, Offermann resembled a giant outdoor snack bar that happened to be above a baseball field. "Hey, cold beer here!" I loved to watch the beer vendor as he set up four big plastic cups on the concrete steps. In a series of quick wrist movements, he'd flip open four longneck bottles. Holding two in each hand, he'd fill the cups to the brim without spilling a drop. All through the game we kept our hands ready, palms up, as beer, soda, hot dogs, peanuts, and various other snacks traveled in one direction, along a conveyor belt of hands, and money flowed the other way, back to the vendor. The phrase "pass it down" would echo through the stadium like a litany. You soon learned to move your hands without looking down, or you'd miss half the game.

Offermann Stadium is long gone now, but it's still there in my memory—and still beautiful. It was an intimate place, where the fans were close to the action; if you called to a player, the chances were good that he'd hear you, and maybe even respond. The emerald green field was beautifully maintained, to the point where fans knew the name of the head groundskeeper, Joe Brown. His young assistant, George Toma, went on to become the head groundskeeper for the NFL Super Bowls. Once, a broadcaster asked him why he worked so hard when the grass he was tending so carefully would soon be trampled. I love Toma's reply: "You do everything you can, and then just a little more."

Between 1956 and 1958, the big draw at Offermann Stadium was the magnificent presence and spectacular power of a first

baseman named Luke Easter. Most International League players were hoping to make it to the major leagues, but a few,
including Luscious (that was his real name!) Luke Easter, had
already been there. Like so many other black players of that era,
he had started out in the Negro Leagues, where he was the first
player ever to hit a home run over the center field bleachers at
the Polo Grounds.

He joined the Cleveland Indians in 1950, and soon hit the
longest home run in the history of Municipal Stadium, a 477-
foot shot to the upper deck. When he came to Buffalo in 1956,
his power hitting and his outgoing, generous personality helped
save the franchise. In his first season with the Bisons, he led the
league with thirty-five home runs, which was all the more
remarkable because he was thought to be forty-one years old.
(Nobody was ever sure of Luke's age.) A year later, he became the
first player ever to hit a home run over the center field score-
board in Offermann Stadium. Soon after that, he did it again.

Whenever Luke came up to bat, the whole crowd would
erupt in a chant of "Luuuuuuuke!" that could probably be heard
all through the neighborhood. It was a high-pitched Luuuuuuuke, much like the one you'd hear years later for Bruuuuuuuce
Springsteen, as opposed, say, to the low growl that often greets
baseball manager (and former player) Lou Piniella. Bill Mazer,
who announced the games on the radio and had a way of making the lowly Bisons sound like the 1927 Yankees, used to say,
lest anyone get the wrong impression, "Folks, they're not boo-
ing. They *love* Luke Easter!" We sure did. And when Luke hit
one out of the park, the Amazing Mazer would call out, "Going,
going, gone! Another White Owl Wallop!" Dad smoked White

Owl cigars, which somehow added to the drama. When the Bisons were on the road, Mazer would re-create the games in the WGR studio, pitch by pitch, although you could hear the Teletype machine clacking in the background. In the early innings of home games, Mazer would urge us to come to the stadium: "Folks, it's a beautiful night for a ball game, so if you're anywhere near the ballpark, keep-a-comin', 'cause there's a lotta great baseball to be played." I spent many nights under the sheets with a transistor radio, listening to Bill Mazer and waiting for Luke Easter to hit another one. I guess you could say it was my intro- duction to the power of broadcasting.

It probably didn't happen this way, but in my memory, at least, every time Dad and I went to Offermann Stadium, Luke Easter blasted another one out of the park. What a beautiful sight it was: in a night game you'd see the trajectory of the ball taking off against the dark sky, still rising as it left the confines of the stadium. People were cheering, of course, but I secretly wished they'd stay silent, just once, so we could hear that ball come down. Luke, however, had his doubts about the coming down part. Once, when a fan bragged that he had witnessed the slugger's longest home run, Luke said, "If it came down, it wasn't my longest." But assuming it did come down, I used to wonder: What happened? Did it shatter a windshield? Hit somebody's roof? The next morning, I couldn't wait to check the sports pages to read how far that ball had traveled. When the game was over and the crowd filed out of the ball park, people were still buzzing about Luke's home run. "Did you *see* that ball?" Fans were smiling from ear to ear.

The Bisons left Buffalo after the 1970 season, but they came back in the 1980s. In 1993, the team invited me to throw out the first pitch on Opening Day, and my son Luke and I did it together. I got a huge kick out of that, not only because of my childhood memories, but also because Luke Russert is named (in part) after the great Luke Easter. On the wall of his bedroom there's a poster of Luke Easter, wearing number 36 for the Rochester Red Wings.

ALTHOUGH I FOLLOWED THE BISONS, the team I really loved was the New York Yankees. Dad taught me early on how to read a box score, and I followed the Yankees every day in the morning paper. My sisters used to laugh when I announced at the breakfast table (as if they cared) that Bobby Richardson had two hits and another RBI in yesterday's game, or that Mantle had homered yet again. I loved the economy and the precision of box scores, and sometimes I'd cut them out and put them in my pocket, carrying the whole team around with me on a tiny scrap of newsprint. I hope I realized how fortunate I was that my childhood coincided with one of the great eras of this remarkable dynasty; by the time I was fifteen, the Yankees had appeared in the World Series thirteen times during my young life. It's an accomplishment that is almost inconceivable today.

In the summer of 1963, when I was thirteen, the Yankees came to Buffalo to play an exhibition game against the International League All Stars, which brought out the largest crowd ever to see a baseball game in our city. I was part of a group of kids who approached the Yankees before the game, hoping to get some autographs. Most of them were nice about it, but one player, Joe

Pepitone, who had a reputation for being a nice guy, walked right past us, pushing the pens and papers right out of our hands. When I came back to our seats and told Dad, he couldn't believe it. "What the hell is wrong with that guy?" he said. "It takes just as much time to be nice as to be a jerk." A big Italian man sitting behind us said, "What's wrong, kid?" When I told him, he too became angry. Every time Pepitone came up, he would yell, "Pepperoni! Pepperoni! You can't see the ball, can you? That's what happens when you don't give a kid an autograph."

This memory stayed with me as I watched my own son grow up and ask for autographs. I never imagined that I would be recognized by strangers, and that I, too, would sometimes be asked for autographs, but it happens, and when it does, no matter how rushed I am, I think of Big Russ's words: "It doesn't take any longer to be nice to a kid." Actually, it *does* take a little longer, but it's worth it.

I was born on May 7, 1950, and every spring Dad gave me a birthday present that was so wonderful it still brings a smile to my face. Yankee Stadium was a full day's drive in each direction, and with Dad working two jobs, a pilgrimage to that sacred shrine was out of the question. But if we planned it carefully, we could see the Yankees on one of their regular visits to Cleveland, a four- or five-hour drive from Buffalo. We'd go on a Sunday, when Dad didn't work, which was fine with me because in those days, Sundays meant doubleheaders—the old-fashioned kind, where you got to see two games for the price of one.

My job was to start the ball rolling while there was still snow on the ground by writing a letter to the Cleveland Indians: "Dear Sirs, Would you please send me a schedule for the upcoming baseball season?" It was a useful exercise: I learned early on that if you write a letter, somebody will answer. When Uncle Fran gave me the addresses of the NFL football teams, I wrote to each one, politely requesting a picture, and they all responded.

When the schedule arrived, I'd look for the earliest weekend series with the Yankees. Dad and I would go to the bank for a money order, and we'd send it off to Cleveland with a request for upper deck seats. For weeks I'd check the mail every day, waiting anxiously for those precious tickets to show up. They would finally arrive, and as the magical date drew closer, I was almost too excited to sleep. It's hard to convey the sheer joy and anticipation I felt as I counted the days until our annual drive to Cleveland. My dad was taking me to see the Yankees, and life didn't get any better than that.

Three of my uncles usually came with us, which made the trip even more fun: Uncle Fran, of course, who was a great fan of the game and Uncle Sonny Seeley, Mom's brother, who served in the Marine Corps. To this day it's Semper Fi all the way. His son, Bernie, became a Marine, too, and so did his stepson, Nick, who fought in Vietnam and was injured when he was hit with a mortar in Da Nang. Uncle Sonny's granddaughter became a Marine, and I recently learned that his great-granddaughter is planning to be one, too. "Some families go to Disneyland," he says. "Mine goes to Parris Island."

Uncle Sonny Rovnak, who is married to my mother's sister, Peaches, was a fireman, a carpenter, and a plumber who could do just about anything. When I was eleven, he put in the entire family room in our basement in about a week. When he was finished, Dad came down and said, "This is great, but where's the bar?"

"What bar?" said Uncle Sonny.

"I'm having a party tomorrow to show off the room. There's gotta be a bar!"

By the next night, the family room had a bar.

When that special Sunday rolled around and it was time to go to Cleveland, Dad and I got up early to make the necessary preparations. We'd pack sandwiches and fruit, but the critical part involved driving over to the Legion Hall, where the ice was free. The routine never varied: each year, we'd fill up our green Coleman ice chest with a few bottles of Vernors ginger ale and a generous supply of Genesee beer in longneck bottles, or if Dad was feeling flush, O'Keefe's Ale from Canada. There was an art to "icing up," as we called it: we'd put down a row of bottles, cover it with a blanket of ice, and build it up in layers. Maybe it's because Dad spent the war years in England, but he's always been a fanatic about keeping beer cold. I'm the same way, to the point where a couple of years ago, on Father's Day, my wife and my son decided that the best gift they could give me was a cooler on wheels that holds a hundred cans of soda or beer, and, of course, a ton of ice.

In the late 1950s, before the New York Thruway was finished, we'd head down Route 5 toward Cleveland. There were five of us in the car—Dad and the uncles in the seats, with me wedged into the back of our green 1955 Chevy station wagon, with a pillow propped up against the freezing ice chest. I was the beer jockey, which meant that I took care of the cooler, opened the beers, and passed them around. On the way home I always fell asleep, only to be awakened periodically by the sound of raucous laughter outside the car when Dad pulled over so the men could take a leak. In those days, nobody thought twice about drinking a good amount of beer during a long drive, and that included the driver.

The ballpark where the Indians played was the complete opposite of our beloved Offermann Stadium in Buffalo. Municipal Stadium was a huge, cavernous arena with seventy-eight thousand seats, and when the Yankees came to town, most of those seats were filled.

We'd arrive early so I could go down near the field and watch batting practice before climbing up to the nosebleed section, where our seats were. From all those games, one scene stays in my mind, and it had nothing to do with baseball. Dad had just opened a bottle of beer, and he must have accidentally shaken it, because a stream of liquid sprayed right into the indented brim of the big Panama hat worn by a large black man sitting directly in front of us. Each time the man lowered his head, the beer would collect in the front of his hat; when he leaned back, it flowed the other way. Dad was afraid that it was only a matter of time before the beer spilled onto his lap and the man in the hat would turn around in anger at what might have looked like a practical joke with racial overtones. But inning after inning, that ever-shrinking puddle stayed pretty much in place, lazily sloshing back and forth until it finally evaporated in the sun. Dad and I still laugh about it.

Although our little party was rooting for the visiting team, I don't remember a single awkward moment from those games. I can't prove that sports fans were better behaved in those days, but that's certainly my impression. People booed the umpire, of course, but they also watched their language and were never abusive—especially in the presence of women or children.

Dad and my uncles were remarkably patient. A double-header can drag on for hours, and for all my love of baseball, I'm not entirely sure that I could sit through one today. On those trips to Cleveland, however, I insisted on staying to the bitter end. This was my first and last chance of the year to see my beloved Yankees, and I was determined to witness the very last out, even if the outcome had been obvious since the middle innings. Only now, as an adult, do I realize how hard eighteen innings of baseball and ten hours of driving must have been on Dad. (He loved to drive, and Dad didn't want anyone else behind the wheel of his car.)

I always brought my glove, and inning after inning I waited for a foul ball, although I knew, even if I couldn't quite admit it, that there was little chance of a wayward hit making it all the way up to the top deck. My dream was to catch one off the bat of Yogi Berra, my favorite player, and although that never happened, I did have the thrill of seeing him swat a couple of home runs. I'd sit there bravely yelling, "Yo-gi, Yo-gi," pounding my fist into my glove as my lone, high voice was swallowed up in a chorus of Cleveland fans. Even then, there was something about Yogi Berra that baseball fans responded to, however they may have felt about the Yankees.

Dad also liked Yogi, and I think he appreciated the fact that I was a Yogi fan when virtually every other kid in Buffalo preferred Mickey Mantle. Mantle looked and acted like a matinee idol; Yogi, on the other hand, didn't even look like a ballplayer, and he certainly didn't run like one. I had learned a couple of facts about him that added to my enthusiasm: that he had grown up in St. Louis in a hardworking Italian immigrant family, which meant (among other things) that he was Catholic; and that he had quit school in the eighth grade to take a job in a shoe factory, which meant that his family didn't have much money. I liked everything about him—from his name to his work ethic to his slightly eccentric but generous personality. Each year I went to Cleveland hoping, somehow, to get Yogi Berra's autograph, but I never came close.

They say you can't go home again, but as an adult I've had the privilege of getting to know Yogi and of interviewing him a couple of times on television. I didn't arrange these interviews just to get his autograph, but that was certainly part of the thrill, and while I was at it, I asked him to sign one for Luke, and for Big Russ, too.

Just about everybody has heard some of Yogi's colorful and unique expressions, but they wear well, and even people who have heard them before still find them funny. This is a man who, when the waiter asked if he wanted his pizza cut into four slices or eight, replied, in all sincerity, "Four. I'm not hungry enough to eat eight." When his wife, Carmen, asked, "Yogi, you were born in St. Louis, you played in New York, and you live in New Jersey. When you die, where do you want to be buried?" Yogi said, "Surprise me."

The first time I met Whitey Ford, I asked him if Yogi had really said all the things he is reported to have said.

"Are you kidding?" said Ford. "It's worse than you think." He told me about a game he was pitching against the Chicago

White Sox. "I had been out with Mantle the night before," Ford said, before adding, in a wonderful understatement, "so I probably wasn't at the top of my game." Leading off for Chicago was Luis Aparicio, who hit the first pitch for a single. Then Nellie Fox did exactly the same thing: two pitches, two men on. The third batter was Minnie Minoso, and Ford hit him with the first pitch. The cleanup hitter, Ted Kluszewski, promptly hit Ford's first offering over the fence for a home run. Four pitches, 4–0.

At this point, Casey Stengel ran out to the mound to confer with his pitcher and catcher. "Yogi," he asked, "does Whitey have his stuff today?"

"How the hell would I know?" said Yogi. "I haven't caught a pitch yet."

Yogi's funny sayings are so entertaining that it's easy to forget what a fierce competitor he was. When I was a boy, every time the Yankees were in the World Series, the broadcasters would show a clip of a particularly dramatic play from the 1955 Series. The Yankees played the Dodgers that year, which was the only time Brooklyn ever won the World Series. In the eighth inning of the first game, the great Jackie Robinson executed one of the rarest and most difficult feats in baseball: he stole home. Yogi was behind the plate, and in the film you can see how passionate and animated he became when umpire Bill Summers called Robinson safe. Now it's clear to me (and to most other observers) that the umpire called it right, but either way, this was a side of Yogi that most fans aren't aware of. On two or three occasions, when I have interviewed Yogi, I have shown him this clip from 1955, and each time I do, he watches it with the same intensity. In 2002, when I interviewed Yogi with his teammate Phil Rizzuto, even Rizzuto, who remembered being on the field with an excellent view of the play, agreed that Robinson was safe because Yogi didn't get his glove down low enough to tag the runner. But Yogi was adamant. Another time, when I insisted on the air that Robinson was safe, Yogi backed off, but only a little. "Well," he finally said in a classic Yogi answer, "he was safe, but he's still out."

After the broadcast, Whitey Ford, who had pitched in that game, wrote me a note saying that Rizzuto wasn't even on the field at the time, so the argument goes on.

LITTLE DID I IMAGINE, as I wrote away for baseball tickets before the 1961 season began, what lay in store for Yankee fans just a few weeks later. That was the year of the great home run race, when both Mantle and Roger Maris were closing in on Babe Ruth's record of sixty in a single season, which had stood for thirty-four years. There were many nights that season when I stayed up late to listen to the Yankees on my transistor radio. Early the next morning, before he went to work, Dad would ask, "How'd we do last night?" I think he already knew, but he realized how much I enjoyed giving him the latest news.

If somebody was going to break Babe Ruth's record, most people wanted it to be Mantle. But I was rooting for Maris. Even at the age of eleven, my friends and I noticed that he was a Catholic from a blue-collar neighborhood. Mantle was a great player, no question about it, but he was going to the Hall of Fame no matter how many home runs he hit in 1961. Maris, on the other hand, had this one chance to achieve baseball immortality, and I really wanted him to make it.

I would have loved to interview Roger Maris, but I never got the chance; he died in 1985, well before I started appearing on television. A few years ago, when I flew in to Fargo, North Dakota, to address a Chamber of Commerce dinner, I remembered that somewhere in Fargo there was a Roger Maris Museum. A driver met me at the airport, and when I told him that I wanted to see the museum on the way into town, he was surprised that I knew about it. A few minutes later, he pulled into the parking lot of a shopping mall. "Not here," I told him. "I want to see the Roger Maris Museum."

"It's in here," he said, and although that sounded odd, I followed him out of the car.

The Roger Maris Museum, I soon discovered, is as unpretentious as Maris himself. It isn't a museum at all: it's a glass case in a corridor of the West Acres Mall, which holds Maris's bat, his glove, and several of his uniforms. There was a notice that Maris was buried in Holy Cross Cemetery, so we drove out there so I could pay my respects.

As we were coming back to Fargo, I remarked to the driver that the traffic seemed pretty heavy.

"Yes," he said, "a lot of people are coming tonight."

"They told me the Chamber dinner was sold out," I said proudly. "More than eight hundred people."

"Oh, this isn't for you," he said. "It's for Garth Brooks. He's at the Fargo Dome for three nights."

"Three nights? How many does the Dome hold?"

"Twenty-five thousand."

"That's seventy-five thousand seats," I said. "How many people live in Fargo?"

"Ninety thousand."

For a fleeting moment, I thought I had made it big in Fargo, North Dakota. But if Roger Maris ended up with only a glass case in a shopping mall, what was I thinking?

8.

Fatherhood

"Never get between a boy and his dreams."

I T'S NO GREAT SECRET that men who might otherwise have little in common are often able to form a connection through a shared interest in sports. I first met George W. Bush in April 1999, when I flew down to Austin to meet with him. As a journalist, I wanted to get to know the governor of Texas, who appeared to be the likely Republican nominee for president in 2000. And as the host of *Meet the Press*, I hoped to persuade him to appear on our program.

I knew, of course, that we might also talk a little baseball. Before he ran for governor, Bush had been one of the owners of the Texas Rangers, and he is often teased for having approved a deal with the Chicago White Sox in which the Rangers traded away a young prospect named Sammy Sosa. (To be fair, Sosa was hitting only .238 at the time.) I also knew that his involvement with the Rangers had been more than a business opportunity, and that George W. Bush had a real love for the game.

When I walked into his office, the first thing he showed me was his collection of autographed baseballs. "Are you a baseball fan?" he asked.

"Absolutely."

"What team did you like when you were a kid?"

"The Yankees," I said.

"Do you remember their lineup?"

"Sure," I said. "For the '61 Yankees, it was Bobby Richardson, second base; Tony Kubek, shortstop; Roger Maris, right field; Mickey Mantle, center field; Yogi Berra, left field; Elston Howard, catcher; Moose [Bill] Skowron, first base; Clete Boyer, third base." Then I named the starting pitchers and even threw in a few uniform numbers. I remembered some from my childhood, and had studied up on the others, just in case.

"So who was better?" he asked me. "Mantle or Mays?"

Now he was playing hardball. This is one of the great ongoing arguments in all of sports, and my friends and I had some heated discussions about it when we were kids, never imagining that the issue would remain unresolved the rest of our lives. But I didn't have a clear favorite in this race, although I'd go to the mat for Yogi Berra over John Roseboro of the Dodgers. I knew, however, where George W. Bush stood on the subject. "I never dreamed of being president," he had said. "I wanted to be Willie Mays."

So I hedged. "Well," I said, "I loved the Yankees, but I'm not an absolutist on that one."

He laughed. "Who's the politician here?"

We soon moved on to other, weightier topics, but I think both of us would have been just as happy to continue talking about baseball. This is a man who, on the campaign trail, asked reporters if they could name an All-Star team made up exclusively of players who had been their league's MVP for two consecutive years, which is not an easy question.

On March 30, 2001, a few weeks after he was sworn in, President Bush hosted a luncheon at the White House for members of the Baseball Hall of Fame. I was fortunate enough to be invited, along with Luke. Of the sixty-two Hall of Famers who were still alive, at least forty came to the White House that day, including Yogi Berra, Hank Aaron, Bob Feller, Tom Seaver, Duke Snider, Bob Gibson, and Carl Yastrzemski. The Marine Band played—what else?—"Take Me Out to the Ball Game," and the president spoke about his childhood hero, Willie Mays.

Luke and I had a wonderful time, and so did the players, many of whom brought baseballs and were asking each other for autographs. Sandy Koufax showed up, which created quite a stir because he doesn't appear in public very often. We also met Buck O'Neil, a Negro League star and chairman of the Negro Leagues Baseball Museum. "I'm the grandson of a slave," he told us, "and I'm standing here in the White House." Luke told him that he and some of his classmates collected caps from the Negro League, including a team known as the Indianapolis Clowns. When we met Nolan Ryan, Luke and I recalled the time we had spotted him a few years earlier in the parking lot at Texas Rangers Stadium. Luke was nine at the time, and when he suddenly ran off to get Nolan Ryan's autograph, I'd had a moment of panic as I remembered that Al and Tipper Gore's youngest child had almost died after being hit by a car outside Memorial Stadium in Baltimore. "Look out!" I had cried as my son sprinted away.

As the White House event was ending, Stan Musial stood up on a chair and played "Take Me Out to the Ball Game" on his harmonica. We were about to leave when the president came over to us and said, "Luke, how are you doing? Have you ever seen the Oval Office?"

"No, sir." The president escorted us to his office, where Vice President Dick Cheney was waiting for him. "Come on in, Veep," the president said. "I want you to meet the famous Luke." (Both men had heard me talk about him, and the president had met Luke during the campaign.) "Let's take some pictures here," the president said, and while we waited for the photographer, he asked Luke what position he played on the St. Albans Junior Varsity team.

"First base."

"Really? That was my dad's position. And what's the name of your team?"

"The Bulldogs."

"Wait a minute, that was my dad's team. What's going on here?"

Back in the car, I suggested to Luke that he write the President a thank-you note. His letter went something like this: "Dear Mr. President, Thank you for introducing me to the Hall of Famers and for showing me the Oval Office. I think that if I work really hard, I'll have a chance for both."

The next time I saw the president, I told him about my son's ambitious plans. His response was beautiful: "Never get between a boy and his dreams."

On our way home from the White House, I thought about how when I was Luke's age, I hadn't been able to get Yogi Berra's autograph. And here my son had met some of the greatest players of all time, and had just been shown the Oval Office by the president himself. I couldn't get over it.

THOSE BASEBALL TRIPS to Cleveland with Dad were so important to me that as soon as Luke was old enough, I started taking him and his friends every year on his birthday to see the Orioles play. Our annual excursions to Baltimore were very different from those long drives to Cleveland: instead of sitting up high, we had seats behind the dugout. I was even able to get the boys onto the field during batting practice.

When Luke was about to turn sixteen, I asked, "Would you like to keep our tradition alive and go to an Orioles game?"

"Dad," he said, "what I'd really like to see is a NASCAR race."

That came as a jolt. My first reaction was, "NASCAR? What about baseball?"

It took me a while to realize that part of being a father is coming to terms with the fact that your son is an independent person, rather than a smaller version of you. In the summer of 2001, instead of going to Baltimore to see a ball game, we went to the New Hampshire International Speedway to watch a NASCAR race. It turned out to be a wonderful experience, because Luke was able to show me around and teach me about one of his interests. It was a gift for both of us, and an important reminder to me that the father-son relationship is a two-way street.

Apparently, though, I needed another lesson. When it comes to baseball, I've always been pretty aggressive. The day Luke was born, I put a little Nerf baseball and a tiny glove in the corner of his crib. When he was able to crawl, we would roll a ball back and forth. As the years passed, we moved on to Whiffle ball, T-ball, Little League, and high school baseball. Luke has loved the game as much as I do, and for six years in a row we went to spring training together.

Early in 2003, he came home from school and said, "Dad, I have to talk to you."

"Sure," I said. My mind was racing. What could it be? What kind of trouble was he in?

"I've decided to give up baseball."

My immediate reaction was a huge sigh of relief. Of all the possible problems he could have brought to me, I was glad it was nothing serious. Then I felt sad, because baseball had played such an enormous part in my life, and with my father, and in Luke's life, and with *his* father.

"How did you come to that conclusion?" I asked.

"I want to explain this and I hope you'll understand," he said. "I just don't have a passion for the game." He had an embarrassed look on his face, and was clearly asking for my support.

"Luke, I understand completely, and I think that's great."

Except that I didn't really say that, or anything like it.

On the other hand, at least I didn't blurt out, "How could you break my heart like this?"

What I actually said was, "Are you sure about this?"

"I really am," he said. "To play the game well, you really have to throw yourself into it. I'm going to stay with football and concentrate on golf."

Golf? I had to laugh. Suddenly the Russerts from South Buffalo were taking up golf? He must have read my mind, because he said, "Moving on up." Wasn't he a little young to know the theme song from *The Jeffersons*?

"Dad, are you okay with this?"

"Sure. I'll miss watching you play ball, but this is about you."

I thought back to the time we had gone to the NASCAR race, and I realized that I was learning that same lesson all over again. Luke was my son, but that didn't mean he was Tim Russert, Junior, or an instrument for Tim Russert to relive his youth. Yes, he's my son, but no, he's not me. Moreover, he was not breaking away, casting me aside, or turning his back on all of our shared memories. He was following his heart, just as I had done in my youth. That was his job, and I, too, had a job to do. My job was to reconcile myself to his uniqueness and his independence, to embrace it and encourage it. I couldn't allow my love as a father to suffocate his individualism. To put it another way, I had to remember not to get between a boy and his dreams.

An hour or so later, I went to him and said, "Hey buddy, whatever you want to do, it's your life and your interests. If you said you didn't want to do anything, I'd give you a hard time. But I can't tell you what sport to choose."

Then I said, "Do you think you can make the golf team?"

"I don't know," he replied. "But I'm going to work hard at it."

That was all I needed to hear. He really was Big Russ's grandson.

9.

Sister Kennedy

"We have to find a way to channel your excessive energy."

I N THE FALL OF 1961, when I was in the sixth grade, our family moved from a modest wood frame house on Woodside Avenue to a slightly larger brick house on the other side of Cazenovia Park. Our old house had been a double, with another family living upstairs. Mom had always wanted a single, while Big Russ may have been influenced by the fact that the new house came with a garage for his car.

Until the move it hadn't occurred to me that our first house had been small, but now we had our own driveway and a real backyard. Officially, our new address put us in the town of West Seneca, but we were only three blocks from the South Buffalo line, close enough to feel that we still lived there. (To this day, I proudly say I grew up in South Buffalo.) I hadn't wanted to move, especially in the middle of the school year, but it wasn't a difficult transition. Kirkwood Drive was filled with boys my age, and I soon made friends with several of them.

One thing that didn't change was that the new house had only one bathroom. This was a point of contention in our family, pitting Mom and especially my three sisters—who always seemed to be in there—against Dad and me. When our turn finally came, we had to hack our way through a jungle of dangling nylon stockings and the deadly fumes of Aqua Net hairspray. Soon after we moved, my Uncle Sonny Rovnak came over and rescued us by building a second bathroom in our basement. We enjoyed our little hideaway, but not for long. When my sisters discovered that the new basement shower was better than the original, Dad and I found ourselves locked out of the second bathroom as well. But now, at least, the lines were shorter.

Unlike our old neighborhood, not everybody on Kirkwood Drive was Irish Catholic. There were Polish, German, and Italian families on our block, and the boys with whom I played basketball in P.J. and Paul Griffin's double-wide driveway included not only Paul McNamara, but Joe Kozak, Patrick DiJoseph, and Don Kubicki.

The diversity we found in West Seneca wasn't limited to ethnic groups. Morgan O'Connell, who lived next door, was very different from the other fathers I knew. Instead of driving off every morning to the steel plant, the post office, or the fire station, Mr. O'Connell kept his own hours. His work had something to do with jukeboxes and pinball machines, some of which were stored in his permanently locked garage. A curious collection of characters, some of them rather seedy-looking, dropped in to visit Morgan: a car would pull up, a couple of men would get out for a brief conversation, and then they'd drive off again. From time to time a delivery truck arrived late at night, and at one point a guard stood watch, pacing up and down the driveway. We didn't know exactly what our neighbor was up to, and although we wondered, we didn't ask.

Two or three times, on a Saturday, he invited me to join him as he drove around to empty out the jukeboxes, pinball machines, and cigarette machines in some of Buffalo's more colorful taverns. I was happy to go, because he gave me a percentage of the take; I always came home with my pockets full of coins. Dad always warned me to be careful in those places, but the people in the bars couldn't have been nicer. When my parents threw a party for my eighth-grade graduation, Mr. O'Connell wheeled an enormous jukebox out of his garage and set it up in the driveway for our enjoyment. I thought of him as mysterious, but in those innocent days it didn't occur to me that there may have been something vaguely sinister going on.

MY NEW SCHOOL, St. Bonaventure, was a lot like Holy Family, but not as large. It too was a parish school, and most of our teachers were Mercy nuns. We had a dress code: the girls wore brown plaid jumpers over white blouses, and the boys dressed in tan shirts with brown clip-on ties and dark pants.

One particular classmate stays in my memory. To some extent Tim Hartnett and I were competitors: we both had the potential to be excellent students, but the other Tim, as our teachers liked to put it, had a more difficult time controlling his behavior. A good-looking boy with dark, curly hair, blue eyes, and tight pants, he was always getting in trouble by making wisecracks, shooting spitballs, or coming to school late, although he lived just a few feet from the building. Often, one of the teachers would send somebody over to wake him up. Tim was bright, bold, and fearless: the other kids liked him, and although he sometimes made life difficult for the nuns, they seemed to have a grudging respect for both his intelligence and his independence.

In December of eighth grade, our class used to walk as a group from the school building to the church next door, where we were rehearsing our Christmas pageant. One morning, we were lined up in the parking lot between the two buildings when a few of us started throwing snowballs. From behind her veil, Sister Lucille noticed a snowball flying through the air, and ordered us to stand still.

"Who threw that snowball?" she asked.

Nobody said a word.

Sister Lucille just stood there and looked at us, waiting for the guilty party to step forward and confess. We didn't have our coats on, and we were starting to feel the cold. Finally, Tim turned to me and muttered, "This is crazy." Then he spoke up and said, "Sister, I threw it."

Several kids protested and said, "No, you didn't," but Sister Lucille either didn't hear them or chose not to. "All right, Tim, come with me," she said. "Everybody else go inside."

Tim was punished in the usual way: he had to wash the blackboard and clap the chalk dust out of the erasers. Later that day, I went to Sister Lucille and said, "Tim took the rap, but a lot of us were throwing snowballs."

"Then why didn't you come forward?"

It was a good question, and I gave her an honest answer: "Frankly, Sister, I wasn't sure which snowball you saw."

She laughed, and I did, too. After school, I told Dad what had happened. "That Hartnett boy did the right thing," Dad said, "and I'm glad you spoke up and told the teacher that he wasn't the only one."

A couple of months later our principal, Sister Edmunda, came in to prepare us for an upcoming visit from the Mother Superior, who was going to quiz us on math problems and state capitals. Sister Edmunda was writing on the blackboard and explaining something or other in an animated way, when, without realizing it, she inadvertently spit on the board.

When she noticed the moisture, she spun around and said, "Okay, who has the squirt gun?"

Of course nobody came forward. There was some nervous laughter, but none of us had any desire to explain what had happened.

"In that case, you're all going to stay right here until I find out who has the squirt gun," she declared.

I was sitting near the back. Tim Hartnett had been mis-behaving that day, and Sister Edmunda had moved him to the front row. He scribbled a note and passed it back to me. "Cover me," he wrote. "I'll get a squirt gun." When I read it, I burst out laughing.

"Timothy, what's so funny?"

"Nothing, Sister." Then, trying to undo the damage, I asked, "Would it be all right if I opened the windows?"

"Go ahead."

I grabbed the window pole and tried to hook it into one of

the large, high windows in our classroom. While the whole class watched me struggle, Tim Hartnett snuck out of the room and ran to the corner store, where he bought a squirt gun. As soon as he returned, he raised his hand and said, "Sister, here it is."

"I knew it! I knew it!" Sister Edmunda felt vindicated. She was proud to have cracked the case, and she soon dismissed the class, with the exception, of course, of Tim Hartnett.

I went straight to Sister Lucille and explained the whole story to make sure that Tim wouldn't be punished. I told Dad, too, and again he was impressed. "Someday that kid will make a great general," he said.

After eighth grade, Tim Hartnett went on to West Seneca Central High School, where he was captain of the football team until he injured his shoulder. He tried to enlist in the Army, but was rejected because of his injury. At the age of twenty-five, he tried again, and this time the Army accepted him. He served for twenty-five years, and spent much of that time flying helicopters into dangerous situations to rescue wounded soldiers. Today, in civilian life, he flies for an air ambulance service out of Buffalo. Although he didn't become a general, Dad wasn't too far off: Tim Hartnett started out as a private and retired as a major.

THREE TEACHERS have had a profound influence on my life, and Sister Mary Lucille Socciarelli, RSM (Religious Sister of Mercy) was the one I met first. A short, stout woman with brown eyes and bright red cheeks that grew even brighter when she was angry, Sister Lucille was a powerful presence in our lives. Youthful, active, and vivacious, she was like no nun we had ever met. She was chatty, she had a sense of humor, she was interested in popular culture, and when we played softball after lunch, she sometimes picked up a bat and started swinging. Soon she'd be rounding first base with her black habit and rosary beads flying in the wind. She did everything with great energy, and that included losing her temper: once, when Laurie Maddigan just wouldn't stop talking, Sister Lucille got so angry that she stormed out of the room and slammed the classroom door with such force that the clock flew off the wall and crashed to the floor. There was absolute silence in the classroom, and it lasted a long time. But as quick as she was to anger, she was equally quick to forgive. Sister Lucille was dynamic and charismatic, and most of us thought of her as the coolest teacher we had ever met.

I still remember our classroom. At the front, above the blackboard, was the alphabet written in script according to the Palmer Method. In the younger grades we used to sit at our desks drawing ovals, trying to create a rhythm and a motion with our wrists that was supposed to lead to good handwriting. Throughout the school day, whenever we looked up, those beautifully drawn letters served as a constant reminder of a certain kind of perfection—one that I was never able to achieve.

Our English curriculum with Sister Lucille included some of the classic stories and poems that millions of schoolchildren learned in the early 1960s, such as Walt Whitman's "O Captain! My Captain!" "The House by the Side of the Road" by Sam Walter Foss ("There are hermit souls that live withdrawn, in the place of their self-content"), and Henry Wadsworth Longfellow's "Paul Revere's Ride," which we liked to recite as,

"Listen my children and you shall hear/Of the midnight ride of a can of beer."

Because our teacher was so intelligent and stimulating, I loved English—or at least the part of English that had to do with literature. I was less enthralled with our grammar textbook, *Voyages in English*, which came in a special edition for Catholic schools in which many of the examples included religious references. What I especially disliked was an exercise that still makes me cringe when I think of it: diagramming sentences. "I don't know why we have to do this," I used to mutter under my breath. I also complained about it to Sister Lucille, but only in private. "Nobody will ever ask us to diagram a sentence," I assured her. I had no idea what adult life held in store for me, but I was pretty sure that this particular activity was not included. And yet I have to admit that diagramming sentences made me a better reader, and, I hope, a better writer.

Like most Catholic schools of that time, St. Bonaventure operated on a tiny budget, which meant that our classrooms were very crowded. It's hard to believe, but there were never fewer than forty kids in the room, and often considerably more. In Sister Lucille's English class, the desks were so tightly packed together that we had to push the back row into the aisle just to open the coat closet. Because we were not divided by ability, every class included a few students who needed extra help. I was impatient when a lesson I had already absorbed had to be repeated because somebody hadn't understood it or wasn't paying attention, and I contributed more than my share of jokes and other disruptions.

One of my misdeeds still makes me cringe when I think

about it. Sister Lucille had a set of rubber stamps with messages ranging from "Excellent" to "Do Over," which she would imprint, as needed, on our homework assignments. Once, when she was in a grumpy mood, I watched her stamp "Do Over" on one paper after another. Out of sheer frustration and Lord knows what else, I picked up the rubber stamp and proceeded to imprint "Do Over" right on her white guimpe. The whole class froze, and I did, too. I couldn't believe what I had done! I turned red and apologized profusely, and my head was filled with visions of being dragged by my ear to the principal, and then to my parents, and of spending the afterlife in a fiery hell for desecrating a nun's habit. God was good to me that day: for whatever reason, perhaps shock, Sister Lucille decided to do nothing at all.

Early in seventh grade, a year or so before this incident occurred, Sister Lucille took me aside and said, "Timmy, we have to find a way to channel your excessive energy. I'm starting a new school newspaper and you're going to be the editor. You'll give out assignments, edit the copy, lay it out, and write the editorials. You'll be the publisher, too. That means you'll have to figure out how much to charge for it, because we'll have to buy our own paper and ink. God has blessed you with a great deal of potential. It's up to you to turn it into something productive."

I loved the idea, although I didn't immediately grasp the full scope of what she was proposing. When Sister Lucille said we were starting a newspaper, my first reaction was, Great, I like to write. It took me a while to realize that this undertaking might be slightly more complicated. Among other issues, there was a bottom line to worry about: we had to take in enough money to produce our product. That, in turn, required some attention to marketing. After all, what was the point of writing a good story if nobody was going to read it?

Today, with the help of computers, even an elementary school can produce a newspaper that actually *looks* like a newspaper. Ours didn't, but nobody expected it would. The articles were typed on a typewriter, and because our school had only one secretary, who was already overworked, Mom or my older sister, B.A., often served as our typesetters. Schools in the early 1960s couldn't begin to afford photocopiers; the *Bonette* was printed on a mimeograph machine that we turned with a crank. It was a long and messy process, and I'd come home with my school uniform covered with ink. "These shirts don't grow on trees," Mom would say, and sometimes we had to buy new ones, which were expensive. After the pages were mimeographed on both sides, we would collate them, staple them together, and set up a table where we sold our little newspaper for a nickel. As the editor, I looked for opportunities to mention as many students by name as we could, which definitely helped our circulation. After the school play, for example, or an appearance by the chorus, we listed everybody who had anything to do with the performance. If Sister Lucille had allowed it, we might have identified everybody in the audience as well.

Her plan worked. I threw myself into the paper, and so did my friends. When Sister Lucille saw how devoted I was, she reminded me that if I didn't keep up my grades, we wouldn't be able to put out the second edition. I took the hint.

The *Bonette* was a success: everybody in our school bought a copy for five cents, and those of us who worked on the paper were very proud of it. I learned a lot, not only about newspapers, but about teamwork. What appeared at first to be an intellectual exercise turned out to be much more: this was my first lesson that a newspaper or a broadcast required not only content, but an effective way of delivering it as well.

After our first couple of issues, I decided to help our paper grow by selling advertising. I was about to approach the owner of Mikoll's, the local delicatessen, when Father Donovan, our parish priest, asked me not to because he was hoping they would buy an ad on the back page of the church bulletin. I realized then that our little newspaper was going to have a tough time competing with the media giants.

A few months later, in November 1963, I learned a very different lesson: that no publication is too small to have an impact. When President Kennedy was assassinated, Sister Lucille, who was devastated by the news, urged us not to be overwhelmed by our grief. "You have a paper to put out," she reminded us, and we immediately got to work on a memorial issue of the *Bonette* in honor of the slain president. I still have that issue, in which I described Kennedy as "that rare and perfect combination of Christian, father, statesman, peace-maker, author, politician, and last but not least, a friend of the common man." It's a telling sentence, full of the innocence and awe of that era, and it pains me that young people today have fewer opportunities to experience that kind of idealism. Where children are concerned, there is such a thing as too much information.

We sent copies of our memorial edition to President Johnson, Robert Kennedy, and Jacqueline Kennedy, and to my amazement, all of them wrote back to thank us. Their responses may have been form letters sent out by low-level aides, but I didn't know that, and I'm grateful that nobody pointed it out. I was thrilled that there was a connection between my insulated little corner of the world and Washington, D.C., where the president, the attorney general, and the first lady had taken the time not only to read our newspaper, but to respond to it. Our little publication at St. Bonaventure School in West Seneca, New York, had been acknowledged at the highest levels by people who appeared on the front page of *real* newspapers.

Looking back, I can see that the satisfaction of putting out a newspaper and the thrill of those responses marked the beginning of my lifelong interest in both government and journalism. I was learning that no matter where you came from, or how distant you might be from the centers of power, it was possible to make an impact with determination and hard work.

In addition to the *Bonette*, Sister Lucille and I shared a couple of other interests that we often discussed during and after school. We were both passionate fans of college basketball, especially the Little Three—a trio of teams from Catholic colleges in the Buffalo area: the Golden Griffins from Canisius College, the Purple Eagles from Niagara University, and the Brown Indians from St. Bonaventure University, about an hour away. (Since 1979 they have been known as the Bonnies.) On Saturday nights, there were doubleheaders in Memorial Auditorium (which everybody knew as the Aud), and the place was usually full.

Sister Lucille, who had graduated from Niagara, was a fan of the Purple Eagles. I liked St. Bonaventure, mostly because Whitey

Martin, their scrappy blond point guard, had grown up down the street from our old house on Woodside. He was an icon in our neighborhood and a basketball star at Bishop Timon High School. Sometimes, when he came home from college during spring break, I'd see him shooting hoops in his driveway. I was only seven when Whitey Martin went to St. Bonaventure in Olean, New York, but from then on I followed the team.

After college, Whitey Martin played briefly for the New York Knicks. He moved back to Buffalo and worked at Father Baker's, where he taught and mentored kids who needed guidance. When I called him not long ago, he told me he often thought about the hardworking fathers in our neighborhood who worked at the steel plants, or the Ford and Chevy plants. "They could have done so much more with their lives," he said, "but there was no one to encourage them, to motivate them, and to let them know there was a life beyond South Buffalo. I realize now that my dad made it possible for me to succeed. He taught me discipline, and you can't have discipline from within unless you have it from without. Because my dad insisted on order, structure, and accountability, I internalized those qualities. And they're the most important things that I've passed on to my own children and the kids at Father Baker's."

When we look back on the people who motivated and influenced us, we often see them as so secure in their identities and professions that it's easy to miss the fact that they, too, had choices to make about their lives and occupations, and that their paths could have turned out very differently. In the case of people who entered the clergy, we often assume that the decision to choose the religious life came easily to them, but that's not always the case.

Sister Lucille had wanted to be a nun, but she had also considered becoming a social worker, a teacher, or a hairdresser. She grew up in Albion, New York, a little town outside of Rochester, where she was the youngest of thirteen children. Her father, an Italian immigrant, died when she was four. He was a railroad worker, and to make ends meet, he went to people's houses at night and cut their hair.

In elementary school, she found herself drawn to the teachers, who were Mercy nuns. "They had something I wanted," she told me, "the life of teaching and prayer." In eighth grade she briefly considered becoming a Carmelite nun, because the cloistered, silent life appealed to her. "But with my mouth," she jokes, "I never would have made it."

I had met Sister Lucille when I was in seventh grade; when Sister Lucille was in seventh grade, she met Sister Mary Carmina, an Italian-American nun from Buffalo who had recently taken her final vows and was "missioned" to the town of Albion. She was a kind, patient, and generous woman who read to her students every day and inspired them with stories of faith and family.

Lucille Socciarelli had wanted to enter the convent right after high school, but her brother was in the service and their widowed mother did not want to be left alone. Their pastor recommended that Lucille work for a year, and she became a telephone operator in the days when people couldn't place a call without going through the phone company. Her mother, who hadn't gone beyond the third grade, wanted her daughter to go to college, but the religious life was too powerful to resist.

When her brother came home, Lucille entered the Mount Mercy convent in Buffalo, and later attended Niagara University to become a teacher.

In the early 1960s, when I met Sister Lucille, the lives of Mercy nuns were highly regimented, to the point where they couldn't even go to the dentist without permission from the Mother Superior. They rarely left the building, and they weren't even supposed to look out the window. Most television shows were forbidden, but they were allowed to watch the news—and Lawrence Welk. When John Kennedy ran for president, however, the rules were relaxed, and the Mercy nuns were given special permission to watch the presidential debates. For some of them, it was the first television show they had ever seen.

Which brings me to the other interest that Sister Lucille and I shared: the Kennedys. A great many nuns liked JFK, and the feeling was mutual. "The bishops are against me," he was quoted as saying, "but the priests and nuns are for me, and there are more of them." Sister Lucille's infatuation with the new president bordered on the obsessional; her nickname was Sister Mary Kennedy. In the summer, she and her friend Margaret Mary Wagner used to drive to Cape Cod so they could be near the Kennedy compound in Hyannisport. They made friends with the man who picked up the family's dry cleaning, and sometimes he let them ride with him in his van. Later, whenever Bobby or Teddy Kennedy came to Buffalo, Margaret Mary and Sister Lucille were always on hand, trying to catch a glimpse of them.

Once, during a visit by Robert Kennedy in 1967, Sister Lucille ran 150 yards after the senator's car to get his autograph. When he noticed her, he waited until she caught up to him.

"Are you on the track team, Sister?" he asked her. "It was worth the run," she replied. When the senator rewarded her with a tour of the *Caroline*, the Kennedys' private plane, she was elated. The next day, when the incident was reported in *The New York Times*, she was reprimanded. Sister Lucille wasn't named in the article, but when a nun was described as running across the field at the Buffalo Airport to meet Bobby Kennedy, there wasn't much doubt about who it could be.

Nuns weren't supposed to talk to us about politics, but when it came to President Kennedy, Sister Lucille just couldn't help herself. That was fine with me. I had a picture of JFK in my room, and my friends and I had Kennedy bumper stickers on our bikes. It was the last thing we were expected to notice, but suddenly a group of ten-year-old boys was excited about politics. Our neighborhood was overwhelmingly Democratic, and we especially loved Kennedy. Although the national popular vote in the 1960 election was almost exactly fifty-fifty, Buffalo voted for Kennedy over Nixon by almost a two-to-one margin. In the second ward, where we lived, the margin was even greater: 7,331 for Kennedy; 3,490 for Nixon; and 7 votes for the socialist candidate, Farrell Dobbs.

We loved Kennedy because he was young and handsome, but even more, we loved him because he was Irish and Catholic. With his Harvard education and his father's wealth, he was, especially to the adults I knew, an important symbol of success at a time when many Irish Catholics still felt themselves to be a step or two behind some of their fellow citizens in their pursuit of the American dream. My own enthusiasm for JFK was less complicated. Father Edwin Dill, my father's old friend, asked me during the campaign, "Timmy, why are you for Kennedy?"

"Because he's Irish Catholic," I replied.

"And if there was a barber who couldn't cut hair, and he was Irish Catholic, would you go to him?"

I was momentarily stumped, and I realized that I hadn't really thought this through. But my feelings for Kennedy were too powerful to be challenged by any rational considerations.

For my friends and me, the fact that he was Irish was almost as important as his religion. "Dad," I remember saying, "he's one of us!" For all I knew, Jack Kennedy could have grown up across the street, and been like any other kid on our block. Dad, who shared my excitement about the Democratic nominee, didn't have the heart to tell me that the Kennedys were nothing at all like us; they may have been Irish, but they certainly weren't working class. Still, there is no question that Kennedy's campaign for the presidency helped to eliminate some of the last vestiges of anti-Irish prejudice in the United States. As the sportswriter Jimmy Cannon once wrote, "I stopped feeling like a mick the day Kennedy was elected."

The Catholic issue was more complicated, and as a boy I was certainly aware of it. People in my grandparents' generation still remembered the campaign of 1928, when Al Smith, the popular Democratic governor of New York, ran against Herbert Hoover; it was the first time a Catholic had run for president. (Smith had planned to run in 1924, but anti-Catholic forces in his own party, including members and supporters of the Ku Klux Klan, had denied him the nomination.) During the Kennedy campaign, we heard some of the preposterous stories that had circulated during Al Smith's run: that if Smith won the election, he would order a tunnel built under the Atlantic Ocean to connect Washington to the Vatican; or that if Al Smith became president, Protestant children would be required to attend Catholic schools. Smith had been roundly defeated in 1928, and we hoped that Kennedy's religion—*our* religion— would not prove to be his undoing as well.

In the fall of 1960, a year before I met Sister Lucille, several Kennedy signs on our block, including the one in front of our house, were torn down during the night. We didn't know who did it, but there was only one Nixon sign on our street, at the house of one of the few Protestant families in our neighborhood, so my friends and I made an educated guess and launched a tactical strike on the Nixon sign. The brothers who lived there were waiting for us, and a brief scuffle ensued, but justice was done. The next day, new signs appeared at both houses.

I didn't have a paper route in 1960, but Billy Clouden, who was four years older than I, sometimes paid me a dime to help him deliver his papers so he would have more time to play baseball. One fall afternoon, I took it upon myself to include a Kennedy leaflet with every copy of the *Buffalo Evening News*. (The leaflets had been given to me by the previous paperboy, who had instructed me to "help get these around" without specifying how, exactly, I was supposed to accomplish that.) When Billy saw that I was inserting something into the newspapers, he said, "What are those?"

"They're Kennedy leaflets," I replied. It hadn't even occurred to me that I might be doing something wrong.

"What are you doing? You can't do that!"

"Why not?" I asked. "They're Kennedy leaflets." As if that made it all right.

"But this is the newspaper."

"Yeah. So?"

"Stop doing that. I'll lose my paper route!"

As a journalist, I try my very best to be objective and non-partisan. As a kid, however, I obviously had a lot to learn.

I stayed up very late on election night, waiting to see if Kennedy had won. But the 1960 election was so close that the coverage went well past midnight, and Dad made me go to bed. I reluctantly agreed, but only if he promised to wake me up early so I could find out what happened. By morning it was finally over, and I remember both my parents smiling. "He won it! He won it!" People in our neighborhood were almost delirious with excitement. There was a huge Kennedy sign at the corner of Tifft and South Park Avenue, where we went to school, and right after the election, somebody attached an American flag to it. In school, the nuns couldn't contain their excitement, and we offered up a prayer of thanksgiving. We weren't supposed to involve God in elections, but when Kennedy won, everything in our lives—faith, education, country, and ethnic identity—came together in an unprecedented moment of triumph.

When the new president was inaugurated, Mrs. Nash, our fifth-grade teacher, wheeled in a television on a chrome stand so we could watch the ceremony. It was a freezing day in Washington, and the commentators noted that unlike President Eisenhower, the new president wasn't wearing a hat. (At least that's how I remember it. In fact, Kennedy merely *spoke* without a hat, but he wore one to most of the inaugural events.) Sister

Clementia was worried that the new president wasn't wearing an overcoat, and she told us that another president had died a month after catching a cold at his inauguration. We all started giggling at this ridiculous story, but Sister Clementia insisted it was true, and she instructed us to find out which president she was referring to. I remember finding the answer: William Henry Harrison, the ninth president of the United States, caught a cold on Inauguration Day in 1841 and died thirty days later when it developed into pneumonia; he was the first president to die in office. But how, exactly, did I get this information? It wasn't from Google, I know that. I probably found it in the *Golden Book Encyclopedia,* which my mother used to buy at Loblaws, our local supermarket, which sold one volume at a time for ninety-nine cents each.

I still remember parts of Kennedy's inaugural address, although some of the lines have been quoted so often over the years that it's hard to know exactly where memory begins. I was especially taken with the final lines, where Kennedy used the word "sacrifice"—a term that especially resonates with Catholics. He ended his speech on a surprisingly religious note: "With a good conscience our only sure reward, with history the final judge of our deeds, let us go forth to lead the land we love, asking His blessing and His help, but knowing that here on earth God's work must truly be our own." It was thrilling to hear a president talk about doing God's work and, if possible, I became even more enamored of Kennedy when I heard those words.

At the time, I never imagined that within two years, for one brief, shining moment, I would have the opportunity to meet President Kennedy, live and in person. In October 1962, when it was announced that the president was coming to Buffalo for the Pulaski Day Parade, the whole city was excited. (Pulaski Day, in honor of the Polish-American general who served under George Washington in the Revolutionary War, is a major occasion in Buffalo, and is to the city's large Polish population roughly what St. Patrick's Day is to the Irish.) Kennedy had been to Buffalo twice before, but this was his first visit as president.

A couple of days before the president came to town, his itinerary was published in the newspaper with a richness of detail that became unthinkable only a year later, after the Dallas trip. Dad was reading the paper, and he told me that President Kennedy was landing at Niagara Falls, and that the motorcade was getting on the thruway and getting off at the Smith Street exit to go downtown. As a driver for both the sanitation department and the *News*, Dad knew every street in the city. "You know what?" he told me. "When the president comes to town we're going to get real close."

"How will we do that?" I asked.

"It's all here," he said, nodding at the newspaper. "He's getting off at Smith Street, and I know exactly where that is. They'll have to slow down on those turns, and that's where we'll see him."

The day of the parade, we drove to the spot that Dad had picked out. The president was due to arrive at 3:05, and we were probably there an hour or so in advance. There were large crowds everywhere, and Dad lifted me up on a mailbox so I could get a better view. At exactly 3:05 we heard sirens, and suddenly there it was, the president's limousine, a convertible with the top down. Dad pulled me off the mailbox, and as the car rounded the corner, he shouted, "Go! Go!" I ran up to the car, reached out, and touched the president's hand. He was looking right at me. "I touched him! I touched him!" I yelled. My whole family was there, and they were as excited as I was. Dad was beaming. "Finally a Russert has met a president of the United States," he said. Our station wagon shook with laughter and cheers as the triumphant Russerts headed home. "Where is the president going now?" I asked Dad.

"He's going to speak at City Hall."

"Are we going, too?"

"No," said Dad, "it'll be too crowded. There will be thousands of people there, and they'll all want to meet him, but we've already done that." We went home and listened to Kennedy's speech on the radio.

The next day at school, I did something Dad would not have liked. I bragged: "My dad is so smart that I shook hands with the president."

"How did you get near him?" I was asked. I explained that my dad had planned the whole thing, that he had read the paper, that he knew the best place to wait, and that we had arrived there early. I was as proud of my father as I was to meet the president.

I learned at least three things that day, and they are lessons that I still think about and follow. First, that a lot of important information is right there in the newspaper, if you only take the time to look for it and read it. I do my work on television, and there are things that television can do better than any other medium. But if you really want to be informed, there is no substitute for reading a good newspaper—or, if possible, more than one. The second lesson from that day is that the key to success is preparation. In journalism, it's absolutely crucial. Like everyone else, I have days when things go well, and days when they don't. But one mistake I have never made is to show up unprepared for an interview. The third lesson is just as important as the other two, especially in the news business: get there first.

Although Dad was sure that I was the first Russert to meet a president, forty years later I learned otherwise. In talking to some distant relatives, I learned that Christian Russert, the younger brother of my great-great-grandfather, had fought for the Union in the Civil War at the battle of Fort Stevens in Washington, D.C. On July 12, 1864, during a Confederate attack, Christian Russert was wounded in the left leg when he captured a Confederate soldier and brought him in as a prisoner of war. According to Christian Russert's soldier's pension form, when he returned to Fort Stevens "he was taken by the hand by President Lincoln and thanked for his courage." This was the same battle in which Captain Oliver Wendell Holmes, Junior, who later served on the Supreme Court, yelled at Lincoln, "Get down, you damn fool, before you get shot"—not realizing that the man he was rebuking was the commander in chief. I see a pattern here: once every century or so, a Russert met a president.

When President Kennedy came to Buffalo for the Pulaski Day Parade, nobody, not even the president, knew that the Soviets had installed nuclear missiles in Cuba. Kennedy was informed on October 16, and eight days later he addressed the nation. He spoke bluntly and warned that a missile attack from Cuba against any country in the Western Hemisphere would cause him to order a nuclear strike on the Soviet Union. It was terrifying. I can't think of any other event in my life, except, perhaps, the terrorist attacks of September 11, 2001, that created as much fear among Americans as the Cuban Missile Crisis. We had always known that a nuclear war was possible, but now, for the first time, it seemed like a military showdown with the Soviet Union might be imminent.

Naturally, my sisters and I turned to Dad for reassurance. Kathy, who was in third grade, asked him, "Daddy, will there be a war? Are we going to die?" Dad did his best to reassure us that everything would be fine, but I wasn't sure he believed it, especially when I overheard him telling Mom, "I just don't know if those bastards are going to turn back." Then, in our half-finished basement, on the black storage shelves that normally held extra toilet paper and lightbulbs, I noticed some cans of food, along with an item I had never seen before: gallon jugs of water. My parents didn't mention it, and I didn't either. I was twelve and a half—old enough to know why these things were there. "This is a tough one," Dad kept saying, but he also kept assuring us that it would turn out all right.

In the middle of the crisis, Dad took me aside and showed me a card that had been issued to all the American soldiers who went overseas in World War II. In the event that they were stopped or captured by Soviet troops who might not be aware of their identity, this card instructed the men to say "*Ya Amerikanets*" (I am an American), and included some basic information in Russian. "I want you to have this," Dad said. "Don't lose it. We're going to get through this, and the day will come when the Russians will be our allies once again, just like they were during the war. They're good people. They just have bad leaders."

It was hard to concentrate on our lessons as we practiced for air-raid drills and said special prayers for peace. On October 26, when a Soviet freighter headed toward Cuba, we were watching a news report when our principal, Sister Edmunda, leaned in to our classroom and asked, "Any news, Sister?"

"They're not turning back," said Sister Lucille.

"Oh my God," said Sister Edmunda. "Pray for us."

During their brief conversation, our entire class was hanging on every word, looking right, then left, then right again, like spectators at a tennis match. When we went to lunch, Sister Lucille stayed behind to watch the news. It was a Friday, and a couple of hours later, as we went home for the weekend, there were anxious jokes about whether we would still be alive on Monday.

I had a paper route that year, and this was the first time that people opened their doors when I approached their houses. Mrs. Watkins, one of our neighbors, saw me and asked, "Do you have any good news for us, Timmy?"

"No, ma'am, not yet."

Looking back on it, one thing that strikes me about those days is that nobody even considered being critical of the president during a time of crisis. And when it ended peacefully on Sunday, October 28, it was such a relief that people were positively giddy. We were proud of our president because he had stared down the Russians and Khrushchev had blinked—or so we believed at the time. In school, the nuns told us that the power of prayer, including our own prayers, had prevailed in the world, and we believed it. Like children all over America, my friends and I matured that week. Suddenly we were more worldly, more grown up than we had been at the beginning of the school year. We had come face to face with the knowledge of our own mortality, and the country had survived. Nobody imagined that thirteen months later, in November 1963, our world really would be shattered.

We were in Sister Mary Austin's history class when the voice of our principal came crackling through the intercom box in our classroom. "Your attention, please. Your attention, please." Sister Austin sighed and rolled her eyes. "Here comes another change in the lunch menu," she said, because we were always being interrupted for trivial announcements. Then Sister Edmunda said over the intercom, "Please pray for the president. The president has just been shot. Please pray for the president." Sister Austin was tall and thin, and when we heard these awful words, I watched her whole mouth drop as the shock of the announcement passed over her.

The next sound I heard was the clanging of rosary beads as Sister Lucille ran into the classroom with tears streaming down her face. "Oh my God, Oh my God. Where was he?"

For some reason I knew. "He's in Dallas, Sister." Somebody wheeled in a television set, and we watched Walter Cronkite report on the shooting. He was handed a piece of paper. He put on his glasses, read the awful news aloud, took off his glasses, and wiped the tears from his eyes. Usually, the school was a little chaotic at dismissal time, especially on a Friday. But that day we all left in silence.

The other scene I remember from that dark Friday was delivering the late edition of the afternoon paper. We had a blue newspaper box where they were dropped off by a driver from the *Buffalo Evening News*, who did for our neighborhood exactly what my father was doing in other sections of the city. I sat on the box with my head down. By the time the driver came by, the neighbors were all lined up outside my house. Instead of delivering their newspapers, I just handed them over, one at a time, without a word.

President Kennedy's death had a profound effect on us. I noticed that although the newspapers and the television anchors said that the president had been assassinated, in our world people said he was "martyred." He was in effect elevated to political sainthood.

In our neighborhood, and probably in other Irish-Catholic areas, a fatalistic feeling developed that perhaps the death of President Kennedy had been inevitable, because the reality of having him as our leader was just too good to be true. A cosmic accident had occurred in our favor and now it had to be undone. An Irish-Catholic president? It couldn't happen. And if, by some fluke, it did happen, it couldn't last. I didn't know it at the time, but Daniel Patrick Moynihan, whom I later came to know very well, had made a similar observation during that dreadful weekend. He was in the Department of Labor in the Kennedy administration, and when he heard the terrible news from Dallas, he said a line that is sometimes attributed to President Kennedy, and that people have repeated ever since: "What's the use of being Irish if you don't know that the world is going to break your heart eventually?"

A FEW YEARS AFTER Kennedy's death, Sister Lucille introduced me to Dave Powers, a close friend of the president who had worked for him ever since Kennedy's first campaign for Congress in the eleventh congressional district of Massachusetts. Powers had been at JFK's side the entire time, from the young candidate's first political appearance in Boston in 1946 to the president's final speech in Fort Worth, Texas, in 1963. He was named Museum Curator of the Kennedy Library, and before it opened he spent years collecting artifacts and memorabilia from Kennedy's life. These items were stored at the National Archives Federal Record Center in Waltham, Massachusetts, where Sister Lucille and Margaret Mary Wagner used to visit Powers on their annual pilgrimages to Cape Cod. I, too, visited Dave Powers there, and I even brought along a couple of Kennedy for President posters that I had saved from the 1960 campaign.

I first met Dave Powers when Sister Lucille brought him to speak at D'Youville College in Buffalo on the publication of the best-selling book about JFK, *Johnny, We Hardly Knew Ye*, that he had written with Kenneth P. O'Donnell. I was home from college at the time, and she invited me to St. Anthony's Convent to meet her pal. It was Powers, by the way, who had given her the honorary name of Sister Mary Kennedy.

"Dave," she asked him, "would you like anything to drink?"

"I'd love a beer," he said.

"Any particular kind?"

"Heineken would be great."

Oddly enough, the convent was fresh out of Heineken, so I foolishly—because it was a Sunday—offered to go out and find some for our visitor. I ended up at the bar of the Statler Hilton, where the bartender said he was sorry, but he couldn't sell me beer if I would be taking it out of the hotel. When I explained that the beer was for President Kennedy's oldest friend who was, in fact, a guest of the hotel and was at this very moment having lunch in a nearby convent, the bartender gave me a sympathetic look as if to say, "I guess it's all right, because you can't possibly be making this up." He was kind enough to let me have a six-pack of Heineken for the astronomical price of $21—a small fortune in the 1970s, which pretty much cleaned out my wallet. When I returned with the goods, Powers treated me like a conquering hero. After a beer or three, he began to regale us with stories about President Kennedy, whom he called "the greatest man I ever met, and the best friend I ever had."

For a couple of Kennedyites like Sister Lucille and me, it was a great treat to have an insider like Dave Powers telling us stories about JFK. A week or so later, Powers sent me a card with a quotation that President Kennedy had inscribed for him on a silver mug, a gift on his friend's fiftieth birthday. It read: "There are three things which are real: God, Human Folly, and Laughter. The first two are beyond our comprehension, so we must do what we can with the third." Amen.

10.

Canisius High School

"What a country!"

HAD SISTER LUCILLE DONE NOTHING MORE than make me editor of our school newspaper, she would have earned my lifelong gratitude. A year or so later, however, she did a good deal more: she put me on a path that ultimately led to far bigger opportunities than I had ever imagined for myself.

By the time we were in eighth grade at St. Bonaventure, my classmates and I were starting to think about which high school we would attend. Most of the girls were going to Mt. Mercy Academy in South Buffalo, which was run by the Mercy nuns. Most of the boys were planning to attend Bishop Timon, a diocesan school in South Buffalo that was named for a former bishop of Buffalo and was run by the Franciscans. With a few exceptions, the rest of our graduating class would be going to West Seneca Central High, our local public school.

When I told Sister Lucille that I expected to go to Bishop Timon along with most of my friends, she shook her head. "You know, Tim, I love the Franciscans, but the Jesuits are known for their teaching. I think you should apply to Canisius."

Canisius? What was she thinking? Canisius was a fancy-pants boys' school on the other side of town. It was named for St. Peter Canisius, the sixteenth-century Jesuit educator who founded a number of schools and universities and wrote the first important catechism during the Protestant Reformation, which our parish priests always referred to as the Protestant Revolution. Canisius was the city's elite Catholic high school, and everybody in Buffalo was familiar with it; the school was so highly regarded that it even attracted some Protestant and Jewish students.

Canisius was known for three things: its classical curriculum, its high academic standards, and its equally high tuition fees. But money alone couldn't get you in: out of a thousand or so eighth graders who took the entrance exam each spring, fewer than a quarter were admitted. It was said that some students took the exam with no intention of attending the school, because if you were accepted at Canisius, that was something to brag about. I, on the other hand, had never even considered applying; it just wasn't something that people like me did. It would be like suddenly applying to Harvard or Yale when you had spent your whole life planning to attend the nearest branch of the state university.

"I don't think so, Sister," I said. "Canisius is for rich people, for kids whose fathers are doctors and lawyers."

"Actually, they have all kinds of students," she said. "If you take the entrance exam, I bet you'll get in."

We both knew that although this conversation might start

with me, it wasn't my decision at all. Sister Lucille was friendly with Mom, who had always heard about the value of a Jesuit education. But even if I did well on the exam, Mom wondered, how could she and Dad possibly afford a school that was clearly out of our league? Dad already had two jobs, and they had my three sisters to consider. Mom had other reservations as well: Canisius was nowhere near our house, and going to school there would mean leaving my friends behind and spending an hour each way on two different buses to reach the north side of the city. In some places that wouldn't seem like much of an obstacle, but to people with a South Buffalo identity, leaving the neighborhood was almost unthinkable. The north side of town? You might as well be going to school on the moon.

But Sister Lucille wasn't easily dissuaded. "I think Timmy should apply," she told Mom. "He'll meet people at Canisius whom he would never meet at Timon. That's where he belongs, and he can do the work. And maybe they'll give him a scholarship."

Big Russ was a tougher sell. He knew Canisius High School as the former mansion on majestic Delaware Avenue where he had dropped off newspapers every afternoon on one of his earlier routes, but the possibility that his son might someday be a student there had probably never occurred to him. "That's a long way from home," he said when we started discussing it, and I had the feeling he wasn't referring only to the length of the commute. He was wondering, as I was, whether Canisius High School was a suitable place for someone from a working-class family. Dad was wary of people whose heads were too big for the doorway, as he liked to say. As I was growing up, he often told me the fable about the greedy dog with a bone in his mouth who, upon seeing his reflection in the water, jumped in after that illusory second bone and ended up with none.

But it wasn't that simple, because Dad also believed in self-improvement, education, and upward mobility. Looking back on it, I think he was caught between two competing perspectives: "that isn't our place" was doing battle with "what a country." In the end, upward mobility won out. Dad understood and appreciated America's great gift—that even if you came from humble origins, you were free to rise as high as your God-given abilities, hard work, and a generous dose of luck could carry you.

What a country is one of Dad's favorite expressions, which he has used to describe everything from a good hot dog to the toppling of Saddam Hussein's statue in Baghdad in 2003. It conveys his love and amazement about the United States, and the freedom of its citizens to achieve whatever they can. He's in constant awe of the miracle of America, and he feels that his life here has been blessed. "What a country" is no idle phrase; every time Dad uses it, with the emphasis on "country," I can hear the feeling and conviction in his voice, and I swear I can almost see his heart pounding.

In a victory for Sister Lucille, and ultimately for me, my parents agreed that I would take the entrance exam at Canisius High School. Mom decided that if I were accepted there and given a scholarship for any amount, it would be a sign from God that I should go. In fact, I scored high enough to be awarded a half scholarship, and if I took a job after school, my parents could almost afford the tuition.

My first few weeks at Canisius were difficult and stressful, and it took time before I felt comfortable there. We hadn't changed classes in grammar school, but now we were on the move all day, walking crisply from one classroom to the next, and from one intimidating teacher to another. Holy Family and St. Bonaventure had been warm, nurturing schools run by nuns, but Canisius was big, cold, masculine, and highly disciplined. The teachers were demanding and had high expectations; there were no excuses here, no second chances. When they gave you an assignment, it had better be done right, and on time. By Christmas each year, Canisius had completed what one of our teachers called its annual clearance sale; students who couldn't keep up soon transferred to another, less challenging school. On the other hand, if you paid attention and did everything that was required of you, by the time you graduated you were definitely ready for college.

Although there were a few other students at Canisius from St. Bonaventure and Holy Family, most of the faces around me were unfamiliar. The Jesuits made a point of splitting up the boys from South Buffalo to prevent us from forming a clique, and to force us to integrate more quickly with the rest of the student body. This plan ultimately worked, but it made the initial adjustment even more difficult.

At first I found the bus rides long and lonely, especially in the morning, when I rode into the heart of the city and back out again in the other direction. On the second bus, from downtown to school, I would stare out the windows at the grand and stately mansions on both sides of Delaware Avenue, the largest homes I had ever seen. Even before I arrived at school I knew that I was entering a very different world, and during my first semester, it felt like a world in which I didn't belong.

Sister Lucille had been right when she said that not every student at Canisius was wealthy. But there were plenty of rich kids,
who moved through the halls with an ease and demeanor that
were foreign to me. Many of my classmates were given their own
cars when they turned sixteen, and went to parties in prosperous
suburbs like Amherst and Williamsville that were difficult to get
to by bus. They dressed differently, too. We were all required to
wear a jacket and tie to school, and South Buffalo guys generally
wore blue blazers and gray slacks. Some of our more affluent classmates took pride in wearing expensive ties, and a few boys actually
came to school each day in three-piece suits.

Dressing up for school each morning took some getting used
to. In August, before classes began, Mom took me to Kimaid and
Mattar, a menswear store on Seneca Street, where we selected a
pair of charcoal gray flannel pants, a navy blue blazer, a gray
sports jacket, three white shirts, and three striped ties. Buying a
new wardrobe for a private high school was an expense that my
parents hadn't anticipated, and it steadily increased as I kept
growing and needing new things. At first I wore clip-on ties, the
kind we had worn in grammar school, but I soon learned how
these were regarded at Canisius when my freshman history
teacher grabbed my tie during class. When it came off in his
hand, he held it at arm's length like a dead skunk, and the whole
class roared as if I were a bald man who had just been deprived of
his beloved hairpiece. One humiliation was enough, and that was
the last clip-on tie I ever wore. It wasn't just the teachers: if you
wore a clip-on tie to school, one of your fellow students might
yank it off, and then you'd be given a detention for not wearing a
tie. Dad showed me how to tie a Windsor knot, going over it

with me again and again until I finally got it right. To this day, I still knot my tie the way Dad taught me in 1964.

Because of our dress code, Canisius students from our neighborhood were easy to identify and even easier to harass. On a cold November afternoon in my freshman year, I was walking down Seneca Street with my Canisius book bag when a car full of kids drove by and pelted me with eggs. The following summer I briefly worked in a warehouse, moving around boxes of frozen beans. I was a couple of years younger than the other guys, all of whom went to Bishop Timon and were well aware that I was at Canisius. "Tim," one of them said, "because you're new here, your job is to wheel these cartons into the freezer room." Before I knew it, they had locked me inside. Forty minutes later they set me free, and to warm me up they were kind enough to throw me into Lake Erie. It wasn't pleasant, but I was careful not to complain. All I said was, "First I was too cold, then I was too hot, and now I'm just right." Nobody had to tell me that I was being punished not for my age, but for my school.

My experience wasn't unusual. South Buffalo kids who attended Canisius were often teased by Timon students, who called us eggheads and Delaware daisies, and thought of us as deserters for leaving the neighborhood. At basketball and football games between the two schools, freshmen at Canisius from South Buffalo were in the awkward position of knowing more students at Timon than at our own school. There was a fierce rivalry between the two institutions, and it wasn't uncommon for fights to break out among the fans. At one football game against Timon in Lackawanna Stadium, the Canisius cheerleaders didn't make life any easier for us when they yelled out,

"Repel them! Repel them! Make them relinquish the ball." Our Timon friends heard this cheer as pretentious rather than ironic, but fortunately for us, Canisius won the game.

Although Canisius High School was justifiably proud of its athletic program, the main emphasis was on academics. Our teachers, most of whom were Jesuit priests, had an intellectual pride that sometimes bordered on arrogance, and an affinity for education that dated back to the time of Peter Canisius. In America, centuries later, Jesuits continue to be associated with higher education, and Jesuit colleges include Boston College, Fordham, Georgetown, Holy Cross, John Carroll, Loyola, Scranton, the University of San Francisco, and a number of other good schools. In a well-known joke, a Franciscan, a Dominican, and a Jesuit are walking along the road. Suddenly, they see an apparition of the Holy Family, with the infant Jesus in the manger and Mary and Joseph standing over him. The Franciscan falls on his face, overcome with awe at the sight of the holy child. The Dominican falls to his knees in adoration. The Jesuit, however, takes the apparition in stride. Instead of being overwhelmed by the vision, he walks over to Joseph, puts his arm around his shoulder, and says, "Tell me, have you given any thought to the boy's education?"

Our teachers were adept at persuading us that we weren't as smart as we thought we were, and that we weren't going to succeed at Canisius without hard work. This was an important lesson, that however successful we might have been in grammar school, where many of us had excelled in our studies, we could no longer get by on pure intelligence. Yes, it was important to think, but first we had to read, study, and learn so we'd have something to think *about*.

One of the first things I learned at Canisius was that contrary to what most of us believed, the Immaculate Conception is not the same as the virgin birth, and that it refers not to the birth of Jesus, but to the birth of Mary. In order to be pure enough to become the mother of Jesus, Mary was conceived free from original sin. Over the years, I've made hundreds of dollars by betting my fellow Catholics in Buffalo, in Washington, and even in Rome that they couldn't tell me the real meaning of the Immaculate Conception. I have a feeling, though, that this wasn't quite what our Jesuit teachers had in mind when they assured us that young people like ourselves would profit from a good Catholic education.

Every Catholic order has its own spirit, and the Jesuits have long been known for a restlessness of mind that tends to make them less dogmatic than other groups. Not surprisingly, this approach was especially noticeable in our religion classes. Whereas the nuns in our grammar schools emphasized fear and guilt and taught us to memorize the fundamentals of our faith, the Jesuits encouraged us to think about these ideas and even to challenge them. They welcomed our questions, embraced our skepticism, and respected our doubts. In the process of teaching us theology, our teachers introduced us to philosophy. When a student brought up the famous *Time* magazine cover story that declared, "God Is Dead," our teacher was neither upset nor shocked by the reference. The next day, he brought in a couple of books that addressed the issue and invited the student to read them.

This was a far more worldly and sophisticated approach to

religion than we were accustomed to, and for most of us, I believe, it was refreshing and even exciting to be in a class where everything was open to discussion and analysis. Faith mattered, of course, but religion at Canisius was also an intellectual endeavor. You came to class with the expectation that you would find the discussion stimulating, and for many of us, those conversations served to strengthen our faith. The Jesuits were especially interested in applying religious ideals to contemporary social issues, and in the 1960s, when young people were increasingly interested in "relevance," their approach happened to mesh nicely with some of the changes in American society.

But religion at Canisius involved more than mere talk. There was an optional Mass each morning, and a compulsory one on Fridays where a faculty member would preach. We also went to confession, which was held in the gym, where we had the choice of an open confession (where you and the priest could see each other), or the traditional closed style, where the confessor retains his anonymity. I opted for the latter; I just didn't feel comfortable unburdening my soul to a teacher from my school.

When I started at Canisius, tuition was $320 a year. During my freshman year, in a kind of work/study program, I had a job in the rectory next to the school, where the priests lived. I ran errands, picked up dry cleaning, and spent a lot of time bringing shoes to and from the shoemaker. Between the homework and my job I didn't have much free time, but Dad was very support-ive, and that made a difference. He thought it was good that I was helping to put myself through school. "You always appreciate things more when you work for them," he said, and as usual, he was right. I knew he was proud of me, and that meant a lot.

During my first year I played for the Acrions, the freshman basketball team that was limited to boys under a certain height, which I believe was five feet, six inches. Our opponents were eighth-grade teams who were a year younger but considerably taller than we were. The best thing about the Acrions was that we played in Memorial Auditorium on Saturday nights, where our games constituted the half-time entertainment during the two intermissions of Little Three doubleheaders. Most of these games were sold out, which meant that we regularly played in front of ten or twelve thousand people, many of whom were actually paying attention and cheering for every basket by either team—a little ironically, perhaps, but it was thrilling nonetheless. We were disciplined and well coached, and most of the time, the shorter guys prevailed.

The game I remember most clearly was against St. Mary's School for the Deaf. Our opponents got off to a quick lead because we were distracted: while we called out our plays like every other team, they were communicating with hand signals, and it was hard not to watch them. It was something to see, and it was impressive, especially at a time when you could almost go through life without ever being aware of a deaf person.

As representatives of Canisius, we came to the Aud in jackets and ties and sat together as a team, watching talented college players go at it from our front-row seats behind the basket. Just by sitting there, like little gentlemen, we made a good impression on the fans. The only problem was that we were expected to root for Canisius College, a Jesuit institution that was affiliated with our school. By this time, however, I had long been a fan of St. Bonaventure, a Franciscan university, and I wasn't about to change my allegiance. At those Yankee games in Cleveland I had learned what it felt like not to root with the crowd, and at the Aud on Saturday nights I held my ground.

Around eleven, when the games were over, a group of us would walk over to White Tower for hamburgers. Looking back on it, I'm struck by the fact that nobody seemed to have any concern about a group of fourteen-year-olds who were wandering around downtown at midnight. Today, in most cities, parents wouldn't dream of allowing it, and they would be right.

Starting in my sophomore year at Canisius, I worked after school at St. Michael's, a big downtown church. Officially I was the assistant to Brother Florian Harter, who ran the office despite the fact that he was blind. A tall, thin, elderly man who had been married and was now a widower, Brother Harter operated the old-fashioned switchboard by feel, plugging the various phone cords into the appropriate places as fast as any sighted person. He was almost ninety when I met him, and I learned later that, at the age of ninety-five, Brother Harter had gone out and bought himself a new suit with an extra pair of pants. Now that's Buffalo optimism.

I was one of a long line of Canisius students who worked at St. Michael's, where the pastor, Father James Redmond, was the brother of Father Frank Redmond, our Latin teacher, who served as a kind of recruiting agent for the church. Giancarlo Lucchesi, my immediate predecessor at St. Michael's, had joined the Marines after his junior year at Canisius, and I took his place. Giancarlo was sent to Vietnam, and in April 1968, a few weeks before I graduated, he was killed in Quang Tri Province. Years later, when I moved to Washington, I went to the Vietnam Memorial and traced his name with my fingers.

As long as anyone could remember, St. Michael's, which was founded in 1851, had occupied a special place in the heart of the city. It was one of the oldest churches in Buffalo, and office workers, retail clerks, shoppers, and businesspeople stopped in to attend one of several daily Masses. Although many of the parishioners had long ago left the area for the suburbs, a number of them still maintained a link to the old church.

Father James Redmond was a short man with white hair that was parted down the middle. Popular, dignified, and a little distant, he looked after his large congregation as well as the church's many visitors. In 1966, when I first started working there, people were still talking about the night in the spring of 1962 when St. Michael's was struck by lightning and burned almost to the ground. When Father Reilly, Father Redmond's associate, noticed flames shooting out of the steeple, he and Father Redmond ran into the sanctuary to save the chalices and other sacred objects. The huge blaze drew hundreds of firefighters, and as the news spread that St. Michael's was burning, people from all over Buffalo came down to watch the fire. Father Redmond told me all about that awful night, and how the only items left standing were two windows, a pair of statues, and some of the walls. The church was then rebuilt in the same style as the old one. "Did you know that Jim Redmond and Frank Sinatra performed on the same stage?" Father Redmond asked me. Immediately after the fire, clergymen and laypeople of all faiths had rushed to help St. Michael's in any way they could. Harry

Altman, who owned a legendary nightclub called the Town Casino, offered his establishment to St. Michael's for as long as it was needed, which was how Jim Redmond ended up celebrating Mass on the same stage where Sinatra had appeared.

I worked at St. Michael's three days a week, from 3:30 in the afternoon until 7:30 in the evening, which made for a very long day. My pay, which sounds like a joke to me now, was seventy cents an hour. Much of my work consisted of answering the phones and providing Mass cards for people who came to the office; the card indicated that a specific Mass was being said to honor a certain individual, usually somebody who had died. The Mass would be said in any case, but now there was a name associated with it, which would be announced during the Prayer of the Faithful. Some people requested Mass cards for other reasons, too, such as a wedding anniversary, a birthday, or a recovery from illness. St. Michael's had its own cards, and I would fill out the time and date and accept a contribution, which was five dollars.

Another of my duties was to count and deposit the money that came in during the collections. We had a machine that not only sorted the nickels, dimes, quarters, and the occasional pennies, but rolled them as well. I operated the coin machine and stored the rolls in a huge safe until it was time to lug them to the bank in cloth deposit bags. We used a big binder to keep track of the Mass cards, and a red vinyl receipt book that allowed Father Redmond to compare that day's collection to the one a year earlier.

At Canisius the rectory had been off limits to students, but at St. Michael's I got to see the priests in their residence, where they didn't wear a collar and were not on duty. About a dozen men lived there: they were retired, or semiretired, but they all heard confession and celebrated Mass at one of the church's several daily services. Before working at St. Michael's I had known priests only in their official capacities, but now I began to see them as normal human beings who joked around, watched TV, and let down their guard. I also saw them in prayer and contemplation, doing the things priests were supposed to do. Some of them ignored me; others talked to me and asked about my studies. When things were quiet I could get started on my homework, and some of the priests in the rectory were former educators who were happy to answer my questions about religion, Latin, or anything else. Several, in fact, had been teachers at Canisius.

Priests from around the diocese came to St. Michael's for confession, and when one of them showed up, I had to notify the on-duty priest that Father So-and-so had arrived. Until then I hadn't realized that priests, too, went to confession, and I found it puzzling when a visiting priest remained in the confessional for more than a few minutes: What sins could a priest possibly have to confess? Some of them, I now realize, had really come for counseling. And others—well, in view of what we know now, I can only imagine.

Although I was never the object of a sexual advance, in both high school and college there were priests who had the reputation of being "a little funny." (Yes, that's what we called it.) It was an open secret that was usually phrased in a euphemism; somebody would say that Father X was known to be "a little too friendly." We even joked about it with the other priests, but as far as I knew, none of my friends was abused. If you felt that a priest was getting a little too familiar, you didn't say anything, and you didn't have to. You just got up and walked away. I don't mean to suggest that priests never behaved badly; there is far too much evidence to the contrary. But either it didn't happen in my little world, or I was too sheltered to know about it. Today, of course, we know all too well what has gone on in the Catholic Church, and it is an outrage. The bishops and the cardinals must reach out to those who have been harmed and take every step to ensure our children will never again be abused.

Sometimes at St. Michael's we had visits from middle-aged women who had developed a crush on one of the priests. I soon learned that rather than notify the priest in front of the visitor, I was better off making that call in private in case he wanted me to say that he wasn't in, or was simply not available. I knew that the priest was trying to avoid an awkward situation, or possibly an occasion of sin, and that he was right to do so. For a former altar boy of sixteen, all of this was a fascinating window into real life.

Real life entered through another window as well. Every day, homeless people came to the church office to ask for a handout. I was instructed not to give out money, but if somebody was hungry, I invited them to come around to the back, where Earl or Pearl, our two cooks, would give them a sandwich and a cup of coffee. I noticed that people would show up once or twice and then disappear, and that even those to whom we gave a sandwich didn't make a habit of it. In time, I learned to tell the difference between a derelict and a person who had suffered a couple of setbacks, between a con man and somebody who was truly in need, although in the language of the day, we referred to most of these people as "bums." We had phone numbers for AA and other forms of treatment and assistance, and I gave them out when it seemed appropriate, hoping that they would be used, but knowing that more often than not, they wouldn't be.

I alternated at St. Michael's with my classmate Mike Hanzly, who became a podiatrist and later treated Dad. Another Canisius student, Danny Richards, worked in the kitchen. Mike once told me that he and Danny kept a bottle of aftershave hidden in a cupboard, so that if they worked late on a Friday evening, they could take what was known as the South Buffalo shower—a shot of Right Guard and a splash of Old Spice—and be on their way to a party or a dance.

After Danny's term at St. Michael's, his brother David took over. After David, their youngest brother, Dennis, came in. After high school, Danny Richards went to Canisius College and married Margie Nash, the daughter of my fifth-grade teacher at Holy Family. They had four children before Danny, a police officer, was diagnosed with leukemia. When he died in 1980 at the age of twenty-eight, Margie's uncle, Father John Nash, S.J., who was then the pastor at St. Michael's, celebrated Danny's funeral Mass. Since 1998, the office at St. Michael's has been run by Margie Richards. That sequence of events, with its family connections, its tragedy, and its loyalty to the church, is a quintessential South Buffalo story.

One of the perks of working at St. Michael's was that I got to eat dinner there. After the priests enjoyed their meal in the dining room, Earl and I would eat in the kitchen. Jesuits are known for living well, and sometimes, when I told Mom what I'd had for dinner, she would ask, "Can you get us invited?" Big Russ loved to hear about those dinners, and if I didn't see him that night, because he had usually gone to his night job before I got home, he often asked me about them the next day, when he vicariously savored every course: "The lamb chops. Were they on the grill or the broiler?" Earl, a compulsive smoker and serious drinker who wore black-framed glasses of the type made famous by Barry Goldwater, was not only an excellent cook, but was able to sniff out good deals on everything from lamb and filet mignon to chicken and veal scallopini, and from time to time, even lobsters. These fine dinners were preceded by a cocktail hour; when the priests were ready for dinner, they would ring a bell and the meal would be served. When it was time for coffee and dessert, they rang it again.

I learned a lot at St. Michael's, and working there helped me mature. Canisius was one way of expanding my horizons, and this big downtown church, where I interacted with everybody from priests and parishioners to shoppers, secretaries, and street people, was another. At the same time, my job at St. Michael's limited my opportunities at Canisius because I didn't have time to participate in sports or other afterschool activities. On balance, though, I'm glad I was there: a job that I took for financial reasons turned out to be a valuable part of my education. As Big Russ's example reminded me every day, not all knowledge comes from books.

II.

Discipline

"If Father said you did wrong, you done wrong."

FOR ALL THE LONELINESS I FELT during my gradual adjustment to Canisius High School, it certainly didn't take long for my teachers to expand my intellectual horizons. On my first day at this big and intimidating new school, during my very first class, Mr. Nochelski, our English teacher, who was studying to be a Jesuit, gave us a simple, straightforward exercise that made a deep and lasting impression on me. After asking us to take out a sheet of paper, he said, "I'd like you to describe what you observed this morning when you walked into this building for the first time."

I was stunned by the question, which was unlike anything a teacher had ever asked me before. In elementary school I had become proficient at mastering facts and taking multiple-choice tests. But this was something completely different, an open-ended inquiry whose answer was not only not fixed in stone, but was presumably different for every student. Mr. Nochelski wasn't asking us to reiterate something we had already been taught or had read in a book; he was asking us to think, to remember, and above all, to *observe*.

I have often thought back to that moment, because since then I have tried never to walk into a room or conduct an interview without an open mind and, I hope, an observant eye. In 1968, around the time I was graduating from Canisius, Mr. Nochelski's lesson was reinforced by a line I especially liked in the Simon and Garfunkel song, "America"—"Be careful, his bow tie is really a camera." For me, that image captured exactly what Mr. Nochelski had wanted us to do: first, to be aware of our environment, and second, to describe it in a way that is clear and meaningful to other people. With that one simple question, he opened up a dimension that I have paid attention to ever since.

I remember writing a rather pedestrian description of a chandelier in the school's foyer. If I had really paid attention that morning, and hadn't been too nervous to notice, I would have described an old Masonic temple on a hill that was attached to an old stone mansion. (Although I didn't know it at the time, the area had some historical significance: in 1901, in what is now the student parking lot at Canisius High School, President William McKinley died after being struck by an assassin's bullet.) We entered the school through a set of tall, blue double doors, each of which was decorated with a cross and the letters CHS. On the other side of those doors was a large, imposing foyer; straight ahead was the auditorium, and behind that, the gym. The foyer floor was black marble, and you knew you had entered the school when you heard the heels of your dress shoes clicking behind you on that hard polished surface.

Most of our teachers were priests, and some were real characters. Father Alvin Hufnagel, an older man with a huge head of
curly white hair and glasses as thick as Coke bottles, could have
passed for Albert Einstein's lost brother. A tall, fit fellow with
broad shoulders and long limbs who liked to swing back and
forth on door frames, he was an early and earnest advocate of
good nutrition and assorted herbal remedies. He chewed sun-
flower seeds incessantly, which he purchased in bulk and resold
to students in little baggies, which I guess made him the health-
food equivalent of a drug dealer.

Father Hufnagel was best known for telling us, forcefully
and at every possible opportunity, "The whiter the bread, the
sooner you're dead." He was concerned about the effects of
sugar and refined flour on our diets, which put him well ahead
of his time and made him a prophet without honor in our community. In the mid 1960s, especially in a city like Buffalo, where
people held strong opinions about food, and where cholesterol
was regarded as one of the more essential nutrients in the food
pyramid, we laughed at his warnings, offered him hot dogs, and
mocked him behind his back by saying, "The wheatier the
bread, the bigger your head."

Our Latin teacher was Father Frank Redmond, whose brother,
James, was the pastor at St. Michael's. A short, white-haired priest
with a grizzly complexion, yellowed fingers, and a persistent
smoker's cough, his beet-red face turned even brighter when
you failed to meet his high expectations. Father Redmond had
been born and educated in South Buffalo, but he didn't volunteer that information, and he was especially tough on Canisius
students who lived in his old neighborhood. He liked to tease

us, offering up sarcastic comments such as, "You can always go to Timon," or "South Buffalo, that seedy Irish place? Don't people ever work out there?" Sometimes, referring to local public high schools, he'd break into song:

You'll do your best at Kenmore West
You'll study hard at Burgard
And you'll make your mark at old South Park.

His point was clear: you won't succeed here at Canisius unless you work harder. Only later, after we had survived Father Redmond's baptism by fire during our freshman year, did we realize that he was actually a loyal friend who was trying to make sure we moved beyond our neighborhood parochialism to become part of the Canisius community.

I HAVE SAVED THE BEST FOR LAST. The teacher who influenced me more than any other at Canisius High School was a short, tough, cigar-smoking, dark-haired priest with a receding hairline who bore the menacing title of Prefect of Discipline. Father John Sturm was a stocky man with huge, Popeye-like forearms; people said he had once been a Golden Gloves boxer, although nobody knew for sure. He roamed the halls like a drill sergeant, which was fitting because Canisius was to other high schools more or less what the Marines are to other branches of the service: difficult, demanding, and proud.

Father Sturm was always searching for signs of trouble, and if trouble was lurking anywhere in the vicinity, he usually found it. More often, though, he discouraged bad behavior before it began. With a mere look, he could stop you dead in your tracks and improve your attitude. First-year students, who were completely unaccustomed to male authority figures after eight years of dealing mostly with nuns, found him especially frightening.

All day long he barked out orders: "Stand up straight." "Fix your tie." "Close your mouth." "Stay in line." "Stand outside my office." And questions: "Are you a smart guy?" "Why aren't your shoes shined?" And my favorite, "Russert, what's your name?" He grilled everyone, all the time. His persistent, powerful, prosecutorial style elicited fast and honest responses even from those who hadn't planned to tell the truth. It didn't really matter whether he actually had evidence of our guilt. What mattered was that we thought he did.

He was smart, earthy, and tough, but he was also fair—at least some of the time. If you were a football hero or the son of a wealthy donor, you were treated the same as everybody else. If you had a problem, he was often sympathetic. Most of the time you had to do something wrong to show up on his radar screen, although he had a sixth sense that alerted him when you were even thinking of breaking a rule. He had an intrinsic sense of proportionality, and saved his toughest tactics for the most incorrigible students. When a big, strong, bruiser type refused to get a haircut, Father Sturm informed him that he had no choice. When the student refused, Father Sturm said, "Okay, here's what we're going to do. You and I will go downstairs and wrestle. If I pin you, you'll get a haircut. If you pin me, you don't have to." It took about six seconds for Father Sturm to win the match. To celebrate his victory, he took a pair of scissors and cut

several large chunks out of his opponent's hair, leaving him no
choice but to get a haircut—and a short one, too.

He tried to make sure that the punishment fit the crime, but
he also knew when you'd had enough. Years earlier, Father
Sturm had himself been a student at Canisius, where he had
probably misbehaved in some of the same ways we did. Whatever tricks we had up our sleeves, he had seen them long ago.

Those of us who were new to Canisius met the Prefect of
Discipline on the first day of school, when he addressed the
freshman assembly with a speech that went something like this:

"Welcome to Canisius High School. Look to your left. Look
to your right. There's a good chance that one of you won't be
here at graduation, unless you apply yourself academically and
conduct yourself like a gentleman. A thousand boys took the
entrance exam and less than a quarter of you were accepted, so
you are fortunate to be here, and I expect you to take full advantage of this opportunity.

"From this day on, you *are* Canisius, you will *think* Canisius,
and you will *act* Canisius, whether you're here in this building,
down the street, or on the other side of town. I went to Canisius High School and I'm proud of it, and I expect you to have
the same pride in this place that I do. In fact, I am so identified
with this place and so proud of it that if you do something
wrong, even if it's outside of school hours or school property, I
will regard it as a personal affront.

"Many of you went to Catholic grammar schools, or other
private schools. Some of you went to public schools. Wherever
you were, most of you were the kings of your classrooms. But
now you're starting over, and you're not the top dog anymore.

You will learn how to survive at the bottom of the totem pole. You will learn to live with other students who are just as smart as you are. And you will be sure to respect each other, whether the other guy is Polish, Irish, Italian, German, black, or anything else.

"You must be at school on time. If you don't have an alarm clock, ask your parents to get you one. With punctuality, as with everything else at this school, you will be held responsible for your actions. Getting here on time is not your parents' responsibility. That is *your* job. There is one excuse that I absolutely will not tolerate, and that is, 'My mother didn't get me up in time.'

"You will be expected to do a certain amount of studying every night. You'll have a lot of homework, and we expect you to complete it. If you don't keep up with your work, you won't be here very long.

"One more thing: a gentleman doesn't go through life on his own. You will need prayer in your life. You will need to ask the Lord to help you and the Holy Spirit to guide you. Without prayer, you're only half educated. You may be smart, but if you're not respectful and you don't take responsibility, you're not a full person. Don't be afraid to ask God's help."

Like Father Redmond, Father Sturm seemed to focus especially on students from South Buffalo. He thought we were cliquish and a little too cocky, and he wanted to make sure we respected authority. One morning, a group of priests, including Father Sturm, were approaching the front of the auditorium to say Mass. As they walked, their hands were folded in contemplation. Out of the corner of his eye, Father Sturm spotted a couple of South Buffalo boys who were clowning around. He swiftly reached out and cuffed them, and immediately refolded his hands and continued his saintly stroll as if nothing had happened. He could quiet an auditorium of noisy boys with a single syllable: when he yelled "hey!" at the top of his lungs, the entire room fell into an immediate and respectful silence.

I had my first personal encounter with Father Sturm a little earlier than most students. On the third or fourth day of the school year I was hungry well before lunch, and between classes I stopped at my locker to get a sandwich. Hiding behind the open locker door, I had taken a bite or two of my peanut butter and jelly when Father Sturm materialized out of nowhere, grabbed me from behind, spun me around, and pushed me up against the wall. "What are you doing?" he demanded.

"Father, I'm hungry."

"You can't eat now. See me after school."

"Father, I'm really sorry. I'm new here. Please, have mercy."

A thin smile crossed his face. "Russert, mercy is for God. I deliver justice."

Word of my transgression spread quickly through the building, and I was afraid Dad would hear about it. When I came home that evening, I fessed up and tried to play the victim. "Dad, you wouldn't believe what happened to me at school."

"What happened?"

I told him the story, but Dad wasn't the least bit sympathetic. His exact words were, "If Father said you did wrong, you done wrong." Case closed. No appeal.

Then Dad told me a story about responsibility and accountability. Shortly after I was born, he was out celebrating. As he was driving home, a tree jumped out in front of him. Fortunately, he wasn't hurt. Just when Dad thought he had avoided any consequences for his behavior, an envelope arrived in the mail with a City of Buffalo return address. He opened it and found an invoice in the amount of $50 for the damage he had done to a maple tree. "I realized that I had to pay the piper," Big Russ told me. "Whatever you do, you must always be prepared to pay the price."

At Canisius, paying the price meant serving a session or more of "jug," which is the term for detention in most Jesuit high schools. People often say that jug is an acronym for Justice Under God, but the word actually comes from the Latin *jugum*, meaning burden or yoke. In any case, it was Father Sturm's chief weapon: if you did something wrong, he'd look at you and say, "Jug, Mister."

You could end up in jug for any number of reasons: For not having cuffs on your pants. For pants that were too short. For hair that was too long. For failing to complete an assignment. For chewing gum. For arriving late to school. For talking in class. For talking back to a teacher. For smoking on school property. For having unshined shoes. For failing to be respectful. For not walking to an assembly in single file. Teachers gave you jug for a specific reason, but Father Sturm might give you jug because he just *knew* you had done something wrong, even if he hadn't yet discovered what it was.

Tony Ragusa, who went to Canisius a few years after I did, had known Father Sturm since the age of six. On his first day in high school, Father Sturm spotted him and immediately sentenced him to jug.

"But why?" Tony asked.

"I want to start you off right."

"But Father, I didn't do anything!"

"I know. This is for the things you're gonna do."

Jug was held after school from three to four-thirty in the afternoon, and the worst part about it was that you couldn't use that time to get started on your homework. Father Greer, a big man who sometimes ran jug and looked like he meant business, might print a Latin sentence on the board and have you write it out a couple of hundred times. Or he might give you the names of a dozen Russian cities on the Siberian Railroad and make you write them over and over until your fingers hurt. One of his favorite assignments was to have you write "Fuzzy Wuzzy was a bear" two hundred and fifty times. With these types of punishment, you were required to space out your writing in a way that he would specify, so it wouldn't help to attach three pens together in an effort to make the punishment go faster. Again and again, you were reminded that the priests at Canisius knew all the tricks, including a few you hadn't thought of yet. One way or another, they were always letting you know that they had seen your type before.

Father Sturm's punishments were more inventive, but that didn't make them any easier. Usually, he'd make you write an essay, five hundred or a thousand words on some oddball topic such as how to grow hair on a doorknob, what your comb was thinking about while you were in jug, a day in the life of a snow-covered fire hydrant, the sex life of a Ping-Pong ball, or the life cycle of a clam. Your composition had to make sense, too. Sometimes he'd make you read your essay to your fellow inmates. Occasionally, he'd send you over to the rectory to read it to the priests.

In jug, as in the rest of school, smart alecks soon regretted their behavior. One jugee wrote his essay on a tiny piece of paper and gave it to Father Sturm, who promptly handed it back and said, "Okay, wise guy, read it." As the student started reading, Father Sturm took a match and lit the paper on fire. "Keep reading," he urged. "I'm enjoying it."

Even on the public bus, you weren't beyond the long arm of Father Sturm's law. Five stops from school, just when you thought you were free of his influence, he might suddenly walk on to make sure that nobody had lit up a cigarette. He also showed up occasionally at Maxl's Brau Struberl, an old German beer house that served the coldest draft beer in town, where you could order a pitcher for two dollars and they weren't too particular about your age. More than once, Father Sturm came in the front door as a group of students scurried out the back.

For all his strength and toughness, it was highly unusual for Father Sturm to draw blood. Normally, if you were out of line, he'd make do with a "love tap," as he called it, a vigorous shove in the shoulder or the chest to get your attention. As strict as he was, he wasn't vindictive. You knew that if Father Sturm hit you, you probably deserved it. Although most of us came to appreciate the man, in many cases our gratitude didn't kick in until we were seniors, or even years later, when most of our other teachers were long forgotten.

A few students never came around; they found him overbearing. When Father Sturm left Canisius, he was assigned to Marriage Encounter, a program that was started by the Catholic Church to improve communication between husbands and wives. The idea that our demanding drill sergeant was now advis-

ing couples on the emotional nuances of their relationship was
something that even his biggest fans found hard to envision. At
our ten-year reunion, one of my classmates went up to the former Prefect of Discipline and teased, "Father, at what point are
you suggesting that we slug our wives?"

TO GET FROM SOUTH BUFFALO (or West Seneca) to Canisius High School, we took one of three buses downtown to
Shelton Square, where Niagara, Church, and Erie Streets met
Main Street in the epicenter of the city. We then switched to
the 25, the Delaware Avenue bus, which brought us to school. In
the morning, as the South Buffalo contingent waited for that
second bus to arrive, two nearby buildings held a particular allure
for us. The Palace Burlesque Theater at 327 Main Street was a
legendary institution in Buffalo. Many eminent entertainers
had played there over the years, including Abbott and Costello,
Phil Silvers, Jerry Lewis, and Sammy Davis, Jr. But the perform-
ers who caught our attention were a little less famous and a lot
more feminine. The marquee at the Palace depicted a dancing girl
kicking to the rhythm of blinking lights, but the real attraction of
the Palace, if I remember correctly, was its magnificent nineteenth-
century architecture, rather than, say, those vivid black-and-
white photographs of the exotic, lightly clad "dancers" who performed there during any given week, and peeked out at us allur-
ingly from behind their prudently placed fans and feathers.
Well, maybe it wasn't the architecture.

The Palace, which was moribund in the morning, was considerably more lively by the time we changed buses on the way

home. The first show of the day began at noon, and was followed by four more during the afternoon and evening. (On Saturdays there was also a midnight show, which we imagined was especially exciting.) As we walked back and forth in front of the theater to keep warm while we waited for the bus, we could hear the band playing with plenty of percussion, followed by sounds of raucous laughter when the comedians came on. When the dancers appeared, they performed under a dim blue light, or so I'm told. And yet it must have been unusually bright inside, because many of the men walking into the Palace Theater were wearing sunglasses, even on cloudy days.

It was sometimes said that no young man growing up in Buffalo could earn his high school diploma without at least one visit to the Palace Burlesque, the point being, I suppose, that such an outing was essential to fill in certain gaps in one's education. (As long as we were in high school, most of us, despite what we may have told one another, were unlikely to learn these lessons in a more gratifying way.) A few of us finally mustered the courage to approach the ticket booth one afternoon, quite oblivious to the fact that we were all carrying our blue and gold Canisius book bags.

"How old are you gentlemen?" we were asked.

"Eighteen," we piped up in our squeaky adolescent voices.

"Tell me," said the clerk, "does Father Sturm know you're here?"

None of us could think of an answer to that one, and we skulked away in defeat.

I was a senior when the Palace Theater finally closed. It had been built shortly after the Civil War, and opened as a burlesque house in 1925. Its owner, Dewey Michaels, opened a new place at Main and Tupper in 1967, which was a little late in the game for burlesque; it may, in fact, have been the last burlesque house to open in the United States. It closed ten years later. Times had changed, but true to the spirit of Buffalo, which doesn't give up easily, Dewey Michaels had tried gamely to hold on. He died in 1982, and one reason his theater hadn't survived was summed up nicely on a bumper sticker on a car at his funeral, which read, "Remember when sex was dirty and the air was clean?"

The other downtown establishment that appealed to us, especially in the morning, was Messina's Coffee Shop at 321 Main Street. This roomy restaurant with long counters was the type of place where you were welcome to sit for an hour or more with a hard roll and a cup of coffee. Messina's served wonderful hot chocolate that was made the right way, with Vitamin-D enriched milk and real whipped cream, sprinkled with chocolate shavings. When the first half of our commute was over, we often ducked into Messina's to warm up, and to fortify ourselves for the second bus ride. On snowy days we sometimes lingered a little longer, which occasionally made us late to school. That was risky, of course, but there was safety in numbers, or so we imagined. One morning we told Father Sturm that we arrived late because the drawbridge had been up at Republic Steel, and although that was sometimes true, it wasn't true that day, as Father Sturm had already determined by calling the plant. It was disheartening to go up against him; all too often, the excuses we worked so hard to invent were investigated and rejected even before we offered them.

But we kept trying to outsmart him, and the more we failed, the more determined we became. One factor in our favor was the indisputable fact that during the winter months, because of the winds blowing off Lake Erie, the weather in South Buffalo was often considerably worse than in the rest of the city. One morning in February 1966, when I was a sophomore, the snow was coming down especially hard. Buffalo, of course, was accustomed to blizzards, and the city buses carried big noisy chains on their snow tires that practically turned them into tanks. A group of us were sitting in Messina's, looking out the window, when Jayce Caulfield said, "It's going to snow like this all day. You *know* nobody else will show up. They'll all chicken out. They'll probably cancel school."

This sequence of events was by no means a certainty, but it fit nicely with our view of the world. We, the hardy few from South Buffalo, liked to think of ourselves as the toughest guys in the school, and certainly more rugged than those pampered rich kids from the northern, wealthier suburbs. "Let's call Father Sturm," Jayce said. "We'll tell him we're snowed in, that the buses can't make it." By now we had our coats off and were savoring our second cup of hot chocolate and our third peanut stick doughnut, which tasted even better when you dunked it into your hot chocolate or coffee.

Messina's had one of those old-fashioned phone booths that used to be everywhere, where you could actually close the door and have a private conversation. (Think of it: if Superman were around today, he'd have no place to change.) For some reason I was nominated to call Father Sturm in an effort to buy us some time until school was called off—or so we hoped.

"We're trying to get there," I said, trying to muffle the mouth-piece so Father Sturm wouldn't pick up any stray restaurant noises, "but the snow is really bad and the buses keep getting stuck. But we're really going to try."

"How did it go?" Jayce asked me.

"Great. He bought it."

It was time for another round of hot chocolate. About twenty minutes later, Jayce turned to me and said, slowly and deliberately, "Oh. My. God." His face was white, as if he had just seen a ghost. In fact, he had seen something worse: Father Sturm had entered the building, causing a dozen or more stu-dents to scatter like cockroaches from a flashlight. Legend has it that one guy actually jumped behind the counter and put on an apron, but I can't vouch for that. All I remember is that Father Sturm said, "Gentlemen, let's go," and marched us toward the Delaware Avenue bus like prisoners of war being led to the gal-lows after an unsuccessful escape. As we climbed the steps, Jayce muttered, "Wait until Sarge hears about this." Sarge was his father, and I had a similar thought: Dad will not be pleased.

It was the quietest bus ride I have ever been on. When we arrived at school, Father Sturm lined us up against the wall. Turning to me, he asked, "Russert, what's this about? What do you mean, you couldn't come to school?"

"Father, I didn't say we weren't coming to school. I said we were *trying* to come to school."

"Forget your cute little word games. Just be a man and fess up."

The Jesuits wore black cassocks, and Father Sturm started rolling up his right sleeve. "Father, please!" I pleaded.

But he wanted to worry me, not hit me. "Russert," he said, "I'm telling you, I've had it. I took the bus downtown and I got there with no problem. Forget the sob stories. You're going to jug for two weeks."

"Two weeks? That's impossible! Father, what about my job at St. Mike's?"

"You owe me two weeks of jug, my friend, and if you can't do it in two weeks, you can do it over five."

That night, I had no choice but to tell Dad what had happened. Once again I portrayed myself as a victim, and once again Dad didn't buy it.

"That guy won't cut me a break," I said.

"He won't, and I won't, either," Dad said. "You're grounded for two weeks."

Being grounded was even worse than jug, and for the next two weeks I was miserable. That's how it was in our house, and in most of the households I knew. When a teacher issued a decree, there was no court of appeals, no second opinion, no parental mercy. My parents backed Father Sturm as they backed every teacher and administrator, and every other adult in our lives. Dad didn't know the expression *in loco parentis,* but he understood the point of it: you behaved at school the way you were expected to behave at home. And if you didn't, you would be punished in both places.

After all these years, that incident is still vivid in my mind. Once again, I broke the rule and paid the price. Teachers often say they give out punishments in order to teach students a lesson, and students rarely believe them. I didn't, either. But often,

these punishments really *do* teach a lesson—in this case, that
actions have consequences.

It's important to have high expectations of children and
young people, and it's equally important to give teachers the
authority they need to impose discipline and teach accountability. In this respect, I believe that parents of my generation have
often failed our kids. We are so eager to be understanding and
sympathetic that we end up being too lenient, even as we further undermine the already diminished authority of teachers,
coaches, and principals.

Does this mean that teachers are always right? Of course
not. Or that they're never too harsh? Sometimes they are. But
that's how life goes: sometimes our bosses and supervisors are
wrong, or too harsh, and we still have to live by their decisions.
Sometimes umpires blow the call, but the call still stands.
Teachers are—or should be—figures of authority, and they need
to know that parents support them. We love our children, but
we do them no favor when we give them the idea, either by
word or by deed, that teachers or other adults are not worthy of
their respect. End of sermon.

As with Sister Lucille, I have stayed in touch with Father
Sturm, and over the years I have come to learn his story. He was
born in 1917 on the East Side of Buffalo, the oldest of three children. His father was a bookkeeper at a slaughterhouse and the
choir director at their church. His mother's brother was a Jesuit
priest, and when John Sturm was eleven, his family traveled to
Maryland for his uncle's ordination. Their host at the seminary
was a theological student named Vincent Hart, who took time
to talk to the boy and treated him like an honored guest. When

John returned to Buffalo, he began to correspond with Vincent Hart, who soon became Father Hart, writing to him about both religious questions and personal issues, and receiving long, thoughtful letters in reply. As it happened, when John Sturm was in his senior year at Canisius, Father Vincent Hart took over as the school's new principal.

At Canisius during the early 1930s, John Sturm was far more interested in football and girls than he was in religion. The idea of becoming a priest first occurred to him during a retreat, and he tried to forget about it, but couldn't. "It got into my head like a song," he says, "and I couldn't shake it. I asked the Holy Spirit to guide me." If he got hurt and couldn't play football, John Sturm decided, he would take it as a sign from God that he should give up sports and enter the priesthood. The summer before he entered Canisius College, he and his cousin drove to Montreal in a brand-new Packard. A bee flew into the car and distracted his cousin, who lost control of the wheel and hit a tree, injuring both boys. John, who couldn't play football for a while, wondered if this might be the sign he was looking for, but he decided that because it wasn't really a football injury, it didn't count. The following season, he hurt his knee in a practice and was forced to miss several games. That settled it.

On a Friday evening at the end of the school year, he was sitting with his parents on the porch after dinner when his mother said, "John, why aren't you out tonight?"

"I have something to tell you," he said. "Today I volunteered to enter the Society of Jesus as a priest." His father was filled with pride at the news; his mother burst into tears of joy. But their son had other things on his mind. "I have a date tonight," he told his parents. "Can I use the car?"

He pledged his parents to secrecy. "I didn't want the word to get out," he says, "because it would spoil all the dates I had lined up for the summer." I love that story, which reminds me of the famous prayer of the youthful St. Augustine: "Lord, grant me chastity—but not yet."

After two years at Canisius College, he left for St. Andrew-on-Hudson Seminary in Poughkeepsie, New York. Father Sturm was ordained in 1950, and was sent to Canisius High School, where he served as Prefect of Discipline for eighteen years. In the 1970s, as I mentioned, he became involved in Marriage Encounter. In 1981, he became an associate pastor at St. Michael's church, where I used to work, and where he still lives. As I was working on this book, Father Sturm published a book of his own, *Life's a Dance, Not a Dress Rehearsal*, becoming a first-time author at the age of eighty-six.

There's a lot in a name. Canisius High School is still there, and it still enjoys an excellent reputation. But things change, and I note with some regret that the school no longer has a Prefect of Discipline. The position still exists, but now it has a more user-friendly title. Today, the man who has Father Sturm's old job is known as the Dean of Students.

12.

1968

"I just don't know what the hell is going on in this country."

W HEN I GRADUATED FROM ELEMENTARY SCHOOL in the spring of 1964, my world was still overcast from the death of President Kennedy seven months earlier. But late that summer, like so many other young people, I found new hope in the Senate campaign of JFK's younger brother. "The torch has been passed to a new generation of Americans," JFK had said at his inauguration, and for many of us, that phrase now carried a new and unintended meaning: the president's torch had been passed to a new generation within his own family.

In late August, my parents and I watched Robert F. Kennedy's appearance at the Democratic National Convention in Atlantic City, where he spoke briefly to introduce a memorial film, a tribute to his late brother. When Kennedy was introduced, the applause and cheering went on and on. It took twenty-two minutes before he could finally speak, and when he did, he had tears in his eyes. So did many of the delegates. We did, too.

When Bobby entered the Senate race in New York on August 25, unthinkably late by today's standards, I volunteered immediately. It wasn't an easy campaign. New York in 1964 had a Republican governor, two Republican senators, and more Republican House members than Democrats. Two weeks before the election, *The New York Times* endorsed the incumbent, Sen. Kenneth Keating, and attacked Robert Kennedy for "attempting to use New York and the Senatorial office in a relentless quest for greater political power." Imagine, *The New York Times* endorsing an upstate Republican over a Kennedy!

During the campaign, Sister Lucille introduced me to Jerry Bruno, an advance man for Kennedy who came to Buffalo to organize high school and college students who wanted to work for Kennedy. Although I had just started high school, Bruno invited me to Syracuse to meet with a group of Kennedy supporters. We then drove to the airport, where Kennedy was flying in for a number of campaign appearances. Bruno had hoped to bring him into town quietly and whisk him off to the various events, but the press knew that Kennedy was coming and had staked out the airport. With his first plan no longer operational, Bruno quickly adapted to the new situation. If the press was going to be there when Kennedy landed, his campaign would look a lot stronger if there was a crowd on hand to greet the candidate. But how do you attract a crowd on ten minutes' notice?

I soon found out. Jerry Bruno walked over to a white courtesy telephone and told the operator, "Would you please ask Robert Kennedy to meet his party at Gate 3?" A moment later, we heard an announcement: "Robert Kennedy, Mr. Robert Kennedy, please meet your party at Gate 3." Immediately, about half the people in the airport converged on Gate 3. Bruno then repeated his request, and the crowd grew. When Kennedy stepped off the plane, a couple of hundred people were there to greet him. I was impressed. So *that's* what an advance man did.

Bruno's deft move made a big impression on me. Sometimes the most expensive techniques and complicated arrangements can't solve the problem at hand, and you just have to step back and improvise, as Jerry Bruno did that day at the Syracuse airport. He didn't mention this little trick in his 1971 book, *The Advance Man*, so to him it was probably no big deal. But it was very big to me, and when I returned home I couldn't wait to tell Dad what Bruno had done. Big Russ nodded in appreciation. "Sometimes you have to play it by ear," he said. "Don't get me wrong: it's always better to plan, but when things don't work out, you gotta think real fast and give it your best shot." It was high praise from a very organized man.

After that trip to Syracuse, I wanted to be an advance man. Forty years later, I can still recall the excitement I felt watching the legendary Jerry Bruno in action. He was only a small cog in the enormous machinery of American democracy, but he made something happen and he moved the process forward. In any large undertaking, whether it's a campaign, a movement, or a newscast, success depends on the many people who attend to the mundane details. Although Jerry Bruno was working for the powerful Kennedy political machine, he served as a valuable reminder that no task is too small or too unimportant to be done—and done well.

When I was in college, I invited Jerry to our campus to talk about his experience in politics. Just as I expected, he held us enthralled for hours as he described the countless details an advance man has to think about, ranging from who should ride with the candidate on the way to the airport to how best to set up a photo opportunity. He told us that great politicians understand that there is a connection in voters' minds between crowd appeal and leadership ability, and that it was his job to make sure there was a good crowd at every political event. He said he had been working for the Kennedys for a couple of years when, at a meeting in Washington, Robert Kennedy said, "I'm going to ask Jerry Bruno to say a few words. Jerry's an advance man, and he'll tell you how it's done." It was not until then that Bruno learned he was an advance man. He had never heard the term before.

Sister Lucille also invited Jerry Bruno to speak, but in her case the results were less satisfying. Addressing the seventh and eighth graders at Our Lady of Sacred Heart School, Bruno told them, "I never even finished high school, and look where I ended up!" Sister Lucille was not amused. "I could have killed him," she told me.

Although Robert Kennedy ran well behind President Johnson, he won the Senate race by 700,000 votes. As I turned my attention away from politics and focused on the demanding curriculum of my new high school, I never dreamed that twelve years later, in 1976, I would volunteer in another campaign for that same Senate seat, or that its outcome would affect me for the rest of my life.

Billy Suchocki and Big Russ. This Polish kid from Chicago saved my dad's life on October 25, 1944. I am forever grateful.

Billy and Big Russ
toasting each other
forty years after surviving
the plane crash.

That's Big Russ on the right with Red and one of his buddies.
Red went overseas with my dad and the 446th Bombardment Group.

Red in full dress uniform.

Big Russ grabs a few winks. Two jobs didn't leave much time for extended sleep.

My first year on Big Russ's lap.

Luke's first birthday.

My sister B.A. and I
in South Buffalo's answer
to a "hot tub"!

The pool on the Russert estate. That's nine-year-old Timmy
being hosed down by four-year-old sister Kathy.

My sister B.A. and I
with Santa (aka Shinyface Collins)
at the South Buffalo American Legion Post 721
annual Christmas party . . .

and in our "finery"
on Easter Sunday 1955.

Mom with B.A. and Kathy
and an obviously pouting
little Timmy.

Mom and Dad
with younger sister Patty
who now calls herself Trish.

That's me in the middle
at my First Communion
in 1957.

Luke celebrates his First Communion in 1994 with Grandpa and Dad.

I'm at the podium reflecting on the "trials and tribulations" of grammar school on graduation day.

More desire than ability on the court and ball field!

Sister Mary Lucille, my 7th grade teacher, who made me editor of our school newspaper to "channel my excessive energy."

Father John Sturm, the Prefect of Discipline at Canisius High School— "Russert, mercy is for God. I deliver justice."

On the campaign trail in 1976 with Ambassador, soon-to-be Senator, Daniel Patrick Moynihan.

Weekend duty during the Ossining prison uprising in 1983 with New York Governor Mario Cuomo and his advisors.

Pope John Paul II
welcomes NBC News
to the Vatican.

The Russert family receives a papal blessing . Luke's T-shirt says "Totus Tuus,"
the pope's personal motto of "all yours" affirming his devotion to the Blessed Virgin.

That's Dad and Mom posing with Aretha Franklin while five-year-old
Luke imitates the Queen of Soul.

A day to remember. Seven-year-old Luke and his dad throw out the first pitch for the Buffalo Bisons.

Big Russ on the set of the *Tonight Show* with Cindy Crawford.

Big Russ on the set of *Meet the Press* being grilled by his grandson.

Vice President Al Gore offers satellite photos which he insists prove the Tennessee Titans beat the Buffalo Bills fair and square.

Father and son in the Oval Office. As Big Russ says, "What a country."

Father, son, and grandson celebrate Thanksgiving Day, 2003.

The last picture ever taken of father and son, in front of the Vatican, 2008.

IN THE SPRING OF 1968, during my final semester in high school, all hell broke loose in American politics. On March 12, in a stinging rebuke to President Johnson's Vietnam policy, Sen. Eugene McCarthy won a surprising 42 percent of the vote in the New Hampshire primary. A few days later, to the delight of his supporters and the understandable fury of the McCarthy supporters, Robert Kennedy entered the race.

The Robert Kennedy of 1968 was a different and more mature individual than the candidate who had run for Senate four years earlier when his campaign had essentially been about resurrecting Camelot. In the years since 1964, Kennedy had turned into a passionate politician who spoke out forcefully against the war in Vietnam, and against racial prejudice and poverty in the United States. His presidential campaign was just getting started when March 31 brought a second shock: at the end of a televised speech, President Johnson stunned the world with a twenty-word addendum that nobody had expected: "I shall not seek, and I will not accept the nomination of my party for another term as your president."

Just four days later, on the evening of April 4, a third shock hit the country when Martin Luther King, Jr., was assassinated in Memphis. Dad took it very hard. South Buffalo wasn't known for its racial diversity, but Dad had made a point of teaching us that there was no place for prejudice in our hearts. The "N" word was frequently heard on the streets, but it was forbidden to be uttered in our house. (Years later, when I was driving Luke to school during the O. J. Simpson trial and the "N" word was mentioned on the radio, my nine-year-old son said, "Dad, what does that mean?" I was so glad he didn't know.) Once, when my older sister repeated a story that included the word "Polack," little Kathy, who was a little unclear on the concept, piped up and said, "B.A., you're not supposed to say that. You're supposed to say 'colored person.'"

Dad had worked with black men all his life, and had no tolerance for bigotry. When he heard that one of his workers was spewing racial insults, he assigned a light-skinned African American to work with him. "Jimmy, you'll take Bobby today, right?"

"Sure, fine."

A few weeks later, Jimmy said, "Bobby is a good, hardworking Italian kid."

"Jimmy," Dad said, "he's not Italian. He's colored. And I hope you learned something."

The murder of King came as an enormous blow to our country. At Canisius, we had a special assembly and a Mass for the slain leader. Riots broke out in many cities, including Buffalo, and when I took the bus from school to my afternoon job at St. Michael's, the area was swarming with police. Fortunately, the church was untouched.

When King was killed, Bobby Kennedy was on his campaign plane, heading for Indianapolis. When he landed, he was told that King was dead from a bullet in the head—a wound similar to the one that killed JFK. Kennedy canceled his campaign appearances, but he went, as scheduled, to a rally in the inner city. The mayor of Indianapolis urged him to call off the event, but Kennedy insisted on appearing. Standing on the back of a truck, he told the crowd what had just happened in Memphis. Then, speaking extemporaneously and from his heart, he asked his audience to pay tribute to King's memory by honoring his great

dream of nonviolence. Although the whole country was explod-
ing after King's death, there were no riots in Indianapolis.

I paid close attention to this speech, and to all of Kennedy's
speeches during his presidential campaign. Although I couldn't
have articulated it at the time, I could feel that Robert Kennedy
had become a different kind of Democrat, one who was speaking out for those who had no political voice—blacks, Hispanics,
children, and the elderly. Where his brother had been cool and
detached, Robert Kennedy was becoming increasingly fervent
and was embracing issues with a passion that JFK never showed.
I noticed that Dad, too, was responding to Bobby, who had the
rare ability to appeal to minorities without alienating white ethnic voters or pitting one group against another. In the 1970s
and '80s, many working-class whites concluded that the Democratic Party had abandoned them, but Robert Kennedy was a
unifier and a coalition builder.

I found it interesting that this son of great privilege was the
politician who spoke out most forcefully about the disenfran-
chised members of our society. But with Kennedy, unlike some
of the liberals who followed him, the message was never about
blaming America. He insisted that we were a great country, but
that we could do better. Kennedy was critical, but he wasn't
negative; he was optimistic and even (at least to me) inspiring.

What impressed me the most was his willingness to challenge student audiences on the issue of the draft. College students were exempt from military service, and although they
were among his biggest supporters, Kennedy attacked this special privilege as elitist and unfair because no such escape routes
were available to the poor. When a student at Creighton Uni-

versity in Nebraska asked him whether the Vietnam War didn't provide a way of helping black Americans escape from the slums of American cities, Kennedy hit the roof: "Here at a Catholic university, how can you say that we can deal with the problem of the poor by sending them to Vietnam? There is a great moral force in the United States about the wrongs of the federal government and how Congress has failed to pass legislation dealing with civil rights, and yet when it comes down to you, yourselves and your own individual lives, then you say students should be draft deferred." At Idaho State University he made a similar point, that the burden of fighting the war fell disproportionately to blacks, Mexican-Americans, and other young people who couldn't afford to attend college. "Student deferments should be abolished," he said bluntly.

I recognized that there was something unusual about Kennedy's willingness to confront, and even alienate, a large segment of his supporters. It didn't strike me as politically smart, but that only raised my opinion of the man. At some risk to his candidacy, Kennedy insisted that his supporters be intellectually and morally honest with themselves.

Of course I had a personal interest in this issue. I had just turned eighteen and was planning to go to college. Vietnam was very much on my mind, and I wasn't sure it was right for someone like me to miss being drafted by going to school. At Canisius, just about everyone in my graduating class was going on to college, but Canisius wasn't the only world I was part of. In our neighborhood, and even on our street, many boys my age were being inducted into the military. And I knew of kids who had already given their lives.

After Kennedy's speech at Creighton University, I asked Dad what he thought about college students and the draft. "Well," he said, "the service was good for me and for my generation," which was a typically optimistic response in view of what happened to him during the war. "If our country was being attacked, I wouldn't have any doubt about what you kids should do. But for this war, right now, if you have a chance to get a college education, take it." I was amazed by his answer, and relieved as well. I saw an enormous difference between World War II and Vietnam, but I wasn't exactly an impartial observer. Coming from Dad, that position carried a lot more weight.

That spring I followed Robert Kennedy's presidential campaign as closely, and with some of the same excitement, as I had once followed the Yankees. Kennedy won the primaries in Indiana and Nebraska in early May, but lost to Eugene McCarthy in Oregon at the end of the month. On June 4, I stayed up late to watch the results of the California primary, where Kennedy won a big, important victory. He ended his victory speech by saying, "My thanks to all of you, and now, on to Chicago." I was thrilled. I turned off the TV and said to my parents, "I told you he'd win." Then I went to bed, because I had a final exam in the morning.

Early the next morning, the phone rang. It was my neighbor, Mike Hanzly, with whom I took the bus to school. "I'm so sorry," he said.

"About what?"

"About Bobby."

"What do you mean? He won!"

"Tim, he got shot!"

"Stop it!"

"No, he got shot in Los Angeles."

I turned on the television and there it was. Somehow I dragged myself to school and took the exam. That night, for the first time in my life, I couldn't sleep. "Go to bed," Dad urged me, but I couldn't.

"Why is this happening?" I demanded. "Why are they shooting people?" We still hadn't gotten over the King assassination, exactly two months earlier.

Dad just shook his head. It was the first time that he couldn't answer my question. I guess that, too, was an answer, that sometimes things happen and you just can't explain them. Another Kennedy was dead, and even Dad didn't know why. He's the most optimistic man I've ever met, but that night, he was really down. "I just don't know what the hell is going on in this country," he said.

After my next exam, I went to see Sister Lucille at Our Lady of Sacred Heart, where she was teaching. In the doorway of the classroom we must have hugged each other for five minutes. We talked about not losing hope, and reminded each other of the things Bobby had said when his brother died, and of his magnificent speech when Martin Luther King was shot. But both of us were devastated by the news. I had a very hard time getting energized again, or persuading myself that the values Robert Kennedy stood for, which included some of the same things that the Sisters of Mercy and the Jesuits had taught me, would endure in American politics without him. I would become involved in politics again, but Robert Kennedy's death ended my interest for some time.

A year later I drove to the Kentucky Derby with some

friends from college. In Kentucky, we were pulled over by a police officer who asked for my license and registration, checked my tires, and performed a mini-inspection on my 1965 Ford. I couldn't figure out why we had been stopped, so I politely said, "Officer, did I do anything wrong?"

"Just do what I tell you," he replied. When he was finished, he pointed to the Kennedy for President bumper sticker that was still on my car from 1968.

"You see that?" he asked.

"Yes."

"We don't want that down here, son. Why don't you and your friends head back to New York?"

It was a grim reminder that not everybody felt about Robert Kennedy the way I did.

13.

Cars

"This is who I am."

IKE EVERY OTHER BOY I KNEW, I couldn't wait to turn sixteen and get my driver's license. Dad and I both assumed that he would teach me how to drive, but although he was an experienced and professional driver, it soon became clear that possessing a certain skill doesn't necessarily mean that you can pass it along to somebody else. Big Russ didn't have the patience to teach me the mechanics of driving, which I had realized a couple of years earlier when he took my older sister out for a lesson. As I watched from the backseat, Betty Ann drove into a traffic circle, and with Dad sitting nervously beside her, she must have gone around it a dozen times because she hadn't yet learned how to ease back into traffic. I found the whole thing hilarious, but Dad failed to see the humor. When we returned home, his face was beet red. "No more!" he announced to nobody in particular. "No more!"

Although I took driver's ed classes at Canisius, I learned

some important lessons from Big Russ as well. To him, driving involved a lot more than knowing how to operate a vehicle. Before I set out, he wanted me to tell him not only where I was going, but exactly how I intended to get there. When we went driving together, half the lesson was a combination of geography test and contingency planning. How do you get downtown? Turn north on Seneca and get off at Church. And if there's an accident? You can also get off at Smith. And if the thruway is backed up? In that case . . .

For every place I might possibly want to go, Dad made sure I knew two or three ways to get there. For him, these alternative routes sprang to mind automatically. He knew the whole city in his head, and during his years of driving for both the Sanitation Department and the newspaper, he had learned to deal with every conceivable impediment: blizzards, hurricanes, icy roads, flooding, detours, heavy traffic, accidents, and fallen power lines. I needed maps to find my way around, and I had to learn how to think about contingencies, but I'm glad I did. When Luke turned sixteen, I made sure that in addition to knowing how to drive, he was able to navigate around Washington, D.C., and its major suburbs.

Another of Dad's lessons, one I didn't learn quite as well, had to do with taking care of a vehicle. Every time I drove home from college, Dad came out to inspect my car. Within moments, the hood would be up and he'd be checking the hoses, the battery, and the fluids. He has always been meticulous about looking after his cars, and makes sure to change the oil every three thousand miles. "If you want something to be there when you really need it," he would remind me, "you have to take good care of it."

He also insisted that I learn how to drive a stick shift. When I pointed out that today's cars mostly came with automatic transmissions, he shook his head: "What if there's an emergency, and a stick shift is all you've got?" Although that struck me as an unlikely scenario, Dad borrowed a car with manual transmission and taught me how to drive it. It didn't come easy: once, when he guided me to a gas station to fill up the tank, the car was bumping along like a crippled camel after a couple of cocktails. "I guess that's close enough," I said, as I pulled into the same area code as the gas pump.

"No, it isn't," Dad said. Two gas station attendants stood there laughing as I jerked and jolted my way in. We filled up the car, and I drove out a little more smoothly than I drove in. Once again, Dad turned out to be right: there were times in college when I was with a friend who was driving a stick shift, and after he'd had a few drinks, I was glad I could take over and get us safely home. Regarding alcohol, Dad reminded me again and again, "If you've had too much, don't drive." But it didn't really hit home, especially when I thought back to all the beer Dad and my uncles had consumed on our way back from those baseball games in Cleveland. It wasn't just Dad; by today's standards, America in the 1960s was shockingly complacent about the dangers of driving while intoxicated. Mothers Against Drunk Driving, which is so deeply embedded into our consciousness that it seems to have been around forever, did not even exist until 1980.

The lack of awareness about alcohol wasn't the only impediment to safety when I was learning how to drive. Cars had no seat belts, and nobody had even heard of air bags. Mandatory inspections, antilock brakes, headrests, and other protective devices were still unknown. The seeds of change had been sown: Ralph Nader's *Unsafe at Any Speed* had just been published, and in Albany, a few years earlier, a young assistant to Governor Averell Harriman named Daniel Patrick Moynihan was thinking about how the federal government could lean on the car companies to make their products less dangerous. But it wasn't until the 1970s that Americans began to get serious about auto safety.

At Canisius High School, Mr. Kuligowski, our driver's ed instructor, grabbed our attention by showing us an unforgettable film called *Mechanized Death*. Made in 1961, this gruesome, thirty-five-minute movie opened with a dying woman in the aftermath of a car crash, and continued with scene after scene of gore, destruction, mangled cars, and ominous warnings. The stark message of *Mechanized Death* was that driving—not drunk driving, or bad driving, but just plain *driving*—was inherently dangerous. There was some truth to that claim: by today's standards, driving in the 1960s really was a risky undertaking. It wasn't just that cars were often unsafe, and especially older cars, which were much more likely to be driven by teenagers, but many roads weren't too safe, either.

Between Dad's warnings and the nightmarish scenes in *Mechanized Death*, I was already inclined to be careful. Then, as my junior year was ending, I received a dramatic wake-up call: a senior at Canisius High School was killed when his car crashed into the guard posts on a bridge as he drove home from visiting his grandparents. Timothy Harmon was probably the most prominent young man in the entire school. He was an honor student, a football star, president of the senior class, and had recently been voted "Mr. Canisius," as well as "senior of the year." A big, strapping redhead, he was such a talented athlete that he was accepted to Hobart College on a lacrosse scholarship even though he had never played lacrosse. If anyone had seemed invulnerable, it was Tim Harmon.

His death reinforced all of Dad's warnings and reminders that I was neither immortal nor invincible. "You're driving a weapon," Big Russ would say, "and unless you're in total control, you could kill yourself. Even the slightest distraction could land you in the hospital or the grave." After Tim Harmon died, I drove extra carefully for a long time.

Although I think I've helped Luke become a better driver, he has helped me as well. "You know, Dad," he told me once, "you sometimes run yellow lights." I hadn't realized it, but I'm sure it was true: when I rode around on a garbage or newspaper truck, a yellow light was a signal to hurry up. I could preach about safety all day long, but if I was running yellow lights, or failing to come to a complete stop at stop signs, what kind of message was I sending to Luke?

When Luke got his license, Maureen and I had a serious talk with him about alcohol. Luke pledged that he would never drink and drive; if he did, he would lose the right to drive my pickup truck. We had been talking to Luke about drinking and drugs since the fifth grade, when Maureen spearheaded an alcohol and drug education program for students and parents at Luke's school. Since then, nearly all the parents of Luke's class had signed a zero-tolerance pledge about alcohol and drug use, and promised to notify one another about unchaperoned parties or a child who was under the influence. It hasn't always worked perfectly, but the pledge has definitely helped lower the amount of drinking that goes on among the students. One thing they seem to have internalized is that they must never drink and drive.

As a father, it's often hard to know where to draw the line. My first instinct was to tell my teenage son, as I did for years, "You will not drink, and you'll never go to a party where there's drinking." That worked for a while, but by the time he was seventeen, it wasn't the prohibition on drinking that Luke objected to as much as how his social life would be affected if he could never attend parties where someone else might be drinking. Then Maureen and I had several frank discussions with him about alcohol, judgment, and common sense—and not just when he was driving.

Today's videos for young drivers focus on the dangers of driving under the influence of alcohol or drugs, and Luke and I watched one together and talked about it at some length before renewing one simple pledge: no drinking and driving—period— or he would lose his driving privileges.

When I was a young driver, so much was left unsaid. I never had detailed conversations about safety with Dad; it wasn't part of the culture, and it wasn't Dad's style. Looking back, I realize that I sometimes acted foolishly and did things that I now know were dangerous. The lesson is clear: *there are conversations you never had with your mom or dad that you must have with your own son or daughter.*

Here, too, the learning has gone in both directions. If we go out to dinner, and I'm driving, Luke will sometimes say, "Remember, two beers in an hour and you're at the legal level"—a valuable reminder from son to father. All the parental

preaching in the world goes to waste if it's mixed with a single
ounce of hypocrisy.

For all my nostalgia and fondness for the good old days, I'm
glad that driving has become much safer, especially for young
people. After Congress forced all states to raise the drinking age
to twenty-one (by making it a necessary condition for getting
federal highway funds), the number of teenagers dying from
alcohol-related car accidents was reduced by half. Drinking and
driving used to be the leading cause of death among teenagers,
but that is no longer the case.

I BOUGHT MY FIRST CAR in 1968, during my senior year of
high school. I paid $50 for a pink 1958 Dodge with push-button
drive and fins, which was definitely a candidate for the ugliest
vehicle of the twentieth century. It was also a lemon, and after I
drove it for a few months, Dad was somehow able to sell it for
$100. My next car was a 1965 Ford that I drove between Buffalo
and Cleveland, where I went to college. One night, as I drove
home in my junior year, it broke down an hour from Buffalo. I
pulled over to a pay phone in a rest area and called Dad collect.
He said, "Stay warm, stay safe, and I'll be there." When he
finally arrived, he opened the hood, saw that a hose was broken,
cobbled it together somehow, and followed me home without a
word of complaint. A couple of months later I had a flat twenty
miles outside the city, and again he drove out to meet me. This
time, however, he was upset. "Are you kidding? This tire looks
like Yul Brynner's head! You've got to be responsible. Part of
owning a car is having good rubber. You know, it's a good thing

this tire blew because it's not safe to be driving on." Another lesson learned.

My third car was a 1967 Mercury Comet, another beauty. It was 1972, and I had just graduated from college when I drove home and told Dad that my car had been throwing off so much smoke I could hardly breathe. "Let's go for a ride," he said. Within a couple of minutes, smoke was pouring into the front seat. "Make a left," he told me, and I turned left. He seemed to have a destination in mind and we soon reached it.

"Pull in here."

"Here?"

"Yeah, straight ahead."

He had taken me to a junkyard!

"How much?" Dad asked the dealer.

"I'll give you twenty-five."

Dad got him up to thirty-five bucks, and we took a bus home.

I had moved back home and I had a job, but now I needed a car. A lot of my friends were buying Volkswagen Beetles, which were cheap, fun to drive, and reliable. When a Volkswagen had problems, it was easy to fix: because the models didn't really change from one year to the next, you could always get parts. But Dad didn't want me driving a German car, or any foreign car, for that matter.

I looked through the newspapers and found a new AMC Gremlin hatchback, a subcompact car that was being pitched to younger drivers, and was selling for $2,295. That was an excellent price even then, because the 1973 models were just starting to appear. It looked to me like a good deal: you could put just 10 percent down and finance the rest, and I had a job and knew I could make the payments. I showed Dad the ad, and he agreed to check it out with me the next morning. This was the first time I had ever gone with Dad to a car dealership, so I had no idea what to expect. As we drove in, Big Russ said, "Just don't be too anxious."

"Okay," I said, "you do the talking."

"Good."

I made a beeline for the Gremlin, and Dad came with me. After a couple of minutes, a salesman came over and introduced himself. "Call me Brownie," he told us. "So you're interested in buying a Gremlin?"

"We might be," Dad said. "We're looking around a little."

"This here is a good-selling model, very economical. The backseat folds down, and it's a great car for a young fellow like this one. Will you be doing a trade-in?"

"No," said Dad, "a straight deal. What can you do for me?"

"Well, $2,295 is already a great price," said Brownie, "but let me ask." A minute or two later, Brownie returned and proudly announced that he could take $50 off the advertised price.

Dad was unimpressed. "You guys must be doing great out here, because you don't need us."

"That's an excellent price, sir," said Brownie, "but why don't you make me an offer?"

"No, no, no," said Dad.

"Okay, let me see if there's anything else I can do," Brownie said. He came back and reduced the price by another $50, bringing it down to $2,195.

"Well," said Dad, "I guess you don't want to move this car."

Brownie pretended he hadn't heard this. "What color were you looking for?"

"What color you got?"

"I have two here."

"The silver one is nice," I said, opening my mouth for the first time since Brownie had introduced himself.

"He likes the silver one, and we can take it off the lot right now. You gotta move these things."

"Sir, I've done the best I can."

Dad thanked him, and we started walking out. Brownie, of course, came after us. "Wait a minute, let me talk to the manager."

Although I could see that Big Russ's method was effective, I was embarrassed to be part of this negotiation. On the other hand, I had never bought a car that wasn't sitting on somebody's front lawn, and maybe this was how it was done. Still, when Brownie left us for the third time, I said, "Dad, should we be pushing him like this?"

"Don't worry about him," Dad said. "Tomorrow, a couple of old ladies will come by, and believe me, he'll charge them the full sticker price."

Brownie came back, and for the third time he reduced the price of the car by $50.

"Now we're talking," said Dad. "But there's no need to rush into this. We'll go home and think about it."

Once again we started walking out, and once again Brownie came after us. "I can't believe you're going to let this one get away."

"I came here to buy a car," said Dad, "and I'm just trying to get a fair price."

"I asked you to make me an offer."

"We're getting there," said Dad.

Brownie suggested that we take the Gremlin for a ride, which I was happy to do. As I drove, I mentioned to Dad that it was too bad the car didn't come with an FM radio, but that I could always have one put in.

When we returned to the dealership, Brownie said, "How did you like it?"

"Not a bad ride for a small car," said Dad. "How about $2,100?"

"I can't do that," said Brownie. "Come up with me a little bit. I guess I could go as low as $2,125."

But Dad wouldn't budge. He held firm until Brownie finally said, "This is it, we're done, $2,100 even."

"I'll tell you what," said Dad. "I'll give you $2,100, but you gotta put in an FM radio."

It was all I could do not to pound my fist into my forehead. I felt terrible for Brownie. "Sir," he said to Dad, "this is not a game."

"No, it's not," said Dad. "I'm trying to buy a car here. All you have to do is take an FM radio from another car and put it in this one, and we'll take it off your hands."

"All right," said Brownie, who knew that he had lost this battle. "But let's shake on it right now."

They shook hands. With a mixture of pride and embarrassment, I added my hand to their handshake. While they prepped the car, Dad and I went off and had a couple of hot dogs. I was a little surprised that Dad didn't ask Brownie to pay for our lunch.

I kept my silver Gremlin until 1982. By then I had put almost 200,000 miles on it, and just about the only thing working properly was the FM radio that Dad had insisted on. I was living on Capitol Hill in Washington, and when I left my apartment one morning, my car was nowhere in sight. I called the police, but they had no record of a stolen 1972 Gremlin. When I called again the next day, the officer I spoke with gave me the phone number of an environmental office whose name I no longer recall, and suggested that I call over there.

When I called and explained that my car was missing, the man on the other end started to laugh. "Was it abandoned?"

"No, it was parked near my house."

"What's the plate number?"

I told him.

"Yeah, we've got it. It's been impounded."

"What?"

"Your car is an environmental hazard. We've had our eye on it for a while."

I could have tried to file a claim, but that would have cost me more than the car was worth.

WHEN I WAS A BOY, Big Russ bought only used cars. I used to say to him, "Dad, someday I'm going to buy you a brand-new Cadillac."

"Yeah, right."

"No, I'm serious."

I *was* serious. Several years ago, a few weeks before Dad's seventy-fifth birthday, I called him and said, "Okay, I'm finally in a position to buy you a new car. When I come for Thanksgiving, we'll pick it up." I sent him catalogs from Cadillac, Mercedes, and Lexus. "Look them over," I told him. "You can have any car you want, with any options. It's a birthday present and I'd love to do it."

I kept calling and asking, "Have you decided yet?" But Dad kept putting me off.

When I came back for Thanksgiving, I said, "Okay, which one did you pick?"

"Let's go for a ride and I'll show you," he said. We got into his Chevy Caprice, and within about four blocks, Dad pulled in at a sign for Jack Adkins Ford.

"A Ford?" I asked. "Dad, what do you want a Ford for?"

"Never mind. I know what I want."

We parked the car, and a tall thin man with polished shoes and a Buffalo Bills windbreaker came out to greet us. "This is Charlie," Dad said. We shook hands. "Charlie, show him the car."

We followed Charlie into the showroom, around a couple of pillars and into a smaller room in the back. And there, all shined up, was a black Crown Victoria.

I couldn't believe it. "Dad, it's a cop car!"

"Isn't she beautiful? Charlie, show him the trunk."

It was huge. "You can get three suitcases in there and two cases of beer," said Dad, "and you've still got room left over." If I hadn't known better, I would have thought that Dad was the salesman and Charlie was the customer.

"Charlie, show him the spare."

Charlie turned the wing nut, pulled out the spare, and bounced it on the showroom floor.

"Look at that," said Dad. He was beaming. "A full spare, not a doughnut. You see these guys with the little doughnuts they try to sell you, and after eight miles they're back on the side of the road. I don't want that. With this one, you've got the same ride for as long as you want. Charlie, show him the CD."

"Dad, you got a CD?" This was a man who had just gotten used to a push-button radio.

"You said I could have anything I wanted. This thing is *loaded*. The CD, an alarm system, everything."

"Dad, if that's what you want—"

"I told Charlie to give you a good deal. He gave me a good number on the trade-in."

I wrote a check and said, "When can we pick it up?"

"It's ready now," said Charlie. "He's been driving me crazy for weeks."

"You want to drive it?" said Dad.

"Dad, it's your car. You drive it."

We had gone about a hundred yards when Big Russ blurted out, "She's a beauty!" He turned right. "God, she handles well. Here, you've got to drive it."

"Dad, I have to ask you something. When I was a little kid I promised you a Cadillac, and you laughed. Now you can have a Cadillac, a Mercedes, a Lexus, or whatever you wanted, and you chose a Crown Vic. Do you really think it's a better car?"

Dad pulled over to the side of the road and put his new car in park, which was a big move for him. "Do I think it's a better car?" he said. "No, of course not. But if I came home with a big fancy Cadillac, do you know what people would say? 'What happened to Tim? He's showing off. He got too big for us. His kid made it and now he's driving a Cadillac.' No, I can't do that. A

Mercedes? A Lexus? Can't do that, either. We beat those guys in the war. This is what I want: a good American car. This is who I am, all right?"

"I get it."

"Are you sure?"

"Yeah, I really do."

"And, uh—thanks."

Dad has always had a strong sense of who he is, and in offering him a Cadillac or a fancy foreign car, I had completely missed the point. At first I was disappointed that he had chosen a Crown Vic, until I realized that buying Dad an expensive car was not just an expression of my love. It was also, in part, my way of showing off. Although Dad was perfectly happy to accept both my gift and my gratitude, he had no interest in stepping out of character or in becoming somebody he wasn't. Even in receiving a gift, Big Russ was teaching me a lesson.

14.

JCU and Law School, Too

"Don't jam yourself up."

I WAS THE FIRST MEMBER OF MY FAMILY to go to college. These days, some form of postsecondary education is pretty much taken for granted in most American families, but in my day, and certainly in our neighborhood, it was far from automatic. Although I didn't realize it at the time, when I took the Canisius entrance exam and was accepted to the school, I was turning onto a big new road on which college followed high school as surely as night follows day. By the time I graduated, the question was no longer whether I was going to college, but where.

About half of our senior class, especially those who were interested in accounting or business courses, went on to Canisius College, just a few blocks from the high school. Some students opted instead for the highly regarded State University of New York at Buffalo. Those of us who were interested in out-of-town schools were encouraged to apply to one of America's twenty-eight Jesuit colleges. I was hoping to go away to school because I thought that living in a dorm, away from my family, would give me a more complete college experience and would help me mature.

But that would be possible only if I found a way to pay for it. B.A. had recently been married, and my parents had gone into debt to pay for the wedding. I had two younger sisters coming along, so I knew that Dad couldn't help me out. The most economical option was to live at home and go to Canisius, and that was my backup plan as I visited Jesuit colleges in Philadelphia, Syracuse, and Cleveland, stopping in at the financial aid office on each campus to see what kind of assistance I might be able to arrange. John Carroll University in Cleveland offered me a partial scholarship, and between student loans, summer jobs, and part-time work during the school year, I was able to accept their offer.

Dad didn't quite see the point of my leaving home when Canisius College was a perfectly good school and much less expensive. He was also concerned that I was planning to take out loans to pay for my education, which troubled him on two counts. Like many men who grew up during the Depression, he has never felt comfortable borrowing money. "You're going to have to pay those off, you know," he told me. He said this not to belabor the obvious, but to point out that at some future date, repaying these loans could prove to be a real burden. His other concern was more altruistic, and I admired it even then: "If you can't repay those loans, that money won't be there for the next kid." That thought stayed with me, and when I got a big salary bump a few years later, I decided to accelerate the repayment of all my student loans. The interest rates were low, so from a financial perspective it was foolish to pay them off early. But I kept hearing Dad's voice: "The sooner you pay them off, the sooner that money will be there for somebody else."

Now that I'm a father, I realize that Dad was concerned about more than saving money. When Luke was a junior in high school and starting to look at colleges, I began to realize that my only child, my longtime companion at sporting events, and in some ways a best friend, was planning to live somewhere else for four years, and possibly longer. How could he do this to me? As it happens, the University of the District of Columbia is just two blocks from my office, and although it's not on anyone's list of top schools, the tuition fees are low and the commute would be a breeze. "Here's a thought," I told Luke. "Instead of going away to college, why don't you go to UDC? I can drive you there every day, we can have lunch together at Taco Bell, and at the end of the four years I'll write you a check for all the money I saved when you didn't go to a private college in another city." He looked at me in astonishment, as if he wasn't entirely sure that I was kidding. I think I was.

Although they might have preferred that I stay in Buffalo, my parents were enormously proud that their son was a college student. The few people they knew from their generation who had gone to college had been very successful, and the fact that I was now walking and studying on a university campus meant a great deal. Right away, Mom asked me to get Dad a John Carroll University sticker for the back of the car window, which was quite a statement because Big Russ has an aversion to bumper stickers or decals. But for his college boy, he made an exception. In the fall, he and Mom couldn't wait to drive to Cleveland for parents' weekend, and they still talk about a local pub called the Lemon Tree, where a group of us would treat our parents to draft beer.

John Carroll University, which was named after America's first Catholic bishop, is a small college in a beautiful section of University Heights, a suburb of Cleveland. It's an idyllic place with stone buildings and big leafy trees that looks like a movie version of a college campus. There were a few of us from Buffalo, but most of the students came from Chicago, Detroit, Pittsburgh, and, of course, Cleveland. I was happy there: I loved the experience of living away from home and making new friends, and unlike Canisius, where it took me a while to settle in, I felt comfortable right away. It's funny, the things that strike you: what I appreciated the most when I arrived on campus were first, the luxury of being able to choose your own courses and, second, that in the school cafeteria you could have as much milk as you wanted—both regular and chocolate. And although I was living away from my family, I could drive back to Buffalo in under four hours.

I majored in political science and received a good education, but when I think about my college days, it's the extracurricular activities that I remember most vividly. Jesuit schools don't allow fraternities, but we had two big service clubs on campus that more or less fulfilled that role. I joined the University Club, and although our official job was to act as ushers for all campus events, we were also in charge of bringing speakers and entertainers to the school. I became president of the U-Club during my junior year, and brought several name-brand acts to JCU, including Sha Na Na, Humble Pie, Richie Havens, the

Beach Boys, Pure Prairie League, and Sly and the Family Stone. Our gym held only two thousand seats, so the trick was to catch groups who were on their way up—or sometimes down.

I couldn't always hire the acts that I wanted to bring to campus. Sometimes, when I called the booking agents, they'd say, "Sorry, but they're playing downtown for the Belkin brothers." Mike and Jules Belkin had started producing concerts in 1966, and had made Cleveland an important stop on the rock concert circuit. I decided to pay them a visit. I told them about our gym and invited them to produce shows in our facility in return for 10 percent of the profits. We started working together: the Belkins gave us advice and encouraged bands to book with us.

Shortly before I graduated, I went back to their office to thank the Belkins for all the help they had given us. "What will you do now?" Jules Belkin asked. I told him I was thinking about law school, but that I couldn't afford it yet, so I was moving back to Buffalo to make some money.

He seemed surprised. "Doesn't your church have a program to help people in your situation?"

"No," I said. "What do you mean?"

"In our community, if a kid wants to go to law school and doesn't have the money, our synagogue gives them a hand."

It was just an offhand remark, but it stayed with me. Years later, Jules Belkin's comment inspired me to establish a scholarship fund for inner-city students who want to attend Catholic schools but can't afford the tuition.

In addition to rock bands, the University Club also brought guest speakers to campus, and although some were very well known, such as Supreme Court Justice William O. Douglas,

New York mayor John Lindsay, and comedian Dick Gregory, Muhammad Ali was in a category of his own. Although Ali had been on the lecture circuit since 1967, when his boxing license was suspended and his heavyweight title taken away after he refused to be inducted into the army, I didn't think we could possibly afford to bring the world's most famous man to our humble school. But for $1,500 plus expenses, he was happy to come; as he liked to say, "Talking is a whole lot easier than fighting." He arrived on a bus with a large entourage, looking bigger than I had expected; in the ring, he was so quick on his feet that I had thought of him as smaller and thinner than he actually was. We were thrilled to have him on campus, and the black students were especially excited; they asked to meet with him privately, and Ali was happy to oblige. Spotting one of our ushers scurrying around before his lecture, he said, "Look at the white boy, breaking into a sweat because we're having a meeting."

"Who's your biggest guy?" the champ asked a group of us before his speech. We pointed to Frank Gerbig, a full-size, burly member of the U-Club; we called him Nitti after Frank Nitti, the legendary Chicago gangster who was immortalized in the TV show *The Untouchables*. When Nitti stepped forward, Ali gave him a shot in the chest—hard enough to rock him back on his heels, but not enough to really hurt him. For the rest of his life, Nitti could brag that he had taken a punch from the greatest fighter of our time, and maybe of all time.

Ali was charismatic and engaging, speaking his mind and answering questions on everything from boxing to Vietnam, from sports to segregation, and mixing serious points with humor until it wasn't always clear when he was kidding. "You see racism every day," he told us. "To show you how prejudiced our country is, when they dish out ice cream, it's always vanilla on top and chocolate on the bottom. Angel food cake is the white cake, but the devil's food cake is chocolate. We've been brainwashed. Everything good is supposed to be white. In Westerns, the good guys wear white hats. Even Tarzan, the king of the jungle in black Africa, he's white!"

At the end of his talk, he asked, "Who's the champ?"

"You are!" we roared, sounding like Baptists in a southern church.

"Can my title be taken away without my being whupped?"

"No!" answered the chorus.

"One more time!"

"No!"

"Who's the heavyweight champion of the world?"

"You are!"

He left us with a little ditty that he had probably recited at a hundred other colleges: "I like your school, I like your style, but you pay so cheap, I won't be back for a while."

ALTHOUGH BEER AND ROCK MUSIC were a big part of my college life, I had more serious interests as well. At the end of my junior year I ran for student union president, and won. With my longish hair and a Fu Manchu mustache that was modeled after football star Joe Namath's, I campaigned on a platform of "student rights and responsibilities." My slogan was, "Make 1972 the year of the student," and I said in my speeches that the most beneficial salesman any university can have is a satisfied

student body. Among other proposals, I wanted to liberalize the
dress code in the Rathskellar, the student-run bar in the basement of the Student Activities Center, which served watered-
down 3.2 beer; to keep the library open twenty-four hours during exam periods; and to extend on-street parking from two
hours to four. (These weren't earthshattering issues, but as Tip
O'Neill used to say, All politics is local.) At the time, the big
issue on campus was "open visitation," which meant the right to
have guests of the opposite sex in our rooms. Our conservative
school had just started to admit women, and in the words of
Mel Brooks's Two Thousand Year Old Man, we were thrilled
and delighted to see them. The trustees of the university had
recently approved a trial period that allowed such visits on
alternate Saturday and Sunday afternoons, but most of the students wanted to go further. I argued for a decentralized
approach in which every dorm would determine its own visitation policy.

Although a small Catholic college in Ohio was hardly on the
cutting edge of the 1960s, no campus was immune from the
huge changes that were rocking American society. Kent State
University was just a short drive from our school, and in May
1970, during a protest against the American bombing of Cam-
bodia, Kent State became known as the place where National
Guardsmen fired on the demonstrators and killed four students. In the aftermath of these deaths there were big, sponta-
neous protests at schools all over the country, including ours.
Three hundred students from JCU marched to Warrensville
Road in University Heights, where we sat down on the street to
block traffic, but other students at John Carroll were so cautious

that they wrote a letter to the mayor of University Heights to apologize for the disruption. At the other end of the spectrum, somebody threw a firebomb through a window of the ROTC building.

That night I called home. "Dad, they're killing us."

"No!" he shouted. "Don't ever say that. A guardsman may have lost his head, but they're not trying to kill you."

"No, they are! Four kids are dead!" It was one of the few times that Dad and I ever yelled at each other. All over the country, fathers and sons were having similar arguments.

The campus was in a state of chaos when a group of students went to the flagpole in the Quadrangle and lowered the flag to memorialize the deaths at Kent State. Before long, a group of ROTC kids raised it back up. At an emergency meeting of the student union, I stood up and with Big Russ's words echoing in my head, said, "Why are we arguing about this flag? It belongs to all of us! Four students lost their lives, and I'm sure the guardsmen who shot them feel awful. They're kids, too, and none of them should be the object of our scorn. Why are we fighting about this when we should be in the chapel saying a few prayers for the dead students, for the guardsmen, and for our country?"

Just before our final exams, Father Schell, the president of John Carroll, led an outdoor Mass on the Quad, which helped to unify the campus at a difficult time. He then announced that anyone who found it impossible to study in this environment was free to go home and take whatever grade they had earned so far. Most chose to leave, and I did, too.

When I came home that summer, Dad and I sat in the garage and talked about the war. Dad had a refrigerator there, where he kept his beer and the fixings for his Limburger cheese, liver sausage, and onion sandwiches, which we refused to let him keep in the house. Just a few months earlier, Dad thought that college students who expressed their opposition to the war were harming the country, but like many Americans, his position on Vietnam was changing. "I can understand why people are wondering about this war," he told me that summer, "because we seem to be pinned down over there. But you can be for peace without supporting the enemy." Although he thought that America was right to be in Vietnam, he could also appreciate the arguments against the war. What he couldn't tolerate were television images of protestors spitting on Vietnam veterans, carrying the Viet Cong flag, or chanting, "Ho, Ho, Ho Chi Minh, the NLF is gonna win!"

Dad's position may seem unremarkable in retrospect, but at the time I found it enormously helpful. When I returned to school in the fall, I found myself repeating what Dad had said and drawing the line between protest and patriotism: "We can be for peace without supporting the enemy. We can be against this war without rooting for the other side."

BY THE TIME I GRADUATED I had pretty much decided to go to law school, not out of any great desire to become a lawyer, but because I realized that without further education, I wasn't going to get very far, whether in politics or anything else. Big Russ may have had his doubts about Canisius and John Carroll, but he was delighted about law school: a couple of his friends were lawyers, and he knew them as upright, honorable men who had "made a good buck." "Education is the key to everything," he said. "Go to law school, and who knows? Maybe you'll become a judge."

First, however, I had to earn enough money to cover the tuition, so I moved back to Buffalo, got myself a small apartment on McKinley Parkway, about three blocks from our old house on Woodside Avenue, and took a job as a substitute teacher, mostly teaching high school history and English. I soon learned that TV shows like *Mr. Novak, Welcome Back, Kotter,* and *Room 222* were not entirely realistic in their depictions of classroom life. After a few months in the trenches, my respect for teachers and the challenges they confront soared even higher.

In January 1973, I went to work at city hall as the administrative secretary to City Comptroller George D. O'Connell, who was known as the best wake-goer in Buffalo. At first I found it odd that anyone would spend so much time going to wakes, but I remembered that Dad had taught me how important it is to be with people in their hour of grief. Families who had lost someone really appreciated it when a high city official showed up to pay his respects.

I shared an office with the deputy comptroller, Frank Szuniewicz, Jr. Nobody could pronounce his last name, so when he couldn't reach somebody on the phone, he would say "Tell him that Frankie Sonovabitch called." Frank was a thin man about ten years younger than Dad, with a ruddy complexion, slicked-back silver hair, and a cigarette dangling from his lower lip. This longtime Democrat and former ward chairman had three great loves: politics, fishing, and pinochle. He liked to take me to lunch at the Roosevelt Bar and Restaurant on Broadway, where, over bowls of homemade soup and beef-on-weck sandwiches, he would regale me with political stories. To Frank, every man was Buddy or Fella, and every waitress was Honey. He lived and breathed politics, and had tickets to every fund-raiser in town. His opinions were simplistic and wildly partisan. "Remember what Uncle Frank tells you," he'd say. "The worst Democrat is better than the best Republican."

He was good to me, and he took an interest in my future. "You really want to go to law school, don't you?" he said.

"Yes, I'm planning on it. That's why I'm working this year."

"How are you doing on that?"

"I'm trying to save enough for the first year, but I still have debts from college."

"Well, don't get too comfortable here, because you'll never go back. I wish I had finished school, but when you get out in the world, one thing leads to another, and you keep putting it off. This is a good job and you seem to be enjoying it, but if you go to law school, you'll have many more options."

In the spring, he brought it up again. "Are you ready to go back to school in the fall?"

"I did pretty well on the law boards," I said, "but I'm still a little worried about the money."

"How much are you short?"

"If I had another two thousand, I'd be in good shape."

"Two grand."

"Yeah, that's my goal."

One night about a week later, the phone rang at my apartment. "Timmy, it's Frank. Where are you?"

"I'm at home. That's where you called me. Where are you?"

"I'm at my sister's joint. Get over here, will you?"

"Why? What's going on?"

"Just get over here." Frank's sister Loretta, known to every-one as Aunt Lory, owned Frank's Grill, a bar on Theodore Street in East Buffalo that was named for their father. I drove over and found Frank in the back room, playing pinochle. When he saw me come in he jumped up. He had a drink in one hand; in the other was a brown paper bag that was twisted at the top. He pushed the bag into my hand and said, "Now get outta here. I'll see you at work."

Back in the car, I opened the bag, which contained more money than I had seen in my life. I drove home nervously and started counting it on my little kitchen table. It was mostly ones and fives, and it added up to exactly two thousand dollars.

I had a moment of panic. Where was I going to keep this money until I could take it to the bank? If somebody came in to rob me, I asked myself, where's the last place he would look? The fridge! I woke up in the middle of the night, worried about the money, and went into the kitchen to make sure it was still there. And of course it was, in a package that gave new meaning to the phrase "cold cash."

When I arrived at work the next day, I said, "Frank, I don't know what to say. First of all, this is a loan."

"You got *that* right."

"I promise you I'll repay every dollar."

"I know you will."

"With interest, too."

"No, no, I don't want any interest. The only interest I have is in you getting a law degree." He paused. "But when I get in trouble, you'll be there to defend me, right?"

"What kind of trouble?"

"Oh you know, some of these saloon keepers, I'd like to throw a brick through their window."

Because the money was in small bills, I assumed that it came from playing cards. "You must have had a hell of a big game," I said.

"Nah, I've been building the kitty."

Frank had dreamed of going to college, but he never had the opportunity, which was probably why my education meant so much to him. He died of lung cancer, and during the time we knew each other, he often warned me against cigarettes. I had tried them, of course, but I'm one of the lucky ones: I didn't like smoking at all.

Thanks to Frank, I had enough money to attend the Cleveland-Marshall College of Law at Cleveland State University. I already felt at home in Cleveland, and because the law school was part of a state institution, it wasn't as expensive as a private law school.

Two or three months into my second year of law school, the president of the John Carroll University Club called to say that he was having a hard time booking entertainment. Because of my experience, he offered to let me produce a concert. Kid Leo, a popular and influential disc jockey at WMMS in Cleveland, had been playing a great new singer named Bruce Springsteen, so I called a booking agent and asked him if this Springsteen guy was available. Yes, he was going to be touring, and for $2,500 I could bring him to John Carroll. I took a deep breath and made the deal. When tickets went on sale, they sold out in a few hours. Bruce Springsteen and his band played for two and a half hours in the JCU gym, and when it was over, I had enough money to pay for my next semester of law school.

When I first met my wife, Maureen Orth, in 1980, I tried to impress her by bragging that I had actually booked Bruce Springsteen before anyone had heard of him. She burst out laughing. "That's nice," she said. "In 1975, I wrote the cover story about him for *Newsweek*."

In 1981, Maureen and I were in a Manhattan restaurant, where we bumped into Springsteen. Maureen knew him, of course, and she introduced us. "You'll never remember this," I said, "but I brought you to Cleveland in 1975."

"Sure, I remember that night because I had a falling out with my manager. That was a college gym, wasn't it?"

"Right. Well, the money I made on that concert helped pay for my second year of law school."

"And how did you pay for your first year?"

"From the winnings of a pinochle game in Buffalo."

"That sounds like one my of songs," he said. "'I went to law school on a rock concert and a pinochle game.'"

After my second year of law school, Dad said, "How did you do?"

"I did well. I made the dean's list."

"And how the hell did you pay for it?"

"A pinochle game and a Bruce Springsteen concert."

"What's that?"

"A pinochle game and a Bruce Springsteen concert."

"Are they legal?"

"Sure."

"Well, don't jam yourself up! What the hell good is it if you get in a jam in law school? You couldn't even defend yourself yet!"

I assured Dad that I was studying the law rather than breaking it. But although I did well in law school, I can't say I enjoyed it. Never in my life have I had to organize and master such a large volume of information. To cover my expenses, I worked half time for the Corporation Counsel of Cleveland, and spent summers back in Buffalo, living at home and working in the welfare fraud unit at the Erie County Attorney's Office.

In the weeks leading up to the bar exam in July 1976, I lived a monastic existence. I ate carefully—no beer, burgers, or pizza—got up early and ran every morning, went to bed early, and studied my ass off. I was completely focused and absolutely determined to do well, because the New York State bar exam, a two-day ordeal covering thirty-five topics, was said to be the toughest one in the country. As the exam drew closer, I began to feel overwhelmed by a fear of failing, especially when I realized how closely my family was watching me. This was a huge event in their lives, too—two days that would determine whether the son of a trash collector would succeed in his attempt to become a lawyer.

This was a hard time for our family for another reason: after nearly thirty years of marriage, my parents had decided to go their separate ways. Mom and Dad no longer together? It was unimaginable. It happens all the time, but this was our family, the Russerts, and we were Catholics. How could this happen to us? Were Dad's two jobs just too much time away, even if they were necessary to provide what we thought of as the basics? Did the fact that Mom was a teenage bride make her feel, now that the kids were grown, that parts of life had passed her by? It may have been both of these, and probably more.

We never really know what goes on between two people, especially when parents are trying to protect their children from unhappiness. My sisters and I talked about it, and we realized that our parents had always been there for us when we needed them. What we didn't yet know was that each of them would continue to be there for us, even if they were no longer together. Thanksgiving, Christmas, and birthdays have continued to be family events, and neither Mom nor Dad has been shy about offering us advice or reminding us to take care of ourselves because, as they both like to tell us, "If you don't have your health, you have nothing." To this day, Mom will call me after *Meet the Press* and say, "You have a sore throat, don't you?" Her maternal instincts are more powerful than any medical diagnosis, and if I'm coming down with something, she often knows it before I do.

At the time, Mom and Dad's separation made us aware that our family was far from perfect. And it certainly made all of us a lot less judgmental of other families who were wrestling with their own problems. That in itself was a valuable lesson.

To cover my anxiety about the bar exam and to lower my parents' expectations, I told them that I was feeling sick, and that if it didn't work out this time, I could take the exam again when I was healthy. Because of the state's painfully slow timetable, it would be five long months before I found out whether I had passed. By the time I got the news—and it was good news—I was in another world entirely.

15.

Daniel Patrick Moynihan

"The smartest man I ever knew."

ALTHOUGH I NEVER TOOK A CLASS with Daniel Patrick Moynihan, he was the greatest teacher I ever had. Sister Lucille taught me the fundamental skills of reading and writing. Father Sturm taught me discipline and accountability. And Professor Moynihan taught me to respect true intelligence, ask good questions, and disagree agreeably.

Now that college and law school were behind me, for the first time since Bobby Kennedy's death eight years earlier, I became seriously interested in politics again. Specifically, I wanted to get involved in the upcoming race for Kennedy's old Senate seat. When Kennedy was shot in 1968, Governor Nelson Rockefeller had appointed Charles Goodell, a liberal Republican congressman from Jamestown, to serve out the remainder of Kennedy's term. In 1970, Goodell ran as the incumbent against both a Democrat, Richard Ottinger, and a Conservative Party candidate, James Buckley, the older brother of

National Review editor William F. Buckley. When liberals and moderates split their votes between Goodell and Ottinger, Buckley, who had been considered a long shot, won the election. New York Democrats had been willing to tolerate Goodell for a couple of years, but the stridently conservative Buckley drove them crazy, and they were determined to replace him in 1976.

By this time I had met Joe Crangle, the New York State Democratic chairman. Joe was that rare creature, an Irish Catholic from north Buffalo; back in the 1950s he had put himself through law school by working in the sanitation department, where he had come to know Dad. Joe had been close with Bobby Kennedy, and looking ahead to the 1976 campaign, he had his own ideas about how to ensure that the Democrats regained what we still thought of as Kennedy's Senate seat.

A few months before the election, there was no shortage of potential candidates: Congresswoman Bella Abzug was expected to run, as were Paul O'Dwyer, the city council president of New York; and Ramsey Clark, the former attorney general in the Johnson administration. But Joe Crangle was a pragmatist who believed that although these well-known liberals would all do well in New York City, they had little appeal upstate and were too far to the left to win in November. Crangle thought the strongest Democratic candidate would be Daniel Patrick Moynihan, who had just left his post as United States Ambassador to the United Nations. Moynihan had worked in the Kennedy, Johnson, Nixon, and Ford administrations, which made him the only person in American history to serve under four consecutive presidents.

I agreed with Joe about Moynihan. I was convinced that for

a Democrat to win in 1976, it would take a centrist who could appeal to mainstream Democrats like Dad, who felt the party had drifted away from them. (In 1980, some of these Democrats would return the favor by voting for Reagan.) Moynihan was intelligent, articulate, and experienced. He was an Irish Catholic with a lot of Jewish support. Although he came from the city, he had a farm upstate in Pindars Corners, not far from Cooperstown. Moynihan had progressive views, but he was far too independent and creative a thinker to be pigeonholed as either a liberal or a conservative. After he was elected, he displayed two magazine covers in his office. One, from *The Nation*, read, "Moynihan: The Conscience of a Neo-conservative." The other, from *The New Republic*, read, "Pat Moynihan: Neo Liberal." His biggest weakness, I thought, was that some Democrats would never forgive him for working for Nixon. There was one other problem: he didn't seem very eager to run.

I first met Ambassador Moynihan in the spring of 1976, when he came to Buffalo to address the Council on World Affairs. Joe Crangle, who had been trying for months to persuade him to enter the race, introduced us at the Statler Hilton. I was excited to meet Moynihan, and I was flattered when he asked me if I thought he should become a candidate. "I'd love to see you run," I said, "but in a Democratic primary, the fact that you worked for Nixon will be seen as a serious liability."

"You think so? You think that working for a president is a liability? I've worked for four of them."

I knew that, of course, but I pointed out that Richard Nixon had resigned in disgrace only two years earlier, and the memory of that traumatic time was still fresh in voters' minds.

"All right, then," Moynihan countered. "What's the worst that people can say about my working for Nixon?"

"They'll bring up Watergate, although you had nothing to do with it. And liberals will accuse you of working for a Republican president who increased defense spending and cut domestic programs."

"Did he, now?" Moynihan picked up a napkin and drew a simple graph that showed domestic spending going up and defense spending going down. "Check it out, Tiger," he said. It was my first assignment from Professor Moynihan.

The next day, I went to the library and found that under Nixon, domestic spending had indeed gone up and defense spending had declined, especially toward the end of Nixon's truncated second term, when the war in Vietnam was winding down. I also learned that under Nixon, social spending had surpassed defense spending for the first time in American history. And I was amazed to find that the health-care program Nixon had proposed, as well as the administration's plan for a guaranteed annual income (which was Moynihan's idea, and had passed easily in the House before being defeated in the Senate), were a lot more progressive than anything the Democrats had come up with—*ever*. Although I didn't know it yet, the subject of President Nixon's surprisingly liberal domestic programs was one of Moynihan's favorite topics. He loved to tell people that Nixon had funded the arts, protected the environment, and pushed for real school desegregation. The Nixon White House, he once wrote, "may well have been the most progressive administration on domestic issues that has ever been formed. It was amazing what he would say yes to."

A few weeks later, Moynihan called to see if I might be interested in working on his campaign. I said, "Mr. Ambassador, I have the numbers right here."

"What numbers are those?"

I reminded him of the assignment he had given me, and I told him what I had learned about Nixon's domestic policies.

"That speaks well of you," he said. "I appreciate a diligent mind." I was still studying for the bar, but I had evidently passed the Moynihan exam.

Moynihan entered the race on June 10, which even in 1976 was very late. I didn't really know him yet, but I'm sure it wasn't an easy decision. For one thing, Moynihan was a man of ideas, a Harvard professor who didn't relish months of campaigning or fund-raising. For another, after his strong defense of Zionism in the United Nations in 1975 won him considerable support in the Jewish community, he had been asked about the possibility of a Senate race. He had answered (on national television), "I would consider it dishonorable to leave this post and run for an office." Moynihan left the UN in the spring of 1976 after repeated differences with Secretary of State Henry Kissinger, and although he didn't quit with the intention of running for the Senate, there was an understandable perception that he was reneging on his pledge. At his campaign announcement, he put it plainly: "The simple fact is that I did not leave the UN to run for political office." And he later joked, "I may have said it would be dishonorable, but I never said I wouldn't run."

Moynihan said later that what finally pushed him into the race was the recent closing of the City University of New York due to the city's severe financial crisis. New York had been the first American city to establish a free college for the children of working people, and Moynihan himself had been one of its graduates. Although the university was closed only briefly, the act had infuriated him.

During the campaign, Moynihan came to Buffalo in a Winnebago, and a few of us drove around with him through western New York. For me, it was like a seminar on wheels. As we rolled down the thruway, the candidate kept up a running commentary on the geography, geology, history, and assorted arcana of the region. He loved information, especially if it was historical or linguistic, or both, such as the nineteenth-century practice of giving Greek names to upstate towns like Marathon, Homer, and Ithaca. When we drove into Afton, the candidate announced that this was where Joseph Smith, the founder of the Mormon Church, had married his wife in 1827. When we entered Batavia, he said, "Ah, Batavia. Do you know the expression, 'a land office business'? This is where it began. This is where the Holland Land Office opened in 1802 to oversee the purchase of three and a half million acres." For Moynihan, a born educator with an endlessly curious mind, the campaign tour was an opportunity to teach, to reflect, and to continue learning about his beloved state. And if he could pick up a few votes along the way, so much the better.

His inquisitive spirit was in no way dampened by becoming a United States senator. Well before the election, he made it known that despite his experience at the UN, he would not be seeking a seat on the Foreign Relations Committee, although this high-prestige position was presumably his for the asking. Having been moved to enter the race by New York's ailing

economy, he was determined to join the Senate Finance Committee, where he could probably do the most good. (There was
some irony in that choice, because it was the Finance Committee, headed by Sen. Russell Long, that had killed Moynihan's
Family Assistance Plan during the Nixon administration. Sixteen years later, when Moynihan joined the committee, Russell
Long was still the chairman.)

Moynihan knew that the last senator from New York to
serve on the Finance Committee had been James Wadsworth, a
Republican, half a century earlier, and he asked my colleague
Dick Eaton to find out the name of the last New York Democrat on the committee. His name was Francis Kernan and,
among other accomplishments, he had nominated Samuel J.
Tilden for president at the Democratic National Convention in
1876. (Tilden lost to Rutherford B. Hayes in a disputed election.) I recently learned an astonishing detail about him that
Moynihan would have loved: Kernan, an Irish-Catholic from
Utica, served in the United States Senate with no less than five
other men who had all worked on his father's farm.

A few of us were having dinner in Utica with the newly
elected senator when, remembering that we were now in Kernan country, I raised my glass and said, "How about a toast to
Francis Kernan?"

"Yes!" said Moynihan. "And since we're in Utica, why don't
we find him?"

We somehow learned that Kernan was buried in St. Agnes
churchyard on Arthur Street, so we piled into the car and drove
down there. Moynihan stood for a moment at Kernan's grave,
crossed himself, and said a prayer.

The next night, speaking at a political dinner in Utica, Moynihan said, "When I went to Washington, I wanted to serve on the Finance Committee, because if you stay off it for a century, your state will go broke. I'm proud to say that I'm the first Democrat in a hundred years to serve on that committee. The bones of my predecessor, the honorable Francis Kernan, lie buried in St. Agnes churchyard just a few blocks from here, and last night I had the honor of visiting the site where he lies in repose." It was a quintessential Moynihan moment. Any number of politicians could have made that statement, but Moynihan would have gone to visit Kernan's grave whether or not anybody ever knew about it.

THE PRIMARY RACE was more difficult than we had expected. Bella Abzug missed no opportunity to link Moynihan to the hated Nixon, and those of us on Moynihan's team had seriously overestimated his name recognition. Most voters paid little attention to foreign affairs, so our candidate's brief but remarkable career at the UN meant little to them. Even so, we ran an effective newspaper ad that showed Moynihan with his hand up in a veto in the Security Council. "He spoke up for America," it read. "He'll speak up for New York State." Almost nobody knew that Moynihan had written that ad, had paid for it, and had personally taken it to *The New York Times*, which ran it.

There were some lighter moments as well. In Utica, the candidate toured a brand-new mental hospital, after which he retired to one of the rooms to take a nap. When he awoke, he found that there was no handle on the inside of the door. He picked up the phone and called the front desk. "Could you please get me out of here?" he said. "This is Ambassador Moynihan."

"Sure," said the desk clerk, "and Winston Churchill was here yesterday."

"This is Ambassador Moynihan," he said again.

"Yes, I'm sure it is, but you can't leave, no matter who you are." Only when Moynihan's driver came looking for him did the desk clerk realize his mistake.

Above all, Moynihan loved meeting with the editorial boards of newspapers, where he could hold forth and discuss public policy with knowledgeable, intelligent people. In the end, it was the newspapers in New York City that made the difference. The *Daily News* endorsed Moynihan, while at the *Times*, publisher Arthur Sulzberger overruled his own editorial board and endorsed the former ambassador with a long and dramatic sentence: "We choose Daniel Patrick Moynihan, that rambunctious child of the sidewalks of New York, profound student and teacher of social affairs, aggressive debater, outrageous flatterer, shrewd advisor—indeed manipulator—of presidents, accomplished diplomat and heartfelt friend of the poor—poor people, poor cities, poor regions such as ours." On September 14, Moynihan won the Democratic primary with 37 percent of the vote. Abzug finished with 36 percent.

Compared to the primary, the general election was a drive in the country. When Buckley started referring to his opponent as *Professor* Moynihan, Moynihan proclaimed, with mock indignation, "The mudslinging has begun." Despite all of Moynihan's campaign travel that fall, the professor continued teaching his Harvard class in social policy, and missed only two sessions all semester. The day after the election, which Moynihan won by half a million votes, the senator elect was back in class.

Shortly after Moynihan's victory, but before the newly elected senators were sworn in, Liz Moynihan called to tell me that some months earlier, her husband had agreed to go on a lecture tour in early December. "I was planning to go with him," she said, "but I think it would be good for the two of you to spend some time together and talk about the Senate office." I accepted immediately. For one thing, it would give me a lot of time with a man I greatly admired. For another, it sounded as if Moynihan was going to offer me a job. And at the age of twenty-six, I would finally have a chance to travel beyond the Northeast.

I flew to Boston, met Moynihan at his house in Cambridge, and drove with him to Logan Airport to begin the tour. We were checking in at the ticket counter when Moynihan pointed to the brown attaché case where he kept his speeches, his reading glasses, several magazines, and a couple of books. "You know," he told me, "a diplomat never lets his attaché case out of his sight."

"I understand, sir."

Putting it on the floor and leaning it against the ticket counter, he said, "This case is everything to me." A few minutes later, we were about to board the plane when my traveling companion said, "Could I have my attaché case, please?"

"Excuse me?"

"You didn't check it, did you? I told you not to let it out of your sight!"

Not only had I not checked it; I hadn't realized that I was supposed to take it. In a panic, I sprinted back to the ticket area, where, to my enormous relief, the attaché case was still on the floor, leaning against the counter. I grabbed it, but the man at the front of the line put his foot on it and said, "Excuse me?"

"Oh," I said, "I didn't realize this was yours."

"It's not mine, but is it yours?"

I mumbled a quick explanation and ran back to the gate. The passengers had boarded—all but one man, who was standing there and waiting. Obviously pleased, he smiled at me and said, "Well now, that's being resourceful."

Still panting, I had just squeezed into the window seat—he preferred the aisle—when I realized that I had left my own carry-on bag at the gate, so I had to excuse myself to leave the plane and retrieve it. By the time I boarded the plane again, I was feeling both foolish and embarrassed. We hadn't left Boston yet, and I had already shown myself to be a total incompetent.

Our first stop was Chicago. As we landed and made our way into the city, Moynihan talked about Richard Daley, who was then in his sixth term as mayor, and who died a few days later. Memories of Daley led him into a description of the 1968 presidential campaign, when he had worked for Robert Kennedy. Moynihan believed, as I did, that if Kennedy had lived, he would have been the nominee, and the country would have experienced a second Nixon-Kennedy race. Moynihan had been sure that Nixon's victory over Humphrey signaled the end of his own White House years, and he was shocked when the new president appointed him assistant to the president for urban affairs. He also told me the real story of the infamous "benign neglect" memo that had been dogging him ever since he had used that phrase in 1970. Moynihan had written that the national conversation about race had become too heated; he had called for a cooling of the rhetoric, not a reduction in commitment. (His exact words were, "The issue of race could benefit from a period of benign neglect.") But some of his fellow Democrats—perhaps deliberately, perhaps not—had responded as if he had advocated a willful neglect of black Americans at a time when he was actually coming up with proposals to help black families. Five years earlier, Moynihan had been widely denounced for saying that a major cause of black poverty was the fact that a quarter of black children were being born to single mothers. Today, in many American cities, that number has tripled, and almost everyone recognizes its terrible consequences. Moynihan was an early victim of political correctness.

Moynihan loved to talk, and I loved to listen to his distinctive, chirpy, pause-filled voice. Later, I learned to imitate that voice rather well, but I gave it up after an important Democratic official hung up on Moynihan because he thought it was me, playing one of my pranks. The senator was not amused.

Moynihan was the smartest man I ever knew, and the best professor I ever had. He taught me phrases like "semantic infiltration" (the tendency to use the language of one's opponents to describe a situation), and "the iron law of emulation" (the process by which organizations that are ostensibly in conflict, such as labor unions and large corporations, increasingly begin to resemble each other). When people called him an intellectual, an egghead, or a professor, Moynihan just smiled and said, "I don't think that's a liability."

During one of our airborne conversations, he asked me what I intended to do for the next few years. I said that if I passed the

bar exam, I was planning to stay in Buffalo and start a law practice, and maybe eventually go into politics. "I'll tell you what,"
he said. "I promised Joe Crangle that if I was elected, I would
open an upstate office in Buffalo. Why don't you run it?" I considered the offer for at least ten seconds before saying yes. A few
days later, I learned that I had passed the New York bar.

AT VARIOUS STOPS ALONG THE TOUR, Senator Moynihan
introduced me to everyone we met by saying, "This is my colleague, Mr. Russert, a young attorney from upstate New York
who has graciously agreed to serve the people of our state." My
colleague? I was thrilled when he said it. After his speech in
Phoenix, Moynihan was surrounded by the usual group of well-
wishers, who on this occasion happened to include two or three
attractive young women. After a few minutes he said, "And now,
if you will excuse me, I will retire to my room and leave you in
the hands of my esteemed colleague—a single, wealthy lawyer
from New York who is making an enormous sacrifice by joining
me in public life." At the word "wealthy," it was hard to keep a
straight face.

On the plane the next day, he stopped reading the newspaper and said to me, while looking straight ahead, "So, nice people last night."

"Yes, very nice."

"You had a nice time?"

"Very nice, Mr. Ambassador." But I wasn't going to provide any
details—assuming, of course, that there were any to give. I was
traveling with a gentleman, and I made every effort to act like one.

At each stop on the tour, people asked if they could meet with Moynihan or if they could bring him to an additional event that wasn't on the schedule. He always refused these invitations, and I was struck by how gracefully he responded. "That's kind of you," he would say, "but there are a few items that I simply must attend to." I was impressed with his courtly and civil way of saying no, and I made a mental note to emulate it. I was accustomed to saying yes to almost every request or invitation that came my way, often because I didn't know how to say no politely. Now I did.

In all of these cities we visited, Moynihan addressed sophisticated audiences about foreign affairs, with special attention to the Middle East and the Soviet Union. He argued that the Soviet Union was a massive economic failure, and that before long they would no longer be able to compete with us. This sounds perfectly logical today, but in 1976, virtually nobody else was saying this. In the first week of 1980, when the Cold War was still very much alive, he predicted on the Senate floor that "the defining event of the decade might well be the breakup of the Soviet empire." It takes a special quality of mind to see the future, and Moynihan had that gift in any number of areas.

As we were landing in San Francisco, he asked, "Have you ever been here before?"

"No sir, never."

"Well, you'll love it. You'll meet the kind of people in local taverns who, anywhere else in the world, you would see only in a private club."

I soon learned what he meant. In Buffalo, just about everybody you ran into had a connection to somebody you already knew. San Francisco was different: half the population had grown up elsewhere. I went on a long walking tour of that beautiful city, and when I met up with him later, he really enjoyed my wide-eyed excitement.

"This is the closest thing we have to a European city," he said.

"I've never been to Europe," I said.

"In good time you'll see that, too." Four years later, he made sure that I did.

Our last stop was in West Palm Beach, Florida, where Moynihan addressed a group of big donors to the United Jewish Appeal. This was the first Jewish event I had ever attended, and I had never seen anything like it. In the churches of Buffalo, giving was a private act; when the collection plate was passed around, many parishioners would fold their contribution so you couldn't see if they were putting in a one-dollar bill, a five, or perhaps something larger. But here, people were making open pledges in a public demonstration of commitment. A shopping mall developer was sitting next to me, and when it was his turn to speak, he stood up and said, "The importance and the dream of a Jewish state are central to our identity as a people. We must make sure that everyone in Israel is cared for and educated." I noticed those words, "cared for and educated," because I was used to hearing the more basic commitment of "fed and clothed." He continued: "The world understands the uniqueness of the only democracy in the Middle East, and tonight I commit 25 percent of my earnings for next year. I pledge two million dollars."

I was flabbergasted. I looked up to the front of the hall,

where Moynihan was leaning back on his chair, his eyes big with amazement. The pledging continued, and by the time it was over they had raised more than $25 million. The money was impressive, of course, but what affected me even more were the reasons people gave for their gifts. Some spoke about their parents, some about Israel's wars, and some about the Holocaust. There was so much dedication, passion, and meaning in that room that I will never forget it. I was riveted by the event, and they, in turn, were riveted by Moynihan. That evening opened my eyes to the Jewish attachment to Israel, which is critical to understanding the Middle East conflict.

As we flew home the next day, Moynihan said, "Well, old friend?"

"Last night was extraordinary," I said.

"Yes, it was. It's important that you understand and feel that fervor and that conviction."

Back home in Buffalo, I described that evening to Dad, and told him how they had raised more than $25 million.

"Did they really raise it?" he said, "or did they just promise it?"

I laughed. "They pledged it, but it was a solemn pledge and a public one." It wasn't until years later that I heard the well-worn joke about the traveler who has been shipwrecked on a desert island. When they find him two years later, he's in remarkably good spirits. "How did you survive this long?" they ask him. "How is it that you never gave up hope?"

"I wasn't worried," he tells his rescuers. "I knew they'd find me sooner or later, because a week before I boarded the ship, I made a big pledge to the United Jewish Appeal!"

16.

Washington

"Stay where you are."

I N EARLY JANUARY 1977, I flew to Washington for Senator Moynihan's swearing in. That same day, the new junior
senator met with his staff and spoke to us about the importance
of behaving ethically and honorably. "I first came here in 1961,"
he told us, "and I've seen so many people come to Washington
with the best of intentions and determined to do the right
thing. Over the years, I've seen some of these same people leave
the city in disgrace. Every mistake in Washington is magnified,
so you can never be too careful." It was good advice, and Moynihan practiced what he preached: twenty-four years later, he
retired from the Senate with an unimpeachable reputation.

I returned to Buffalo to set up the senator's western New
York office. After hiring a secretary, I paid courtesy visits to the
mayor, the county executive, and the local offices of veteran
Republican U.S. Sen. Jacob Javits and the three area congress-
men. I started to represent the senator, speaking for him and

"delivering greetings" at Kiwanis lunches and similar functions. Together with his staff in Washington, I began to map out a schedule for Moynihan's visits to western New York.

Until spring arrived, his trips to the Niagara area would depend to some extent on the weather, and even by Buffalo standards the winter of 1977 was especially bad. We had had twenty-eight consecutive days of snow, and this was the coldest January in the city's history. So when snow started falling yet again in the early morning hours of Friday, January 28, nobody paid much attention. Within a couple of hours, however, the winds started whipping and the sky grew dark. Huge snowdrifts blew in off the lake, forcing schools to close, businesses to shut down, and drivers to abandon their cars. Some people stayed in their cars and froze to death.

The weather quickly grew worse, and the city was soon paralyzed, with snowdrifts reaching as high as twenty-five feet. Yes, twenty-five feet! Some residents, whose houses were almost entirely covered over, could get out only by digging tunnels from their front doors to the road, where they could walk only by trudging over the tops of cars. (One snowplow driver was quoted as saying that smaller cars weren't much of a problem: "Volkswagens are okay," he said. "They go through the rotary blades.") At the zoo, the snow was so high that three reindeer stepped over their restraining fence and strolled around the city. Mail delivery was suspended for almost a week. And for the first time in 143 years, the *Courier Express* was unable to publish the morning paper.

All across the city, people pitched in to help one another, proving that Buffalo deserved its slogan as the "city of good

neighbors." National Guardsmen, with the assistance of soldiers flown in from Fort Bragg, North Carolina, began to clear
the snow and deliver food and medicine to people in need. That
week, at least, government worked as it should: officials from
both political parties and a variety of institutions pulled together
to care for the sick, the elderly, and the many families who were
trapped in unheated houses. The blizzard of '77 made front-
page news across the country and sealed Buffalo's reputation as
the snow capital of America, although as every Buffalonian is
well aware, that honor rightfully belongs to Syracuse.

That Friday, I went to work as usual at the federal building
downtown. As the blizzard grew worse, I called Dad and told
him I wasn't sure I could make it back to my apartment.

"Don't go home," he said. "We're going to need a lot of help.
Stay where you are."

He recognized immediately that we were in the early hours
of a real crisis, and that Senator Moynihan's involvement would
be critical in helping the city respond to it. As usual, I listened to
Big Russ, and as usual, he was right. Ironically, though, his advice
to "stay where you are" turned out to be my ticket out of Buffalo.

I walked over to City Hall to meet with the mayor and his
advisors about the possibility of getting help from the federal government. When the phones were working, I spoke to Moynihan's
staffers in Washington and gave them updates on how the blizzard was affecting the city. None of us had any experience with
this sort of problem, so I began researching the laws on federal
assistance that might apply to Buffalo's predicament. A snowstorm had never led to the declaration of a disaster area, but we
thought this one might qualify. Meanwhile, I was pleased to hear

that Moynihan's staffers were in touch with their counterparts in Senator Javits's office, and that the two senators were resisting any temptation to grandstand or to allow party differences to over-shadow the emergency. I told everyone I spoke to that I thought both senators should fly to Buffalo as soon as possible, to see the damage for themselves.

Moynihan's Washington staffers were extremely intelligent, but they were city people who had little understanding of Upstate New York. At one point, when Stuart Gordon, Moynihan's chief of staff, couldn't reach me, he called Dick Eaton, who ran the senator's office in Oneonta, near the Moynihans' farm in Pindars Corners. "How's Tim doing?" Gordon asked. "How the hell should I know?" Dick replied. "He's five hours away, and the thruway's closed." Dick and I used to joke that the senator's Washington staff seemed to believe that all of Upstate New York consisted of one small town of apple growers.

That first evening, just about everyone who was stranded downtown gravitated to the Statler Hilton. By the time I got there, the bar had run dry, the hotel was completely sold out, and they were setting up cots in the lobby. One man refused to believe that every room in the hotel was booked. "If President Carter showed up," he said, "you'd have a room for him, wouldn't you?" Everybody within earshot started laughing at the old joke, but the question actually led somewhere: the manager opened the presidential suite and filled it with additional cots. I decided to sleep in my office, and as I left the hotel, I overheard a woman on a pay phone saying, "Honey, tonight *I'm* not coming home."

As I had hoped, Moynihan and Javits flew up to Buffalo to see how the blizzard had affected the area. I toured the city with them and before they left, Moynihan asked me to join them on the flight back to Washington. With no time to pack, I boarded the plane in my parka and my Timberland waterproof boots. I claimed the middle seat, between the two senators, and during the flight I took notes for a letter asking President Carter for disaster relief. When we landed, we went straight to Moynihan's office to get the letter typed. The office driver took me over to the White House, where I hand-delivered the letter to Hamilton Jordan, President Carter's chief of staff. The president acted on it immediately.

I spent the night in a hotel above the Dubliner, a great Irish bar. I took my first shower in days and showed up at Moynihan's office in the morning, where I called in the Buffalo reporters and helped arrange interviews for Senator Moynihan with every radio and television station in Buffalo.

After a day or two, Liz Moynihan turned to me and said, "You know, you're pretty good at this. Why don't you stay here and help us out with the press?"

"That's a capital idea," her husband said. "Why don't you move down here to Washington?"

"I've never really thought about it," I said.

"Well, you just did," the senator told me. "We could use you here, and you can look out for the interests of Buffalo. It will change your life, and you'll never look back."

It didn't take much persuading. I flew home, packed up all my belongings, and loaded them into my 1972 Gremlin with a coat hanger for an antenna until I looked like the Buffalo version of the Beverly Hillbillies. Before I left, I drove over to my parents' house to tell them the news. Dad, who hated to see me leave, asked how long I would be gone. I wonder if he knew, or suspected, that I was leaving Buffalo for good. He may have realized it, but I didn't.

"I don't really know," I told him.

"What will you do down there?"

"They want me to help with the press."

"What about your job here? Can you do them both?"

"No."

"Well, if you want your old job back, will they give it to you?"

"No, they'll get somebody else."

"Are you sure this is what you want?"

"Dad, I'm going to try it. It's a great opportunity, and I'll let you know how I'm doing."

"Okay" was the best he could offer. I was trading security for challenge, which always made Dad uneasy. It's something I've tried to explain to him, that sometimes in life, especially when you're young and single, it makes sense to take a risk in order to get ahead and become more fulfilled. It was Dad, of course, who made it possible for me to be in this position. His fulfillment came from raising and educating his four children.

In time, Dad and Moynihan would come to know and like each other. Moynihan always treated Big Russ with real respect, which Dad noticed and enjoyed. When I used Dad's car to drive the senator to a speaking engagement in Skaneateles, he sent Dad a thank-you note on a sheet of old White House stationery; Dad appreciated the note, and held on to it. Moynihan took Dad seriously, and asked his opinion on the issues of the day, and when the senator came to town, Dad made a point of going to see him. During the 1982 campaign, when I accompanied the senator on a barge down the Erie Canal, Dad showed up in Lockport to meet us in his *News* truck. To this day, Big Russ considers that some of the highest honors he has ever received are the times when Senator Moynihan asked Dad to escort him to the stage, as is the custom at statewide American Legion conventions. When I saw the two of them coming down the aisle together, I was deeply touched to see my real father and my intellectual father matching each other step for step.

IN WASHINGTON, I moved into a small and modest apartment on Third Street, Northeast, right behind the Supreme Court. When I told a reporter from the *Buffalo News* where it was, he made it sound as if I were enjoying the good life in a swank bachelor pad. I was actually living like a graduate student, with a mattress on a frame, a burlap rocking chair, and a black-and-white television resting on an old lobster trap.

In some respects, starting work on Capitol Hill reminded me of starting school at Canisius: here, too, I was lonely, anxious, and unsure whether I had made the right decision, whether I really belonged in this place. During my first few months in Washington, I often took refuge in the office of James T. Molloy, a former firefighter from South Buffalo who had succeeded the legendary Fishbait Miller as doorkeeper of the House of Representatives. Molloy's office was a meeting place for Buffalo natives and visitors, and he would regale us with colorful stories from home—like the time on St. Patrick's Day when he stopped in at Frank and Teresa's Anchor Bar, which has since become famous as the birthplace of Buffalo wings. While Jimmy and his partner were enjoying a few beers, a fire broke out, and nobody could find Jimmy—or, more important, the city's only amphibious fire truck, which Jimmy had been driving in the parade and which was now sitting behind the Anchor Bar. "A fire truck is a difficult thing to lose," Jimmy would say, "and I didn't enjoy the reputation of losing one."

It is the House doorkeeper who announces, as the president enters the hall for the State of the Union address, "Mr. Speaker, the president of the United States!" When I joined NBC News, I always made sure that Tom Brokaw put in a good word for James T. Molloy of South Buffalo. In 1994, in honor of Jimmy's final announcement as doorkeeper, I asked Brokaw to crank it up a little, and he was happy to do it. The president's arrival, Brokaw told the viewers, "will be formally announced, as it always is, by James T. Molloy, who is the House doorkeeper. He's been in that job for some twenty years now. He will be a familiar voice and face to all of you. He is a true Renaissance man from South Buffalo."

The next morning, Jimmy called me and said, "What the hell did Brokaw say last night?"

"What do you mean?"

"The guys in the firehouse told me that Brokaw said I was gay."

"What?!"

"Brokaw said I was gay."

"No, Jimmy, he said you were a Renaissance man."

"A what?"

"A Renaissance man."

"Well, they couldn't find that word in the dictionary, so they decided he was calling me gay."

Only in South Buffalo.

UNLIKE SOME POLITICIANS, Moynihan liked reporters and was usually able to see things from their perspective. But there were limits to his tolerance. When a writer whose views he found too conservative converted to Catholicism, Moynihan made a point of congratulating the man. He then added, with a smile, "Now, if we can only find a way to make you a Christian."

I too enjoyed dealing with the press. Reporters have a job to do, and when you're straight with them and accessible, they tend to give you the benefit of the doubt. I worked hard to understand the legislative issues well enough to explain them to reporters, and sometimes I'd ask our legislative point man to write out the key provisions of a bill as if he were sending a letter to his father. Whenever possible, I gave reporters other information that might be useful to their story, even if it had nothing to do with Moynihan. I tried to see things from their perspective, and a few times, when a reporter wasn't able to reach a source, I would provide that person's phone number. "Here it is," I'd tell them. "If he asks you where you got this number, tell him it was in the files. So make sure to put it in your files, and then take it out and call the guy."

My difficult moments came not with the press, but with a few of Moynihan's other staffers. They were serious, high-powered intellectuals, Ivy League graduates whose idea of a good time was a two-hour argument over the intricate details of arcane left-wing factions in the City College cafeteria. I didn't always follow their conversation, and I was sometimes intimidated in their presence.

One afternoon, when I was alone with the senator, I told him that I wasn't sure I fit in with the rest of the staff. "I think a little differently from these guys," I said. "We have meetings and discuss the votes, and the conversation veers off into theoretical discussions about socialism. I have a Jesuit education and a law degree, but half the time I have no idea what they're talking about!"

Moynihan burst out laughing. Just then the bells rang in the office, which meant it was time for the senators to cast a vote. "Walk with me," he said, and I followed him into the elevator and down to the Senate subway, the little underground rail system that links the Senate office buildings to the Senate chamber. When we reached the Senate floor, Moynihan put his arm around me and said, "Ideas are important and words matter, but so does getting elected. Let me tell you something: what they know, you can learn; but what you know, they will never learn. Remember: none of these guys has ever worked on a garbage truck."

That was all I needed to hear, and after the senator's vote of confidence, I walked back to the office a couple of inches above the ground. I now knew that he understood and valued my abilities. Maybe I didn't have the intellectual style of my colleagues, but common sense and street smarts were important, too. These days, whenever I'm asked to give a commencement address, I remind the students that success is not just reserved for rich people or those with Ivy League educations, but is also available to the sons and daughters of working people, immigrants, and pioneers. What a country!

Moynihan was one of the few men I've ever known who was at home in both worlds. In addition to teaching at Harvard, he was a widely published and influential social thinker; George Will once quipped that Moynihan had written more books than some senators had read. And during his four terms in the Senate, he spent every summer at his farm in Pindars Corners, where every morning he would walk over to the local schoolhouse and work on his latest book, not allowing himself to look at a newspaper until he had reached his daily word quota. At the same time, he had grown up in a single-parent household and knew what it meant to be poor. Although he sometimes embellished the amount of time he had spent in the Manhattan neighborhood known as Hell's Kitchen—in Moynihan's case, former New York mayor Ed Koch joked, it was more like Hell's Condominium—he had certainly known hard times. He and his brother had been shoeshine boys in Times Square, and young Patrick had gone to high school in East Harlem. More than most intellectuals, the new senator had a realistic view of how the world actually worked.

Not long after his reassuring comment, I said, "Senator, I appreciate what you said to me the other day."

"You know," he said, "some people think that just because somebody holds a high position, they have a monopoly on good ideas." I wasn't sure where he was going with this comment, but then he started telling me about the day President Kennedy was killed. When he heard on the radio that Lee Harvey Oswald, the presumed assassin, was being held by the Dallas police, Moynihan just *knew*, somehow, that this was a disaster waiting to happen. "I knew Dallas," he said. "At least I knew it well enough to assume the police might be incompetent. And I knew Texas well enough to worry that somebody there might shoot the guy who was accused of killing the president. And that terrified me, because we would never know for sure what had happened, and people would start believing in conspiracies. We had to get custody of that man."

In November 1963, Moynihan was a Labor Department official; he had no power, but he had access to people with power. Although he called everybody he could think of, he was unable to persuade anyone who mattered that it was essential for the federal government to take protective custody of Oswald.

Why was he telling me this now? Because Moynihan wanted to reinforce his earlier reassurance. He wanted to make sure I knew that education was not the same as knowledge, and that there were things, important things, that regular Americans knew and educated people—especially highly educated people—often did not. "You can be very learned and successful in this country," he told me, "and still not understand that the world is a dangerous place. The Kennedy people were very smart, but none of them had ever seen the inside of a city jail."

Moynihan described that awful weekend in his own book, *Coping*. "I was right that night at Andrews Air Force Base," he wrote, "and others, with far greater reputations, had chosen to be wrong." *Had chosen to be wrong?* I was struck by that formulation, because Moynihan used words very carefully. (He hated it, for example, when somebody in the office said that the White House had called. "No, it didn't!" he'd say. "Houses don't talk. You spoke to a person. Who was it?") He was saying that these intelligent, educated, and seasoned officials had not only made an egregious mistake in allowing the Dallas police to keep Oswald, but had done so knowingly, even after the possible consequences of their inaction were pointed out to them. They had been warned, and they had ignored the warning. Given

what happened, Moynihan was entitled to his righteous indignation.

A few months after this conversation, I was telling Tim
Moynihan, the senator's son, how his dad had put me at ease during my early weeks in Washington. "That's nice," he said, "but
make sure you know who Charles Parnell was." I had heard the
name, and I thought I remembered that Parnell had played a role
in Ireland's independence, but I couldn't really identify him. Tim
Moynihan told me that when he was about ten years old, he and
his father were out cutting firewood together. Neither one was
very good at it, and Tim's father was critical of how the boy was
stacking the logs. When Tim started to argue the point, his father
pointed at him and demanded, "Who was Charles Parnell?"

When Tim couldn't answer, his father said, "Aha, not as
smart as you think you are!"

Ten years later, Tim snuck into one of his father's lectures at
Harvard. When a student challenged him on something he had
said, Professor Moynihan looked around the room and asked,
"Who was Charles Parnell?"

Out of a couple of hundred students, maybe thirty raised
their hands. "Aha," said their teacher, "not as smart as you think
you are!"

When Tim told me that story, he said, "I realized that at the
age of ten, I was as ignorant as most Harvard students. And I
sure as hell had learned who Charles Parnell was."

So of course I immediately read up on Parnell, a nineteenth-
century Irish nationalist leader who was jailed by the British
after organizing an important rent strike against a prominent
British landowner. And then I waited for Senator Moynihan to

ask me about him. But he didn't mention Parnell's name during the rest of 1977, or the following year, or the year after that. One of my duties for the senator included monitoring the Sunday talk shows, and in January 1980, I was watching *Meet the Press* when President Carter announced that if Soviet troops didn't withdraw from Afghanistan within a month, he would not allow American athletes to participate in the upcoming summer Olympic games in Moscow. Moynihan had been urging Carter to take this step, and I called the senator to let him know that the president had just threatened to boycott the Olympics.

He thanked me for the call, and said, "By the way, do you know where the word 'boycott' comes from?"

Uh-oh. A familiar, sinking feeling came over me whenever Moynihan was reminded of all the things I didn't know.

He continued: "It comes from Charles C. Boycott, a British land agent in Ireland. But to know about him, you'd have to know who Charles Parnell was."

Bingo! "Charles Parnell was jailed after organizing a rent strike in 1880," I said. "He was an important figure in the movement for Irish independence."

"Good for you!" he said. "There are students at Harvard who don't know that name."

I didn't bother to tell him that I had been prepped for that question in 1977, and had been waiting two and a half years for the chance to answer it.

But Charles Parnell was just a drop in Moynihan's ocean of knowledge. Whether the subject was American or world history, arms control, ethnicity, international law, trade policy, public architecture, or urban planning, he had thought about the issues and read deeply in the literature. Sometimes I had the feeling that he had read and memorized just about everything. When Moynihan got up to speak, even extemporaneously, he would treat his audience to quotations—always cited accurately—from Shakespeare, Yeats, or Dylan Thomas, or, if the occasion demanded it, from Churchill, Jefferson, or Disraeli. Whatever the topic, you could count on him to provide an appropriate historical or literary comment.

He liked to say that the key ingredient in learning the truth was to ask the right questions, and I absorbed that lesson, never imagining that I would later spend most of my waking hours preparing to do just that—ask the right questions—in public on Sunday mornings. "You can't solve a problem until you can measure it," he often said. His approach reminded me of law school, where we were always being asked, What's the issue here? What, exactly, are we arguing about? And yet Moynihan was one of the few senators who wasn't a lawyer. He was a social scientist, with the emphasis on *scientist*.

A lot of people were surprised by how hard he worked to save New York City from bankruptcy. They had expected him to come into the Senate as a lofty orator, perhaps even a windbag, who paid little attention to details. They certainly didn't expect this worldly intellectual to focus on the nuts and bolts of legislation or to make sure New York received its fair share. But he knew how to deliver the dollars. He got federal aid to restore the Erie Canal and, in a major coup, he was able to persuade the federal government to award the state $5 billion for the New York Thruway, despite the fact that it had been built decades earlier.

Only rarely does a senator attend a hearing held by a committee on which he does not serve. But Moynihan and Javits attended virtually every session of the Banking Committee, and they questioned every witness. They made quite a pair: this large Irish Catholic Democrat, and this short Jewish Republican, who looked so different but worked as partners for the good of their state. William Proxmire, who chaired the Banking Committee, said later that any senator who voted against aid to New York had to feel that he was letting down two of his colleagues who really cared.

I can recall only one Banking Committee meeting that Moynihan missed. He had planned to attend a gathering of his old friends in New York the night before, and when several of us reminded him that the next day's hearing was especially important, he assured us that he would take the 7 A.M. shuttle and make it to the morning session in plenty of time. One of us went to the airport to pick him up, and when he wasn't on the 7 A.M. shuttle, we began making frantic phone calls, trying to find him. He finally called in just before eleven. "Good morning," he said. "Missed the seven. I'll be on the noon." Click.

Although Moynihan relished a good argument, he was never rude or cynical. He believed that public discourse should always be civil, and he did his best to keep it that way. He considered government a noble calling, and he believed in raising the level of public conversation, culture, and architecture. He was cheerful and witty, but not always patient—especially with cynicism. When he encountered it, he loved to quote Prince von Metternich, the nineteenth-century Austrian foreign minister who, upon learning of the sudden death of the Russian ambassador at the Congress of Vienna, said, "I wonder what could be his motive?"

NO MAN KNOWS EVERYTHING, and Moynihan was remarkably uninformed about sports, which is rare among male politicians. But on October 16, 1977, the senator showed me that even in this area I shouldn't underestimate him. He was a guest that morning on *Eyewitness News Conference*, a Sunday talk show on WABC in New York, and as we were driving over the Triborough Bridge on our way into the city, I said, "They're going to ask you about the borough president race, and why you endorsed Wagner, but try not to get into a long discussion about it." (A few days earlier, Moynihan had endorsed Robert F. Wagner, Jr., who was running as the Republican-Liberal party's candidate against Andrew Stein, the Democrat, which had caused some consternation among the party faithful.) "There are other issues to talk about," I said, "like the fiscal situation, but what people really care about right now is the World Series."

"Oh, really? And where are they holding it this year?"

I couldn't help but laugh. "Senator, it's not a moveable feast. It's the Yankees and the Dodgers, and Game 5 is today, in Dodger Stadium, and it will be on ABC. The Yankees are ahead three games to one, and they could win it all today."

Moynihan had other things on his mind, and he probably resented my tone. "I'm a serious man," he said. "I loved baseball in my day, but at the moment I'm thinking about saving New York from bankruptcy."

"I understand, sir."

We went to the studio, and Moynihan disappeared into the makeup room. When the interview began, it wasn't long before somebody said, "Senator, you got yourself involved in a big race here in Manhattan . . ."

He didn't even wait for the end of the question. "There's only one race that people here in Manhattan, and in Queens, Brooklyn, the Bronx, and Staten Island care about," he said. "The Yankees will do it today. And if they don't do it today, Mike Torrez will do it on Tuesday."

I was stunned. Our driver, who had heard the conversation in the car, turned to me and said, "How the hell did he know that?" I was wondering the same thing.

As we left the building, Moynihan turned to me and said, "So what did you think, Tiger?"

"That was amazing. How did you know about Torrez on Tuesday?"

"First of all, who's Mike Torrez?"

I couldn't believe he didn't know, because he had just talked about Torrez on television, but I answered him anyway: "He's the Yankee pitcher who won Game 3. He'll be pitching again in Game 6 if the Yankees lose today."

"Okay, that makes sense."

"But how did you know —"

"I was sitting in the makeup room, and as they were putting powder on my nose, a ten-year-old boy with a Yankees hat and a baseball glove said, 'Hi, Senator.' I said, 'Hello there, young man. Are the Yankees going to do it today?'"

"'It doesn't matter, Senator, because if they don't do it today, Torrez will do it on Tuesday.'"

I paused for a moment to take it all in, but I still couldn't believe it. "Senator," I said, "how could you go out on live television and not know exactly what you were saying about the World Series?"

He put his arm around me and said, "Old friend, if you can't trust a wide-eyed ten-year-old with a Yankees hat about the World Series, you can't trust anybody."

17.

Politics

"If the guy doesn't have a serial number,
then the guy wasn't in the army."

IT MUST BE OBVIOUS BY NOW that I greatly enjoyed
working for Senator Moynihan. I guess the feeling was
mutual, because in 1979 the senator asked me to be his chief of
staff. At twenty-nine, I became the youngest administrative
assistant (as the position is formally known) in the Senate. I felt
honored by Senator Moynihan's confidence in me, and delighted
with my new salary of $57,500. My only regret was that the
details of my income appeared in a Buffalo newspaper. It was
excellent pay for government work, and Dad was astounded—
and maybe even a little offended—when he read about it. "Fifty-
seven thousand? Jeez, you're just a kid!" I quickly repaid my student loans and my $2,000 debt— he would call it a marker—to
Frankie Sonofabitch. For the first time in my adult life, I was
debt-free.

I remembered how Dad had felt when he became a foreman; he appreciated the promotion, but he had enjoyed driving a truck more than he liked his new position. "Being a boss can be a real headache," he used to tell me, and now I learned what he meant. It's nice to have the top job, but it's also a real burden to find yourself responsible for hiring and firing people and supervising a staff. Although I'd had no administrative experience, I was now in charge of a million-dollar payroll and all the employees in the senator's offices in Washington, New York City, Oneonta, and Buffalo. I was also fortunate enough to continue doing what I loved, which was working with the press.

It's an old complaint in Washington, but it's true: the day after you win an election, you have to start planning for the next campaign. I had encouraged Moynihan to visit all of New York's sixty-two counties, because I wanted him to become so well-known and so popular around the state that it would be difficult for any challenger to unseat him. In 1981, the year before he was up for reelection, we ran him ragged with countless speaking engagements and local TV appearances. He complained about the heavy schedule, but he went along with it. Although Moynihan was an old-fashioned gentleman, he was also a realist who understood that politics had changed enormously during his lifetime and that campaigns were now won or lost on television. In fact, he used the media as well as almost any politician in the country. Looking ahead to a Senate race in which I could finally play a substantial role, I took a temporary leave of absence from my chief of staff job to become Senator Moynihan's campaign manager.

A year before the election, a lot of people thought Moynihan was destined to be a one-term senator. Liberals who had

distrusted him in 1976 were unhappy with his bipartisan ten-
dencies and his hawkish views on foreign affairs, while conser-
vatives, naturally, found him too liberal on domestic issues.
There wasn't much I could do about hard-core Republican voters, but I arranged for Moynihan to meet with as many Democratic groups as possible. "You may not always agree with him," I
told them, "but you have to concede that he's doing a hell of a
job for the state, and that you share many of his views on social
issues." That was even more true after President Ronald Reagan
came into office, when Moynihan positioned himself as the leading defender of Social Security. When Rep. Elizabeth Holtzman
thought about challenging Moynihan in the Democratic primary, some of her fellow liberals persuaded her not to run
because from their standpoint, though Moynihan wasn't ideal, he
was acceptable. More important, he was also electable.

At the other end of the spectrum, when the National Conservative Political Action Committee announced that they
planned to spend hundreds of millions of dollars on TV ads that
accused Moynihan of being a big spender, we recruited a retired
chief justice of the New York State Court of Appeals to inform
stations that they were not required to accept these ads, and
that if we believed they were libelous, we might sue the stations
that aired them. Only a handful of stations ran the ads.

Looking ahead to the November election, we had a pretty
good idea that the senator's Republican opponent would be
Bruce Caputo, a good-looking and well-spoken former member
of Congress, who was also an excellent fund-raiser and capable
of running a strong campaign. Because I have always been a
research maniac, I started tracking down everything I could

find about him. LexisNexis didn't exist yet, and the Internet was well beyond our imaginations, so I relied mostly on blurry, photocopied newspaper clippings from small towns around the state and from Westchester County, the district Caputo had represented in Congress. As I read through one profile after another, I noticed some differences in the various accounts of Caputo's military service. In one article, Caputo said he had served in Vietnam during the late 1960s, but the reporter could find no evidence that this was the case. Another article said Caputo had been a war hero. According to a third one, he had worked at the Pentagon as a second lieutenant, while a fourth article indicated that he had worked there as the *equivalent* of a second lieutenant. I wasn't sure yet, but I had the growing impression that something about this story just didn't add up.

Around this time—it was early 1982—Dad asked me, "Who's the Italian kid who's going to run against the senator?"

"I'm glad you mentioned him," I said, "because I've been reading up on this guy." And then I told Dad what I had found.

"Trust me," Dad said. "If you were a second lieutenant, you would *know* you were a second lieutenant." He then rattled off the date he had entered the army, the date he had left, and his serial number. We both laughed, and then moved on to other things.

A couple of days later, I told Moynihan that Caputo was speaking around the state and attacking the senator's voting record.

"I wouldn't worry about that," Moynihan said. "The election is a long way off."

Then I mentioned the inconsistencies I had noticed about

Caputo's military record. I told Moynihan that when I had mentioned this to Dad, he had blurted out his serial number.

Moynihan laughed, and proceeded to rattle off *his* serial number from the navy.

A couple of weeks later, I was chatting with Harrison Rainie of the *New York Daily News* and Martin Wald of the Associated Press, who were regular visitors to our office. They asked me about Bruce Caputo's recent attacks on Moynihan, and one of them mentioned that they were scheduled to have lunch with him in a couple of hours. I said, "Really? Why don't you ask him what his serial number was?"

"What are you talking about?" they said.

I described the discrepancies I had noticed and told them about my conversation with Dad. And I repeated something else Big Russ had told me: "If the guy doesn't have a serial number, then the guy wasn't in the army."

When the reporters asked Caputo about his military service, he gave a fuzzy, convoluted answer. They checked with me to see what I could tell them, but all I knew was what I had read in the newspapers. The two reporters went to work on the story, and before long, both the *Daily News* and the Associated Press ran articles alleging that Caputo had exaggerated his military record.

Then the *Times* weighed in with a devastating opening sentence: "Former Representative Bruce F. Caputo, a Republican candidate for U.S. Senator from New York, has described himself as a Vietnam-era 'draftee' and an Army lieutenant although he was neither." The article also noted that Caputo's distortion of his military record had been called to the attention of reporters "by the staff of Senator Moynihan." When the *Times* reporter, Michael Oreskes, had asked me about this, I told him the truth—yes, I had pointed out what looked to me like inconsistencies. We also released a statement from Moynihan: "This is a startling revelation, and I ought not to comment on it just now." In refusing to get involved, the senator was adhering to a fundamental rule of politics: never get in the way when your opponent is in the process of self-destructing. Privately, Moynihan was outraged. "A man who lies about his military record," he said, "will lie about anything."

If any of Caputo's supporters were tempted to blame his downfall on the liberal media, George Will put an end to that excuse. In his column of February 28, 1982, Will reported that he had asked Caputo flat-out if he had ever been drafted into the army. "I treasured his reply," Will wrote. "*Not exactly.*" He blasted Caputo for dissembling—not only about his military service, but about Moynihan's voting record as well. If Caputo's campaign had any remaining life, George Will had just killed it.

But you can't please everybody. While Caputo's campaign was unraveling, I heard from Meade Esposito, the well-known Democratic power broker from Brooklyn who was later convicted on bribery charges. "Hey kid," he said, "why are you taking this guy out now? They'll just find someone else to run against your man."

Esposito was upset that Caputo had been attacked too early; as an old political warrior, he would have preferred to undermine his opponent in the final month of the campaign—as in "October Surprise." But the reason the story had credibility was that it had come up naturally, in a conversation with the two reporters. When they asked me about Caputo, I told them what

I had noticed, but they investigated and reported the story on their own. I didn't know what they would find, but if our side had made these charges against Caputo, they might have been dismissed as typical partisan ploys. As it played out, Caputo had only himself to blame. Although he had been careless with the facts (to put it kindly), he could have saved his campaign by giving the two reporters a truthful answer at their lunch. All he had to say was, "It's true that there have been differing reports about my military record, and maybe I haven't always been clear about it, so let me set things straight. I worked at the Pentagon, where they gave me a rank-equivalent, but I never served in the army." End of story. Once again, the great Watergate cliché proved to be true: the coverup was worse than the crime.

When Caputo withdrew from the race, several other Republicans stepped forward, and a conservative candidate named Florence Sullivan won the primary. By then we were ready with some unusual campaign commercials. A few weeks earlier, five of us— Liz and Pat Moynihan, television consultant David Sawyer, his assistant Mandy Grunwald, and I—had met together and made several decisions. First, we would start running our ads immediately after the other side chose its candidate. We expected the Republicans to take some quick polls to determine how strong Moynihan was, and if they detected any trace of vulnerability, they would pour a lot of money into Sullivan's campaign. But if our ads appeared early enough, before the other side was ready, the polls might indicate that Moynihan was unbeatable, in which case the Republicans would spend their money elsewhere. There was another advantage to starting early: although Moynihan's campaign was actually little more than a mom and pop operation, a flurry of ads at the start of the election season would give the impression that we had a ton of money to spend, which would further discourage our opponents.

The ads we ran were distinctive in their simplicity. As a boy, I used to watch news shows with Dad on our black-and-white TV, and in 1982 I was reasonably sure that I wasn't the only American adult who associated black-and-white television with a higher level of honesty and credibility. In addition, black-and-white seemed entirely appropriate for an old-fashioned candidate like Moynihan and was also cheaper and faster to produce. Finally, because we were the only ones not using color, our ads stood out amid all the noise and clutter that saturates the airwaves during election season. We produced a number of these ads, some of which included images of newspaper articles or editorials that supported what Moynihan was saying.

The candidate himself suggested many of the topics, and he rewrote every commercial we made. He also insisted on two key points. First, we would run no negative advertising: no matter what happened during the campaign, we would conduct ourselves with civility. Second, we would run ads only about legislation that the senator had either authored or had helped to pass. This was setting the bar rather high, but Moynihan's staff adhered to these rules not only in 1982, but in the senator's subsequent campaigns as well. I don't believe he ever ran a negative ad, and he deviated from his second rule only once, when Mandy Grunwald persuaded him to appear in an ad about the Clinton Crime Bill, which he had neither authored nor worked on.

In the 1982 election, Senator Moynihan was reelected by a

million and a half votes. At the time, it was the biggest margin of victory in any statewide election in American history.

When you win that big, people notice. Politicians and journalists were astonished at how quickly Moynihan's major opponent had disappeared, and Andy Logan wrote in *The New Yorker* that Bruce Caputo had been "russerted." A little later, when Gary Hart was looking for someone to run his presidential campaign, he was quoted as saying, "Get me a Russert!" I was flattered that my name had become both a noun and a verb. My only worry was that Sister Lucille might put it all together and ask me to diagram the sentence.

As much as I loved working for Moynihan, I didn't want to spend the rest of my life as a Senate aide. Well before the 1982 campaign, I told the senator that I was going to leave after the election, probably to practice law. I was tempted to stay: the civil-service voice in my head, the one I had inherited from Dad, whispered, *Don't leave. You have a wonderful job with a man you respect, and it's secure.* But although I'd had a great six years on Capitol Hill, another, louder voice within me—the same impulse that had prompted me to leave Buffalo for college, for law school, and most recently, for Washington—was encouraging me to move on and try something else, where I could be my own boss. I had become friendly with Leonard Garment, a lawyer I knew through Moynihan (and whose wife, Suzanne Garment, came from Buffalo), and he and I discussed the possibility that I might take a job with his firm. Sixteen years earlier, Garment had changed Moynihan's life by bringing his ideas to the attention of his law partner, Richard Nixon. Would he now change mine? I was also thinking about opening my own law practice.

Although Moynihan would have been happy to have me stay on, he understood my restlessness and gave me his blessing. As Liz put it, "Everybody has to grow up and leave home."

People say that life is what happens to you while you're making other plans. During Moynihan's 1982 reelection race, we often ran into another Democratic candidate on the campaign trail—a lawyer and former baseball player who was running for governor, and who won in a close contest. Right after the election, I heard from Andrew Cuomo, Mario's son and campaign manager. "I understand you're leaving," he said. "Would you consider coming to Albany and working for Mario?"

Although I hadn't intended to stay in politics, Mario Cuomo was a very appealing figure. For one thing, he was a serious and thoughtful Catholic who was equally serious and thoughtful about public service. For another, people said he might run for vice president in 1984, or for president in 1988, which gave Cuomo an even greater allure. But even if he didn't run, after six years in the legislative branch of the federal government, I was excited by the possibility of working in the executive branch of the state I cared most about: it was new, it was different, and it would certainly be a challenge. The day Cuomo was elected, his mother, upon hearing that the state had a $2 billion budget deficit, told her son, "I knew they wouldn't let you win anything too good."

The problem facing Cuomo was a big and important one. Now that New York was committed to fiscal responsibility, the new governor had to balance the budget and reduce the size of government without abandoning the people who needed its help. Another factor in my decision was that although I would be working out of Albany, the job would include a lot of time in New York City, where I could be closer to a smart, attractive writer named Maureen, whom I had been courting for two years. Of course I discussed the Cuomo offer with Moynihan, who encouraged me to take the job. He pointed out with some pleasure that if I went to Albany, I would be doing exactly what he had done when he went to work for Governor Harriman in the 1950s.

It happened very quickly. In early December, I signed on for a two-year stint as a counselor to Mario Cuomo. Despite the title, I wasn't a legal advisor; most of my work would be with the press—especially the national press, because part of my job was to serve as a link between Albany and Washington.

When I called Dad to tell him about my new job, he couldn't understand why I had taken it. "Moynihan was just reelected!"

"Yes, Dad, I'm aware of that."

"So why would you give up a six-year term with the Irishman to take a four-year term with the Italian?" As usual, Dad was thinking about job security.

A few days later, he read in the paper that I was one of five key aides hired by Cuomo, and that each of us would earn $75,000 a year. Dad called and said, "Okay, *now* I get it. Seventy-five *thousand*. Now I get it!" In fact, my decision to go with Cuomo had nothing to do with money. If that had been my goal, I would have given up on public service and started practicing law.

Most elected officials get to enjoy a bit of a honeymoon, but just days after Cuomo was sworn in, a riot broke out at Ossining

Correctional Facility—the prison formerly known as Sing Sing—where the inmates took dozens of guards hostage to dramatize their complaints about overcrowding. Cuomo's five-man brain trust had been focusing on the budget; the last thing we expected was a hostage situation in a maximum-security prison. As soon as it happened, we moved into a command post on the fifty-seventh floor of the World Trade Center and installed a hotline to the prison. The governor's initial instinct was to go there himself, but we were able to persuade him that this would be a big mistake: his appearance would signal to the prisoners that they had already won a major concession, which would only encourage them. Instead, Cuomo stayed in a conference room during the fifty-three-hour crisis, and even slept there. Until it was over, he refused to meet with the press. That was my job.

When I had a free moment, I called Big Russ to tell him what was going on. Like everyone else in Upstate New York, he was afraid of another Attica. (In 1971, when inmates took over the Attica State Prison, Governor Rockefeller sent in troops; when it was all over, forty-three people were dead.) "I hope this one won't be another bloodbath," said Dad. "But these guys might come to their senses if they knew what could happen."

A couple of hours later, we were meeting in the conference room when the governor said, "I think we have to demonstrate some show of force to let the prisoners know what could happen here if they harm any of the guards."

"Governor," I said, "I was speaking to my dad just now, and he thought it might be useful for the prisoners to know what fate might await them."

Cuomo nodded. "Here's what we'll do," he said. "Tim, go

out and tell the press that we're determined to negotiate this. We're not granting amnesty, but if the prisoners want to air their grievances, we'll give them a chance to be heard. And it wouldn't hurt to say that we're trying to avoid another Attica."

As I walked to the podium, I took comfort in the fact that Dad and the governor had come to the same conclusion. Almost as soon as I mentioned Attica, the television stations began to replay the awful pictures of that gruesome event. The prisoners at Ossining were watching TV, and it soon became clear that this footage had a sobering effect on them. The governor's strategy was starting to work, and we were all praying that we could bring this uprising to a peaceful conclusion.

And because of Cuomo's creativity, we did. To our enormous relief, the situation ended with no deaths or injuries. It lasted only a couple of days, but those fifty-three hours felt like an eternity. The Ossining hostage crisis was a defining moment for the new governor, who passed his first major test with high marks. Politicians seldom get credit for the disasters they were able to prevent, and today almost nobody remembers Ossining. Because he avoided bloodshed, this was one of Mario Cuomo's finest hours.

A year and a half later, I had the good fortune to witness another great Cuomo moment. Unlike Ossining, which was handled quietly, this one was a very public event in American political history. In his unforgettable keynote address at the 1984 Democratic Convention, Cuomo reminded Democrats what their party believed in. The part that most resonated with people, Republicans and Democrats alike, was Cuomo's moving description of where he had come from. He spoke about his

Italian-born father, who had worked in a little grocery store so his American-born son could get an education and move up in the world. "I watched a small man with thick calluses on both hands work fifteen and sixteen hours a day," the governor said. "I saw him once literally bleed from the bottoms of his feet, a man who came here uneducated, alone, unable to speak the language, who taught me all I needed to know about faith and hard work by the simple eloquence of his example."

And now the grocer's son was the governor of a great state in a great nation, being seen by a television audience of close to eighty million people. As Cuomo spoke, I could see him reacting to the energy of the crowd, leaning back on his heels and gesturing. It was as if he were having an animated conversation with the whole country about lessons from our fathers and the values that made us great.

DURING MY TWO YEARS WITH CUOMO, I stayed in close touch with Senator Moynihan, and our friendship continued all through my subsequent career with NBC. Both before and during my time on *Meet the Press*, Moynihan was a regular guest on the program; only a handful of politicians appeared more often than he did. (Bob Dole holds the record for the most appearances.) Moynihan, who first appeared on *Meet the Press* in 1965, had fond memories of Lawrence Spivak, who cofounded the program back in 1947 and served as its moderator from 1966 through 1975. In the Spivak era, Moynihan recalled, the program ended at noon, "whereupon a silver tray laden with Bloody Marys appeared and anxiety evanesced accordingly. Now you get orange juice at ten o'clock in the morning, as if you had just given blood."

Whenever Moynihan was a guest during my term as moderator, I had the opportunity to apply one of the many lessons he taught me, this one about fair disclosure. In introducing him, I always made a point of telling the viewers that I had worked for the senator during his first term in office. One of my favorite on-air moments with him came in 1993, when I asked him whether the Democrats' proposed energy tax would be a fight to the death, or whether he might be willing to compromise a little. "Fight until death over taxes?" he said. "Oh no. Women, country, God, things like that. Taxes? No."

Most politicians are good at coming up with long-winded, circuitous answers, and Moynihan had that gift as well. But he could also be brief, concise, and blunt. When I asked him in 1994 what he thought the United States should do about North Korea's efforts to develop nuclear weapons, he said, "If they go ahead with what they have done, in defiance of the world and the clear understanding of what is going on, you bomb them."

"You bomb them?" I asked, not entirely certain that I had heard him right.

"Bomb them," he repeated.

He died on March 26, 2003, and he was as dignified in death as he had been in life. In political circles, there is a tendency for funerals to take on the form of political theater, a trend that reached its low point at the memorial service for Sen. Paul Wellstone in the fall of 2002. Moynihan's funeral had none of that: it consisted of a solemn Mass in the old Washington church that he had walked to every Sunday, which is known, appropriately enough, as St. Patrick's. There were no eulogies, just a homily by the pastor, Monsignor Peter Vaghi, who noted that toward the end of Mass the senator used to leave his pew and stand on the side so he could see the choir. Sometimes he helped with the collection, and when he did, he would thank each person individually for their contribution. It was a lovely touch, the pastor noted, although it slowed down the service considerably.

After the funeral, the hearse made its way down Pennsylvania Avenue, as if to thank Moynihan for making sure that Washington's most famous street became a source of pride, rather than shame. When he had started working on the restoration of Pennsylvania Avenue back in 1962, the District's central artery, flanked by the White House at one end and the Capitol at the other, was tacky and seedy during the day, and dark and abandoned at night. Moynihan was supposed to present his plan for the improvement of Pennsylvania Avenue to congressional leaders in November 1963, as soon as President Kennedy returned from Dallas. Decades later, his dream of a revitalized boulevard was finally realized. In his honor, a stretch of Pennsylvania Avenue, near Thirteenth Street, is now known as Moynihan Place.

At Arlington Cemetery, a navy band played the "Navy Hymn," and led a horse-drawn caisson that for me, at least, brought back memories of President Kennedy's funeral. Seven sailors fired three rifle volleys and a bugler played "Taps." The band played "America the Beautiful," and Maura Moynihan, Pat and Liz's daughter, read the famous poem by Dylan Thomas, "Do Not Go Gentle into That Good Night." She chose it in part because her father had known Thomas, and sometimes drank with him at the White Horse Tavern in Greenwich Village.

I was one of the pallbearers, along with several other graduates of the University of Moynihan. When we arrived at the grave site, the navy honor guard took over for the final few steps. In respectful silence, they removed the flag that was draped over the coffin and folded it precisely. The commanding officer and the navy chaplain walked over to Liz Moynihan and presented the flag to her, and she hugged it. It was such a touching moment. It was painful to see somebody as wonderful and loyal as Liz Moynihan having to say good-bye to her life partner.

The honor guard fired the salute, three final shots, and a navy man picked up one of the shells and handed it to me. It was the first time I had held a rifle shell since my childhood, when I stood next to Dad outside the Legion Hall on Memorial Day. I brought it to work the next day and put it in a small Lucite box on my desk that Robert Kennedy had given to the people who had helped him in his 1964 Senate campaign. Pat Moynihan's name is etched on top of the box; below it is an outline of the state of New York, and in the map it says, "Kennedy, '64." When her husband retired from the Senate in 2000, Liz Moynihan had sent it to me with a note: "Tim dear, This box has been on Pat's desk—wherever the desk was—since Bobby sent it to him in 1964. As a memento of your years together, he thought you might like to have it. Love, Liz."

She must have known how much that little box would mean to me, with its connections to two senators from my own state, both of whom I admired, and one of whom I loved.

18.

Totus Tuus

"Speak their language."

A VERY IMPORTANT THING HAPPENED during my time with Governor Cuomo: I got married. Appropriately enough, given the nature of my work in those days, I met Maureen at a reception at the 1980 Democratic National Convention in Manhattan. Maureen Orth was covering the convention for the *Village Voice*, and I was working for Senator Moynihan. It was a Saturday night, and we walked to a pub on Columbus Avenue, where we talked and talked until they finally put up the chairs and threw us out. At four in the morning, I offered to walk her home. When we passed an all-night newsstand, Maureen stopped to pick up the Sunday *Times*. I bought the *Daily News*.

When we got to her building, she said, "There's something I have to ask you. If you're such a political hotshot, why did you get only the *News*, and not the *Times*?"

"Because you bought the *Times*," I said hopefully.

"Not a chance," she said, closing the door in my face. I went home and slept with the *Daily News*. But I called her again, and one thing led to another, until in 1983 we went to Spain and got married. It sounds simple enough, but we had to go through the rigors of convincing the Catholic Church in that country that we were two American Catholics in good standing who had never been married before. Maureen's fluency in Spanish led us to a meeting with two priests on the second floor of the chancery of the diocese of Madrid, where she tried to persuade them that I was all right. "Look at him," she said. "He looks like a choirboy, he's a former altar boy, and he studied under the Jesuits for eight years."

Hearing this, one of the priests dropped his prayerbook and exclaimed, in Spanish, "I thought you said he was a good Catholic!"

Even so, we received the necessary permissions and were married at the Basilica of San Miguel. When we got home and told my family that we were married, they were of two views: overjoyed at the news, but disappointed that there hadn't been a grand wedding, which was precisely the sort of event we had wanted to avoid. I was thirty-three, and my sisters had begun to think that I was going to be one of those holiday fixtures in South Buffalo, the Irish bachelor uncle.

The most important thing that happened to me after that was the birth of our son in 1985. We were living on the Upper West Side of New York, and at 3 A.M. on August 22, 1985, Maureen went into labor. I hailed a gypsy cab, a vintage white Oldsmobile with no shock absorbers, and brought her to Lenox Hill Hospital. It was a long, difficult labor, and the doctor told us that Maureen might need a C-section. After a few hours I went outside for a breath of air. When I found myself in front of a church behind the hospital, I went in and knelt down at a little shrine to St. Ann, the mother of Mary and the patron saint of mothers. I prayed for a healthy baby and a healthy mother, and vowed that I would never again miss Sunday Mass. When I returned to the hospital, the doctor explained that Maureen would indeed need a C-section. She was deeply disappointed, but there was no choice.

When they brought me our nine-pound, thirteen-ounce baby and put him in my arms, I burst into tears. Although I had known for months that this moment was coming, I just couldn't believe it. Luke's eyes were barely open, and I counted his tiny fingers and toes and held him tight. *I'm a father!* I told myself. *I'm a father! And I have a son!* Maureen and I thought we were having a boy, and I was secretly hoping for a son. It wasn't much of a secret, though, because long before he was born I had started referring to the baby as Luke. It must have been the right name, because whenever I said it, the baby answered with a kick. And now, holding this little gift in my arms, I knew that something magnificent and miraculous had happened, and I felt honored and humbled to be part of it. But there was so much I didn't yet know, and couldn't possibly know. I whispered to Luke, "Never has a Papa loved a baby so much." I'd had no idea how much love I was capable of feeling for another human being.

We chose the name Luke for three reasons: for St. Luke the Evangelist, whose name means "the enlightened one"; for Luke Easter of the Buffalo Bisons, who gave me so much joy when I was young; and for the tough and stubborn character played by Paul Newman in my all-time favorite movie, *Cool Hand Luke*. After a few years I added a fourth reason: I told Luke's little friends that he was also named for Luke Skywalker, the Jedi hero of *Star Wars*.

As a father, I've certainly made my share of mistakes. But one mistake I refused to make was to miss out on any of the important moments of my son's childhood. I've known any number of men who have put their careers ahead of everything else, and have told me, with genuine regret, that they couldn't remember what it was like when their children were young, because they weren't home very much. Although it can't possibly be true, I sometimes feel that I can remember every single day of Luke Russert's life.

I don't mean to suggest that I didn't also care deeply about my career. During my second summer with Governor Cuomo, when I was a recently married man who was no longer enjoying the weekly commute between Albany and New York City, Moynihan's old friend Len Garment asked me what I wanted to do when I grew up. I told him that I was still planning to practice law, but he had something else in mind. "Do me a favor," he said. "My friend Larry Grossman has just been made president of NBC News. He's talking to people about the news business, and I'd like you to meet him."

Garment, a born matchmaker, had also been talking to Grossman about me. A week or two later, Larry Grossman and I had dinner at a Japanese restaurant on the Upper West Side. At the end of a long and engaging conversation, he asked, "Have you ever had any interest in working in a news division?"

"Not really," I said. "But I was editor of my school paper, and I do like hanging around with reporters. I even married one."

"You should give it some thought," he said. "I'd love to bring you with me to NBC."

The next day, I called my friend David Burke, the assistant to Roone Arledge, president of ABC News. David had previously worked for Ted Kennedy and Hugh Carey, and when I told him in confidence about Grossman's overture, he assured me that television news, with its constant energy and the need for quick decisions, was not all that different from politics. "You would enjoy doing what I do over here," he said, "assistant to the president with a wide-open portfolio." Larry Grossman and Roone Arledge had gone to college together, and I took that as a sign that this was an idea worth exploring. I called Len Garment and told him I had enjoyed the dinner, and that Grossman seemed interested in hiring me. Once again, my new job fell into place very quickly: in September 1984, I moved to NBC News as Larry Grossman's deputy and began a new chapter in my life.

Governor Cuomo was gracious about letting me go. "There are just two things Tim has to do," he told a reporter. "Get his weight under control, and never, never lacquer his nails." When I signed a three-year contract with NBC, some people, looking for an angle, noticed that the agreement would expire just in time for me to jump on a Cuomo-for-President bandwagon in late 1987. In fact, I signed a three-year deal with NBC for a very unexciting reason: that's how their contracts were structured.

My first assignment was to focus on the *Today Show*, which was doing quite well with Jane Pauley and Bryant Gumbel, but was lagging behind ABC's *Good Morning America* in the hotly competitive breakfast-show ratings. My mandate was to work with

Steve Friedman, *Today*'s executive producer, to come up with ideas and improvements that would boost the show's audience. "We'll spend money if we have to," Grossman told me, which was a phrase I certainly hadn't heard very often in the public sector. The size of the show's audience wasn't just a network concern; I soon learned that NBC's many affiliates cared a great deal about *Today*'s ratings. The local stations receive half the show's advertising revenue, and most have news windows to fill at 7:25 and 8:25. And the more people tune in to *Today*, the more viewers the affiliates are likely to retain for their nine o'clock programs. Although it took me a while to get used to the idea, like everything else on commercial television, news is a business with millions of dollars at stake.

Shortly before I joined NBC, new developments in the technology of broadcasting had made it much easier for *Today* and its competitors to go out on the road. In September 1984, the same month I joined the network, *Today* went to Moscow, where Bryant Gumbel received excellent reviews for his news-making interviews with top Kremlin officials. (He had majored in Russian history at Bates College.) "Let's plan another big trip for the spring," I told Steve Friedman. "It's a great way to attract new viewers."

"Good idea," said Friedman, who was kind enough not to mention that the new guy had just pointed out the obvious. "Where do you think we should go?"

"How about Italy?" I said. "The music, the art, the fashion, the food, the vibrancy—and if we could somehow get behind the walls of the Vatican at Easter, people would be fascinated."

"Good idea," said Friedman. "Let's get the Pope."

"The *Pope?*" I burst out laughing. "Friedman, in my church that's a very big deal. I used to be an altar boy, but there are a few steps in between!" We were both laughing now, but I soon realized that only one of us was kidding.

What the heck? I thought. Why not give it a try? I learned that the Pope does not grant exclusive interviews to journalists, so that approach wouldn't work. But maybe he would agree to lead a special Mass in his private chapel during Holy Week, and we could film it and include it as part of our coverage. It sounds absurd, I know, but I actually sat down and wrote a letter to the Pope, asking if he would appear on the *Today Show* when we traveled to Rome. I sent the letter to the papal nuncio in Washington, and asked him to kindly forward it to the Vatican.

Writing that letter was a first step, but I couldn't imagine that something this big could ever happen without some serious, high-level intervention. A few days later, I read in a church newspaper that Archbishop John Foley of Philadelphia was the head of the Pontifical Commission for Social Communication, so I sent him a copy of my letter to the Pope. He liked the idea of the Pope appearing on American television, and he told me that his friend, John Cardinal Krol of Philadelphia, was also a good friend of the Holy Father. Pope John Paul II had grown up in Poland, and Cardinal Krol's parents were Polish; when both men were bishops, Karol Joseph Wojtyla (as the Pope was then known) used to visit Joseph Krol when he came to America. So of course I asked the archbishop if he could help me meet the cardinal, so I could make my appeal in person. Archbishop Foley made some calls, and before long I had an appointment to see Cardinal Krol in Philadelphia.

Around this time I was on the phone with Dad, and as usual, I told him what was going on at work. I mentioned that I was looking forward to meeting Cardinal Krol, but that my letter to the Pope had gone unanswered.

"You wrote a letter to the Pope?" he said. Dad thought that was pretty funny. "Let me know if you hear back from him," he roared. When I mentioned that I was hoping to get some help from Cardinal Krol, who was Polish, just like the Pope, Dad laughed again and said, "Maybe you should write that letter in Polish. I have some friends in Cheektowaga who could help you." We were both laughing. Then he said, "I'm serious. When you talk to people, speak their language. It shows respect." When I hung up the phone, I thought, *Actually, that's a pretty good idea.*

At work the next day, I faxed my letter to our Warsaw bureau and asked them to translate it into Polish. When I went down to Philadelphia to see Cardinal Krol, I brought the letter with me. "I wrote an appeal to the Holy Father," I said, "and I would be grateful if you would present this to him."

I handed him the letter, and the cardinal looked at it. "This is written in Polish," he said.

"Yes."

"And it's very good Polish, too."

"Yes?"

"This is excellent. The Pope loves to receive letters in his native language. Tell me, are *you* Polish, Mr. Russert?"

I paused—probably a bit too long. For a moment I was actually tempted to slip one by the cardinal, but that would be wrong. "No," I said, "but I come from Buffalo, and some of my best friends . . ."

We both laughed. "I'm flying to Rome next week," he said, "and I'll be happy to bring your letter. But right now I'm going to the cathedral for a rehearsal of the Archdiocesan Boys' Choir of Philadelphia. Would you like to join me?"

I've been asked a lot of questions in my life, but I can't think of many that were easier to answer. "There's nothing I'd rather do," I told the cardinal, "than listen to those little cherubs." And they *were* good. As we sat there, listening to those angelic voices, the cardinal said, "You know, Mr. Russert, my dream is to one day have them perform—"

"For the Holy Father?"

He laughed, and I smiled. When I told Archbishop Foley about the cardinal's wish, he thought it was an excellent idea. "The Pope loves young people," he said, "and if they come with you, he'll really enjoy it." Back in New York, I added an extra paragraph to my letter to the Pope. If His Holiness accepted our invitation to broadcast live from St. Peter's Square, I wrote, we would be accompanied by—who else?—the Archdiocesan Boys' Choir of Philadelphia. I revised my letter and sent it, translated into Polish, to Cardinal Krol in Philadelphia.

Evidently I had found the right man, because a couple of weeks later a couple of us from NBC were invited to fly to Rome to discuss our proposed plans for Holy Week. I was very excited: I didn't think the Vatican would invite us unless they were seriously considering our idea. Throughout my time in Rome, I was constantly writing letters to the various officials I met, which were translated into Italian by the NBC News Bureau in Rome. *Speak their language*, I kept reminding myself, just as Dad had reminded me. *Reach out to them and respect them by speaking their language.*

The trip was going well—so well, in fact, that I was even promised a private audience with the Pope. I was nervous, of course, but I reminded myself that I had come to the Vatican for a specific purpose, and that I mustn't allow my excitement about meeting the Pope to stand in the way of my mission.

On the appointed day, I was led into a huge, empty room and instructed to wait there. A few moments later, the door opened and the Pope walked solemnly in, dressed in white. I was awestruck: there I was, a former altar boy from South Buffalo in the presence of the Vicar of Christ. I liked to think of myself as a tough news executive, but any such illusions crumbled immediately in the presence of the Holy Father. My heart was pounding, and my mind quickly shifted from NBC's ratings and Bryant Gumbel's career to a far more personal and immediate concern: the prospect of salvation. "Bless me, Father," I blurted out. I was looking for a little holiness, an ounce or two of extra protection against the forces of evil.

The Pope put his arm around my shoulder and said softly, "So you are the one called Timothy from Enn Bee Chee?" I wanted to say, "Don't ever forget this face. I am your guy." But the best I could manage was a simple, "Yes, Father."

"They tell me you are a very important man."

Me? Important? Here? Now? I said, "Your Holiness, with all due respect, there are only two of us in this room, and I am a most distant second."

He smiled, looked me in the eye, and said, "Right."

In that humble spirit, I made my pitch. "NBC wants very much to come here for Easter," I told him.

"Yes, yes, with Philadelphia. Philadelphia!"

I took that as a yes.

That same day, I wrote another letter to the Pope, this time to thank him for seeing me. I had it translated into Polish, and I brought it back to the Vatican, hoping to give it to somebody who would give it to the Pope. I showed the letter to one of the Swiss Guards, who have been protecting the Pope for the past five hundred years. When the guard saw that the letter was in Polish, he brought me to an elevator that leads directly to the Pope's apartment. When I got up there, I noticed that on the wall next to the door was a plaque with the Latin words, *Totus Tuus*. I recognized the phrase: it's Latin for "totally yours" and is known as the motto of Pope John Paul II. In 1981, when the Holy Father was shot and almost killed by a Turkish gunman, he had said, "Blessed Mother, if I live, I will rededicate my life to you. *Totus Tuus*."

At the door to the Pope's apartment, I was greeted by a distinguished-looking gentleman in a black suit and a white shirt. "I have a letter for His Holiness," I told him. When he noticed the Polish writing on the envelope, he picked up a silver platter and held it out to me. I dropped the letter and left.

Archbishop Foley was with me in the Vatican, and of course I told him about my meeting with the Pope. The next morning he called me at my hotel and said, "Come and see me." When I arrived, he said, "The Pope has agreed to say a private Mass for your group in the Pauline Chapel. He will then come out and greet everybody who was in the chapel." I wanted to cry out,

"Yes!" but that just didn't seem appropriate. We were going to base the show in Rome for an entire week, and now there was no question what the high point of our visit would be. Needless to say, I was a very happy passenger on the flight back to New York.

ON THE APPOINTED DAY during Easter Week, our group from *Today*, which included my wife and several other spouses who didn't want to miss this once-in-a-lifetime opportunity, left the hotel before dawn to attend the private Mass in the Vatican. Just before it began, Archbishop Foley asked me to do one of the readings. I said yes, of course, but I couldn't imagine how I could possibly calm my nerves enough to get through it. The Pope entered the chapel. *This is really happening*, I told myself, but it was still hard to believe. Suddenly it was my turn to approach the lectern and read. I knew the drill: you walk to the center of the altar, and you bow to the Pope, who lifts his hands in the classic papal gesture. My mind was racing as I walked toward him, and my mouth was dry. *I can't do this*, I thought. *I have no voice.* But when I opened my mouth and started reading a letter of St. Paul, the voice that came out sounded a lot like Charlton Heston. I can't explain it other than to say that the Holy Spirit seemed to have descended on me.

When the Mass was over and the Boys' Choir of Philadelphia had sung, we all went outside. When the Pope came out to greet us, the choir sang "Stolat," a Polish song that means, "May you live a hundred years." I had also arranged for a traditional Polish Easter basket (which generally includes eggs, horseradish, ham, kielbasa, salt, cheese, a candle, and a mound of butter in the shape of a lamb) to be flown over from Poland. With the cameras rolling, Bryant Gumbel and Jane Pauley presented it to the Pope.

He was clearly delighted. "Where did you get this?" he asked in English.

"From Warsaw," said Bryant.

"But *you're* not from Warsaw," said the Pope, which broke everybody up. Although Dad hadn't specifically advised me to find a Polish Easter basket, it was exactly the sort of thing he would have done. When you go to visit somebody, he taught me long ago, give some thought as to what they might enjoy. If we were going to see Aunt Mary, he'd pick up some strawberries. If we were going to Uncle Fran's, he'd stop at Quality Bakery to buy his brother's favorite cherry pastries. And if Dad were visiting the Pope during Easter, he would definitely show up with a traditional Polish Easter basket from Warsaw.

I was looking at Bryant and nodding, as if to say, *Go ahead. This is your chance! Ask him something!* "Your Holiness," he said, "I brought some pictures of my children. Would you bless them?"

"And I have twins!" Jane said.

After the Pope wished the American people a happy Easter, I said, "Your Holiness, these are for the wonderful boys from Philadelphia." I had brought along a stack of black NBC baseball hats, and the kids put them on.

"For Archbishop Foley, I have a red hat. And for the Papa—" and I handed the Pope a white hat. He didn't put it on, but he hung it on his wrist as he waved, and the audience exploded.

As the Pope made his way toward Maureen and me, I said to her, "Speak to him in Italian." (Although the Pope is Polish, he speaks Italian and several other languages.) Maureen was halfway through her pregnancy, and she was showing a little bit. The Pope made the sign of the cross on her forehead, and she said, in Italian, "Would you bless my baby?"

The Pope smiled and said, "Ah, Italiano." He put his hand on her womb and blessed it. Then he said, in Italian, "When your baby is born, bring him back for another blessing."

Our week in Rome was an enormous hit, both spiritually and commercially. Archbishop Foley called to tell me that a young man from Milwaukee had decided to enter the priesthood because of the show, and I doubt that he was the only one. "Many Americans may have been late to work last week, fascinated by the visit of NBC's *Today Show* to Rome for Holy Week," noted an editorial in the *Boston Globe*, and other newspapers were equally effusive. Some writers were amazed that the Holy Father had even recorded a promotional spot for us. No, he didn't come out and say, "Hi, I'm the Pope, this is *Today* on NBC." But he did convey that same basic message—with full papal dignity. We couldn't have asked for more.

After Luke was born, Maureen and I began to think about the Pope's invitation to bring our baby to the Vatican for a blessing from the Holy Father. In April 1986, a year after the *Today Show*'s visit, the three of us flew to Rome. A private audience was out of the question: we would stand with the crowd and take our chances. But how could we be sure that the Pope would give Luke his promised blessing?

And then it hit me: I had contacted the Pope the first time by taking Dad's advice and speaking his language. This time, I took one of Luke's white T-shirts and had the words *Totus Tuus* printed on it in papal red lettering. Thanks to Archbishop Foley, our family was standing in the front row of the papal audience. When the Pope moved through the line, I held Luke up so the Holy Father could see his shirt. Sure enough, he spotted Luke, gently took him out of my arms, held him high, admired both the baby and the shirt, and said, in perfect English, "Very nice. Very, very nice." Then he kissed Luke on the forehead and handed him back to me. We went to Rome for a papal blessing, but it turned out to be a papal hug and kiss.

I had come prepared: an NBC crew was standing by, taping the entire event. I had the tape dubbed into slow motion, and sent a copy to my Italian mother-in-law. When she saw the Pope kissing her grandson, she was finally willing to admit that maybe there really was some value in having an Irish son-in-law. As for me, I've watched the video any number of times. But even today, when I see that picture of the Pope kissing our little boy, I still get choked up. At Dad's suggestion, I had spoken his language. And now the Pope was speaking ours.

19.

Meet the Press

"Pretend you're talking to me."

I N 1986, I experienced what millions of American workers went through during that decade: the company I worked for was taken over, and some people lost their jobs. In our case, the world's oldest television network (NBC) was acquired by one of the world's largest corporations (General Electric). Two years later, Larry Grossman was ousted as president of the news division, and a new executive, Michael Gartner, was brought in. As Larry's right-hand man, I expected that I, too, would be let go, and that I would finally get the chance to dust off my law degree.

But Jack Welch, G.E.'s chairman, came to my office with a different idea. "You're thirty-eight years old," he said, "and you have a bright future here. You'd be a good person to head our news division, but first you'll need to demonstrate that you can run something. We know you're a good deputy, but are you also a good manager? Let's find out. What would you like to run?"

This was all a bit sudden. "I haven't thought about it," I said, "but I'm comfortable with news."

"Well then, what's the most important news bureau?" he asked.

"Washington."

"Would you like to run Washington?"

"We already have somebody there," I said.

"I didn't ask you that. Would you like to run Washington?"

"Can I think about it?" I asked.

The next day, Michael Gartner brought me upstairs to the Rainbow Room for lunch and asked me to run the Washington bureau. I accepted the offer, and in early 1989, Maureen, Luke, and I moved to Washington.

When my new job was announced, several media reporters wrote that I was on track to become the next president of NBC News. Whenever I was asked whether this was part of my thinking, I answered honestly: yes, it was. I didn't realize that acknowledging this would make me seem overly ambitious, but I'm afraid it did. Sometimes it's better to say nothing.

Our Washington bureau had problems, and after analyzing the situation, I decided to make a number of changes all at once. "In for a penny, in for a pound," Senator Moynihan used to say. I didn't enjoy reassigning people, but my job was to improve the bureau, and I did what I believed was necessary.

Even before I took the new job, I was concerned about *Meet the Press*, which was produced by our Washington bureau and had been through several different moderators in the five years since Bill Monroe left in 1984. For that and other reasons, the longest running network television show in history was languishing in third place in the ratings. David Brinkley pretty much owned Sunday morning, and CBS's *Face the Nation* was a distant second.

Every morning at 9:30, the bureau chiefs at NBC News participated in a conference call with Michael Gartner. In 1990, Gartner said to me, "You know, I'm learning a lot from you on these phone calls. I've thought about this, and I'd like you to be one of the panelists on *Meet the Press*." (At that time, the program included a rotating panel of journalists who all participated in the questioning of the guests.)

He must be kidding, I thought. Me, on television? I have a perfect face—but for radio. When my boss made it clear that he was serious, I tried to reason with him. "Michael, this is crazy. First of all, I don't belong on television. People on TV look and dress a certain way. They have chins, not cheeks. Second, I don't have any experience, or any media training, or voice lessons, or anything like that. And third, I don't want our Washington correspondents to think I'm trying to take away their air time. I'm their boss, and I'm being paid to be a manager."

"Don't worry about any of that," Gartner said. "I want you to give it a try."

My first appearance as a panelist on *Meet the Press* was on September 16, 1990, when the guests were House Speaker Tom Foley and Senate Majority Leader Robert Dole. On Saturday I called Dad: "I'm going to be on *Meet the Press* tomorrow. Any advice?"

"Just be yourself," Big Russ said. "Pretend you're talking to me. Don't get too fancy. Don't talk that Washington talk.

You've got to talk so people can understand you. Ask questions that my buddies at the post would want to know about."

It was good counsel, and as usual, I took it. I still do. A mention of Senate Bill 1482 may send hearts pounding on Capitol Hill, but it doesn't mean squat at the Russert dinner table in Buffalo.

In the fall of 1990, people in Washington were concerned about the budget deficit and its effect on the federal budget and taxes. In my very first question to Senator Dole, I said, "Senator, let's talk political reality. If you were back in Russell, Kansas, this morning in the coffee shop and someone said, 'Senator, you're going to tax my beer, you're going to tax filling up my gas tank, you're going to tax buying an automobile—and now I read you're giving a tax cut to those who make over $50,000. And I ask you one question: Why shouldn't those who make under $50,000 have a tax cut?'"

"I think you ask a good question," Dole responded. "If you're going to increase taxes if I drive, drink, or smoke, then somebody else maybe ought to pay a tax increase, because that's not going to hit the rich as much as it hits somebody in Russell, Kansas. So I think we have to have a balance . . ."

In fact, Congress did change the tax code to give more of a break to the little guy. In Washington, it's easy to get caught up in ideas and terminology that make no sense to regular people. Big Russ had reminded me to bring the conversation down to earth, to make it practical. When I asked Senator Dole about the likely reaction of regular people in his hometown, people very much like Dad, he was reminded that their concerns had to be considered in the budget and tax negotiations.

It wouldn't be the last time that Dad gave me helpful advice about *Meet the Press*. And over the years I've noticed that just about every time Dad calls a guest a "phony," he turns out be right.

A year later, in 1991, NBC CEO Bob Wright decided to expand the *Today Show* to seven days a week, all of which would be produced in New York. At the time, Garrick Utley was both the moderator of *Meet the Press* and the weekend cohost of *Today*. Now he had to choose. He opted for New York, which meant that we had to find yet another moderator for *Meet the Press*. Michael Gartner asked me to draw up a list of possible replacements, and I started thinking about appropriate candidates both from within our bureau and outside it.

A few days later, in New York, Gartner said, "I looked at your list and I'd like to add one more name." He wrote it on the page I had given him, and handed it back to me. The name he had written was mine. "I think you should do this," he said.

I had the same reservations as before—only more so.

"Michael, I'm not sure I'm suited for this job."

"I think you are."

"This would be quite a risk."

"I don't agree. It's a big step, but I don't think it's a big risk."

"But I have no experience, and people don't know me. We don't even know if I'll be able to draw and hold an audience."

"There's only one way to find out, isn't there?"

I gave the matter a lot of thought, and decided to give it a try. I started paying extra close attention to Tom Brokaw, Ted Koppel, David Brinkley, and Dan Rather to see what I could learn, but I finally realized that Dad had been right, that I just had to be myself. The camera really does capture reality (more

or less), and people would either like me in this new role or
reject me.

But there was one thing I knew for sure: if I failed, it wouldn't
be for lack of preparation. Just as Dad had prepared fully for
President Kennedy's arrival in Buffalo, and just as I had worked
my head off when I was studying for the bar, I knew I would
walk into each week's program knowing as much about our
guests and their positions as I possibly could. As a news executive, I had seen correspondents on all of the networks who
weren't prepared, or who just "phoned it in." I wasn't going to
be one of them. This job would take time, I realized, because
there are no shortcuts to preparation. I would have to discipline
my mind to read everything, talk to everyone, and really understand the issues.

The first person I called was Lawrence Spivak, the cofounder
of Meet the Press and its moderator from 1966 through 1975, to
ask his advice. "Learn everything you can about the guests and
their positions," he told me, "and then take the other side on the
air. If you do that in a civil way each week, you'll have a fair and
balanced program, you'll get good answers, and you'll make
news." In 1997, for the fiftieth anniversary book about Meet the
Press, we asked Bob Dole, who had appeared on the show more
than anyone else, how a guest should prepare. Dole advised them
to read their briefing books and the Sunday newspapers, and,
when possible, to show up with a newsworthy statement. "If all
else fails," he added, "try to read the questions upside down
across the table."

My first show as moderator was December 8, 1991. I was
nervous, of course, and on Saturday night, to take my mind off

the show, Maureen and I and some friends went to Blues Alley, a Washington music club, to see Junior Walker and the All-Stars. I had a lot to drink that night, but all of it was water.

I was especially nervous on my first day as moderator because of what had happened four weeks earlier, on November 10. The guests on *Meet the Press* that morning were the two candidates for governor of Louisiana—former governor Edwin Edwards, who had twice been tried and acquitted on federal racketeering charges, and David Duke, who had been both a Nazi sympathizer and a grand wizard of the Ku Klux Klan. Edwards was a Democrat and Duke was running as a Republican, although neither the national Republican Party nor the White House wanted anything to do with him. It had been a close and contentious race, with its share of bizarre moments. At one point, Governor Edwards, who was known as a ladies' man, said that the only thing he had in common with David Duke was that both of them were wizards under the sheets. And now the candidates were appearing together on *Meet the Press* just six days before the people of Louisiana would make their decision.

When it was my turn to question them, I looked into the camera and asked Governor Edwards, "Will you promise that if elected governor, no more gambling, no more womanizing, no more cronyism—all part of your past?"

"Well," he began, "I'm not a gambler." It was that kind of campaign.

Then I turned to David Duke and asked, "What was it about this country, this society, that you chose to become a Nazi? What did you find so offensive and so objectionable

about the United States of America that you found Nazi Germany to be preferable?"

Duke denied being a member of the Nazi Party, and gave a
vague, rambling answer that included references to Vietnam
and forced busing. After a commercial break, Duke was shown a
picture from that morning's *New York Times* that showed him, in
his youth, wearing a Nazi swastika and carrying a sign that said,
"Gas the Chicago 7."

When the questioning returned to me, I returned to his
Nazi past. Then I asked him to name the three biggest employers in Louisiana. When he couldn't, I kept after him. When I
saw that he was floundering, I became more aggressive, jabbing
my finger in the air. Instead of letting his ignorance stand on its
own, I went in for the kill.

The next day, Duke's inability to name the three leading
employers in his own state made headlines in Louisiana. But
there was some discussion at NBC that perhaps I had crossed
the line from being an objective questioner to behaving more
like a prosecutor.

I called Dad and said, "What did you think of the show?"

"I thought it was great, just great. You really nailed that
guy."

I mentioned that some people at NBC thought I had moved
from objective questioner to overzealous prosecutor.

"What are they saying, exactly?"

"That I may have made a mistake by going after him so hard."

Big Russ was silent for a long time. Then he said, "I'll tell
you something: if you're going to make a mistake by being too

tough, make it with a Nazi." Dad's comment put my aggressive posture in a context that I could live with.

FIVE DAYS AFTER THE TERRORIST ATTACKS of September 11, 2001, I drove to Camp David for an exclusive interview with Vice President Dick Cheney. This was going to be the first time since September 11 that the nation had heard from the vice president. In effect, he was going to brief the country about what he, the president, and the national security team had decided after their weekend meetings. On Saturday, I called Dad and told him I was going to interview the vice president.

"This is very important," he said in a tone I hadn't heard before.

"How so?" I asked.

"People want to know what was going on behind the scenes on September 11. What kind of decisions were made that day? And what does the president have in store for the people who did this to us? Just let him talk. Let him help get us through this."

Dad was so right. Without his advice, I would have focused mostly on the future, on our response to terrorism. Dad was reminding me to pay attention to what had happened that day. "This is an opportunity to capture a moment in history," he told me. That morning, the vice president explained in great detail what had happened at the White House on September 11, how he had turned on the television in his White House office when his secretary said that a plane had hit the World Trade Center, and how, as soon as the second plane hit, he had realized that this had to be a deliberate attack. Moments later, as he described it,

Secret Service agents ran into his office, grabbed him—"hoisted me up and moved me very rapidly down the hallway, down some stairs, through some doors and down some more stairs into an underground facility under the White House" because they had received a report that a plane was headed for the White House. This was Flight 77 out of Dulles, which crashed into the Pentagon. Cheney also revealed that he had urged the president, who was in Florida, to delay his return until it was safe to come back.

I asked the vice president what he thought was the toughest decision that the president had made on September 11. Cheney said that he and the president had discussed whether or not the military should shoot down a commercial airplane that appeared to be headed for the White House or the Capitol. "You've got an airplane full of American citizens, civilians, captured by terrorists, are you going to, in fact, shoot it down, and kill all those Americans on board?" The president's answer was yes—if all else failed, they would shoot down the plane.

It was, I felt, a riveting interview. We ended the program with a tribute to those who had died on September 11, and especially Father Mychal Judge, the chaplain of the New York Fire Department, who raced to the World Trade Center to comfort the injured. Father Judge died of a heart attack after administering the last rites to a dying rescue worker. And we showed the extraordinary photograph of the New York firefighters raising the American flag at Ground Zero, which was eerily similar to the famous photograph from Iwo Jima in 1945. I may be a journalist, but I'm also an American citizen.

Driving home from Camp David, I called Dad. He answered the phone and said, "That was great. Thank you." This was the first time he had ever thanked me after watching *Meet the Press*, so I knew the program must have affected him deeply. And if that was Dad's reaction, I was reasonably sure that the rest of the country was going to respond overwhelmingly. And they did. Later that day, for the first time, NBC aired *Meet the Press* again; our total audience was over fourteen million people—far more than usual.

Big Russ is the least expensive and most accurate focus group around, which is why I call him every Monday morning for his reaction to Sunday's show. He gives me his honest assessment, and it isn't always what I'm longing to hear. On more than one occasion he has concluded his review by saying, "I still can't believe they pay you all that money to bullshit."

During the 2000 campaign, I once again became involved in a New York Senate race. On September 13, in Buffalo, I served as the moderator for a debate between Hillary Clinton, the Democrat, and Rick Lazio, the Republican. After the debate, most of the news coverage centered on the moment when Representative Lazio demanded that Mrs. Clinton sign a document that would ban the use of soft money. There were a couple of other dramatic moments in that debate as well, when I asked each candidate about truth and character. I asked Mrs. Clinton about her charge that critics of her husband were part of a "vast right-wing conspiracy," and I asked Mr. Lazio about a campaign commercial that showed him walking down the hall with Senator Moynihan, who was retiring from the Senate, when the two men had never actually been photographed together. (Moynihan had called it "soft-money fakery.")

Immediately after the debate, I began talking to Dad about

these three dramatic moments. Big Russ shook his head. "No," he said, "that's not the most important thing that happened here tonight."

"What do you mean?" I asked.

"The most important part of the debate was when Lazio was asked about the upstate economy, and he said it had 'turned the corner,' that great progress had been made. I'm sorry, but he doesn't get it. We're in trouble up here, and if he thinks we have turned the corner, he's got a lot to learn."

The next day, the coverage in the Buffalo paper took note of what the candidates had said about the economy, but it focused on the tough questions about character that I had asked each of them. Over the next week or so, however, the issue of the upstate economy began to take hold. Eight days after the debate, when Hillary Clinton returned to Buffalo, the *Buffalo News* headline read, "Clinton Claims Lazio Ignores Reality of Upstate Economy." The article quoted the *Republican* county executive, who said that while the upstate region had made noticeable gains, "it has a long way to go." He also said it was time for Lazio to give voters a reason to vote for him.

All of us in the media were focusing on the heated exchange between Hillary Clinton and Rick Lazio about soft money, but Big Russ wasn't fooled. The Buffalo debate, Senator Clinton wrote in her memoir, "was another turning point in the race that helped push some voters in my corner, although I didn't realize it right away." Maybe she didn't, but I know somebody who did.

20.

Loss

*"I will give you a son for seventeen years,
but then it will be time for him to come home."*

M ICHAEL GARTNER, my former boss at NBC News, had
a teenage son named Christopher, who used to visit his
dad at the office. Christopher was a big kid—well over six feet tall
and built like a defensive tackle. He was warm and very likable,
and whenever I ran into him at NBC's headquarters in Rockefeller Plaza, we would always chat for a while in the hallway. In
1993, at the Super Bowl in Pasadena, seven-year-old Luke sat
next to Christopher, who couldn't have been nicer. Luke clearly
admired him: when Christopher stood up, so did Luke. When
Christopher ordered a hot dog, so did Luke.

A year and a half later, Michael's former secretary called to
tell me that Christopher Gartner had suddenly died of acute
juvenile diabetes, and that Michael was in very rough shape. I
didn't know how to respond to this devastating news, but I called
him the next day and said, "Michael, I'm so sorry, and I just

wanted you to know that." He thanked me for calling and said he was having a terrible time. How could it be otherwise? I wondered. "I just don't understand this," he said. "I don't know how to deal with it. I had a wonderful, robust, healthy boy on Tuesday, he got sick on Wednesday, and he died on Thursday. No matter what people say, nothing seems to help."

"Well," I said, "let's talk about this a little bit," and because Christopher was adopted, what I had to offer might have been a little easier for Michael to hear. "Think of it this way," I said. "What if God had come to you and said, 'Michael, I'm going to make you an offer. I will give you a beautiful, wonderful, happy, and lovable son for seventeen years, but then it will be time for him to come home.' You would have made that deal in a second, right?"

"Of course," he said. "I wouldn't even have to think about it."

Michael called a couple of days later to say that my words had helped him. "Rather than thinking of what was taken away," he said, "I've been trying to focus on what God had given me."

"That's where you draw your strength," I told him. "This wasn't your decision, and Christopher's death wasn't any retribution against you. This is God's design, God's plan. He blessed you with Christopher for seventeen years."

Michael wrote about Christopher's death in his column in *USA Today*. He noted that words were of little comfort, but that what I had told him on the phone had been helpful. He repeated my words, ending with, "You would have made that deal in a second."

"And that was the deal," Michael wrote. "We just didn't know the terms."

A couple of weeks after the column appeared, Michael

wrote to tell me that he had received hundreds of letters, including many from other parents who had lost a child. He was especially grateful to a reader who added another dimension to what I had said: "Mr. Gartner, after reading your column I want you to know something else. If God went to Christopher and said, 'Here is our arrangement: you will go and be with Michael and his wife and the Gartner family in Iowa for seventeen years,' Christopher would have taken that deal, too, because you are a hell of a father."

Michael told me he had started running a few miles every morning because it's impossible to run and cry at the same time. "Give Luke extra hugs," he urged me at the end of his letter, and you can be sure that I did.

I also received a few letters after that column appeared. I felt a little awkward about that, because I never imagined that Michael would make my words public. I hadn't thought them out, and although I was offering a kind of religious counsel, I hadn't gone over it with my parish priest. On the telephone with Michael, the words just poured out. They came from my heart.

But they also came from my memory. A few weeks before my eleventh birthday, Paul Lawrence, the older brother of my Woodside Avenue neighbor, David Lawrence, who lived across the street from us, was killed in a car accident. Paul had joined the navy a couple of years earlier, so he was something of a local hero. When he was killed, a heavy cloud hung over our neighborhood. I was confused and distraught: this was the first time that somebody I knew personally had ever died.

I can still remember sitting down with Mom and Dad at the kitchen table, with Paul Lawrence's obituary in front of us. My parents spoke to me about how this was a difficult test of faith, how Paul had lived a short life, but a good one, how his parents had loved him deeply, and how they would always remember the years they'd had together. They told me that all the neighbors were bringing food to Paul's parents and were stopping by to tell them how much joy their son had provided and how much they had appreciated him. The family's pain was still beyond measure, but my parents stressed how important it was for a community to respond in their hour of grief.

And then Dad gave me another way to understand this terrible event. Would it have been better if Paul's family had never known him? Or should they be grateful, even in their grief, for nineteen years of love and memories? Mr. and Mrs. Lawrence had suffered a terrible loss, but if they had been offered the possibility of having Paul in their lives for nineteen years, they would have taken that deal without question. Dad's words had been locked up inside me all those years, until one day, on the phone, they came pouring out.

I really believed what I told Michael Gartner. The importance of faith, and of accepting and even celebrating death, was something I continue to believe as a Catholic and a Christian. To accept faith, we have to resign ourselves as mortals to the fact that we are a small part of a grand design.

But it's one thing to believe these things, and quite another to have them quoted in a major newspaper. Who was I to be talking about God's plan?

Three years later, I happened to be seated next to Cardinal John O'Connor at the annual Al Smith dinner in New York, which raises money for Catholic hospitals. We were talking about a mutual friend who had died at a young age, and I told the cardinal about Christopher Gartner, and what I had said to Michael. "I hope I'm getting my theology right," I said. The cardinal smiled. He asked me if I could send him all the details, so back in Washington I wrote it all up. In the letter, I added some thoughts of my own: "We can't withstand major crises and the huge changes they bring about alone. We are not strong enough. We really aren't. When people are confronted with a crisis, particularly with the death of a loved one, the most important thing is to reach out to them. Help them, because they can't go through their loss alone. It is inexplicable in their lives at that time. You have to be there for them and help them to understand, *There is something here to accept. This is out of your control; this is a power far beyond yours.*" The words may have been mine, but the ideas came from Dad.

A few weeks later, Cardinal O'Connor read my letter at Sunday Mass in St. Patrick's Cathedral, so I have to assume that the theology really was all right.

Tragedies continue to occur and young people continue to die. Not long ago, the daughter of some good friends took her own life. I called her parents, and as we talked, that kitchen table conversation with my parents came roaring back again, even more powerfully this time.

I know that Dad's words aren't right for everybody, and that we all respond to grief in our own way. I also know that it's much easier to talk about acceptance than to accept, and much easier to discuss faith than to have faith. I am the first to say, and weak enough to know, that God forbid, if anything like this ever happens in my own family, to my own son, I don't know how I

would cope. I would in the end; I know that. But I know I would
need other people to support me and to remind me about strength,
acceptance, and faith.

In the fall of 2003, when a high school football player whom
Luke had played against died in a car accident, I found myself
passing on Dad's wisdom to my own son. Acting on their own,
Luke's entire football team went to the funeral service as a group,
which brought some comfort to the grieving family. I have tried
to teach my son, just as Big Russ taught me, that as much as we
wish it were otherwise, grief and loss are central to our lives, and
when somebody near us loses a loved one, we have a duty to show
up, to be there, and to help them remember; to offer a hand and a
shoulder, and yes, to celebrate a life. And if Dad's way of looking
at it brings some consolation, so much the better.

21.

The Bills

"Wide right."

ANYONE WHO WATCHES *Meet the Press* knows that I try my best to be objective and nonpartisan, but that when it comes to the Buffalo Bills, I just can't help myself. I think of them as more than a football team. To me, and to so many people in Buffalo, they represent our city and the tough times it's been through. When the team loses, the whole town feels it. And when they win big—well, we're still waiting to find out what that's like.

I can remember a time before people made jokes about the Bills. I even remember a time when the Bills didn't exist. In 1960, when the American Football League was born and Buffalo was awarded a franchise, we were thrilled. It wasn't the NFL—not yet, anyway—but an AFL team was still something, and we were thrilled to have it. At the impressionable age of ten, I had the good fortune of being able to root for my home team from its very first game.

In those years the Bills played downtown in War Memorial Stadium. The arena had been built as a WPA project during the Depression and was known as the Rockpile because it seemed to be falling apart. Tickets were only three dollars if you sat in the end zone, as Dad and I were more than willing to do. You could bring anything you wanted into the Rockpile, and some fans from South Buffalo even lugged in their own kegs of beer. Dad and I would arrive with a basket of sandwiches and fruit, enough for three or four days, and an ice chest full of cold drinks. I'd sit with a thermos of hot chocolate, while Dad's was filled with coffee. At least that's what he claimed, but by the fourth quarter I had my doubts.

My favorite player was Cookie Gilchrist, who fit the profile of Buffalo: when you gave him the ball, sod flew, dirt splattered, mud exploded, and he got you six yards and another first down. Legend had it that Cookie drove a pink Cadillac and that written backward on the hood, so you could read it in your rear-view mirror, was the phrase, "Lookie, Lookie, Here Comes Cookie." The Cadillac was real, although some say it was actually red, but I'm still not sure about the writing on the hood. As a boy I spent a lot of time looking for that car, but I never found it.

In 1964, with Cookie's help, the Bills beat the San Diego Chargers to become the AFL champs—the first time in my life that a major league team from Buffalo had gone all the way. (The Super Bowl didn't exist until 1967.) A year later, in 1965, the Bills won another AFL championship. The AFL existed for only six years before the Super Bowl began, and during that time the Bills won two titles. Too bad they didn't win a third one in 1966, because the winner of *that* game (Kansas City) went on to play in the very first Super Bowl.

I can't discuss the Buffalo Bills of that era without a word about the greatest running back of them all. To watch O. J. Simpson play football was a little like watching Michael Jordan play basketball: he was that good. Off the field, O. J. was known for his warmth and his charm. He handled celebrity with grace and struck everybody as a genuinely nice person. All of us in Buffalo were grateful for the pride and attention he brought to our city.

In January 1994, Luke and I went to the Super Bowl in Atlanta. Luke, who was eight, got up early that morning and said he would meet me in the hotel's breakfast room. When I came down a few minutes later, he was having a conversation with O. J. and Nicole Simpson, whom he had met in the elevator. O. J. couldn't have been kinder, and he even invited Luke to join them for breakfast. (Luke declined, because he was waiting for me. I felt honored.) "You've got a fine young boy there," O. J. told me, and the feeling seemed to be mutual. "Dad," Luke told me excitedly, "I asked him if he drinks orange juice—and he does!"

A few months later, this seemingly gentle man, who had invited my eight-year-old to breakfast, was charged with the murder of his wife and her friend. At first it was hard to believe, and it was probably even harder for those of us from Buffalo. "It hurts a lot," a friend told me. "Even though we keep losing the big games, at least we had those wonderful memories of O. J. left, O. J. right, and O. J. up the middle. And now we can't even keep our memories."

In 1998 I was invited to speak at the Pro Football Hall of

Fame in Canton, Ohio, and I brought Luke with me. We walked through the building, and when we came to a bust of O. J. Simpson, Luke turned to me in a mixture of astonishment and disgust: "*He's* still in here?"

I looked at this portrait of the man I had cheered for, a man who had done so much for our city. I could have told Luke what a wonderful player O. J. had been, and how much he had meant to the people of Buffalo, but Luke didn't want to hear that, and I can't blame him. For Luke there was no question, no ambiguity, and no doubt about it: O. J. Simpson no longer deserved to be honored. And he was probably right.

IT WASN'T UNTIL 1991 that the Bills finally made it to the Super Bowl. They got there by beating the Oakland Raiders in a 51–3 pounding that nobody in Buffalo will ever forget. As the Oakland game ended, Buffalo fans were as happy and optimistic as we had ever been. The team's potent no huddle offense led by Jim Kelly was almost unstoppable, and we were confident of beating the New York Giants in the Super Bowl.

With eight seconds to play, the Giants had a one-point lead. But Buffalo had the ball on the Giants' 29-yard line, well within field goal range. As Scott Norwood prepared to kick the game winner, a total distance of 47 yards, the whole city held its breath. The snap was good, the hold was fine, but the kick, which started off well, veered off to the side and missed by three or four feet. *Wide right*, the announcers said, and nobody from Buffalo will ever forget that phrase. To come so close to winning it all was a crushing disappointment of the sort that Red Sox fans had experienced a few years earlier when Mookie Wilson's ground ball rolled under Bill Buckner's glove.

But even to have lost the Super Bowl was quite an achievement, and the next day, Luke and I flew to Buffalo to welcome the team back home. We picked up Dad and drove to City Hall, where we joined twenty-five thousand other fans, an amazing turnout for a team that had just lost the biggest game in its history. Even more amazing was that the crowd started chanting, "We want Scott!" As bad as we felt about the loss, we knew there was one man who must have felt even worse. Scott Norwood came to the podium with tears in his eyes and guaranteed that the Bills would be back in the Super Bowl next year.

The outpouring of compassion for Scott Norwood seemed all the more remarkable when I remembered another Bills kicker, Booth Lusteg. When I was sixteen, Lusteg missed a twenty-three-yard field goal against San Diego that would have won the game; earlier that day, he had missed two others. When the game ended, Lusteg was so upset that he decided to walk home from the Rockpile. A few minutes later, three men got out of a car and beat him up. When Lusteg was asked why he hadn't reported the incident or asked for help, he said, "Because I deserved it." For the rest of the season, every time Lusteg went in to kick, the stadium was filled with boos. That's how demanding Buffalo fans can be. But in Scott Norwood's case, we were willing to forgive, in part because we were grateful that the team had finally made it to the Super Bowl.

Several years ago, I was walking through Reagan National Airport when somebody tapped me on the shoulder and said,

"Excuse me, Tim, my name is Scott Norwood and I just wanted to introduce myself."

"I know who you are," I said, as pleasantly as I possibly could. I had to restrain myself from telling him that I still wake up in the middle of the night, screaming, "Wide right!"

But Scott Norwood kept his promise: he said that the team would return to the Super Bowl the following year, and they did. This time their opponents were the Washington Redskins, which was a little awkward for me because I was living in D.C. I had watched the 1991 game in a bar with some Buffalo friends, including my old Canisius pal, Jayce Caulfield. This time we watched at my house. I was at the supermarket loading up on snacks when a well-dressed woman came up to me and said, "Mr. Russert, I just want you to know that you're not alone. I'm rooting for the Bills, too."

I quickly ushered her over to the empty produce section. Even so, we spoke in hushed tones because the whole town was Redskins' territory. "Are you from Buffalo?" I asked.

"No," she said, "but Jack Kent Cooke is my former son-in-law." Cooke was the owner of the Redskins and her comment made my day. It also showed what I was up against: the only person I could find to root for the Bills was the former mother-in-law of the Redskins' owner. But I was feeling confident: last year we lost by forty inches on the Norwood kick. This time we were going to run right through the Redskins.

The first loss had been painful. This one was not only painful, but expensive, too. I must have had a bet going with every member of NBC's Washington bureau. The day after the game, the line outside my office seemed to stretch forever as my colleagues stopped by to offer their condolences and take my money.

The following year, in the playoffs, the Bills were trailing Houston 35–3 in the third quarter when they mounted a miraculous comeback and won the game in overtime. This had to be a sign! If the Bills could overcome a 32-point deficit, they would surely make it to the Super Bowl. And they did.

Third time's a charm, right? But maybe the Bills couldn't win if I watched on TV. Maybe I had to be there. For the 1993 game I decided to take *Meet the Press* to Pasadena, where the game was being played. At the end of the program, I looked into the camera and said, "It's now in God's hands, and God is good, and God is just. Please, God, make three a charm. Our time has come. Go Bills!"

When he saw that, Tom Brokaw said, "You Irish Catholics are shameless. You can't pray on the air."

"We can't?" I said. "I think I just did."

A few hours later, when I trudged back to the hotel after the Cowboys had squeaked by Buffalo, 52–17, the first person I saw was Brokaw. He put his arm around me and said, "Well, Russert, I guess God is a Southern Baptist."

The following year, amazingly enough, the Bills reached the Super Bowl for the fourth consecutive time. The game was in Atlanta, and once again we were playing Dallas. I brought Dad and Luke to the game because we couldn't possibly lose for the fourth time. I ended *Meet the Press* by saying, with Dad at my side, "Well, it's another Super Bowl with my Buffalo Bills. You remember last year I prayed, and that didn't work—an unworthy petitioner, I guess.... So now, America, I ask for your understanding one more time. Let the Bills have this one. Dallas doesn't need another Super Bowl. They've already won three. They have all that big oil, big bucks, and big hair. Why in the world do they need another Super Bowl? I'll make you a deal. You cheer for the Buffalo Bills and they win, I will not mention them on *Meet the Press* for one year—I promise. And, most important, you'll make this guy, my dad, the happiest guy in the world. So for Big Russ, his buddies back in Buffalo who helped make this country great, for the city of Buffalo, and for all the other underdogs in this country and around the world, go you Buffalo Bills. Pull off the biggest upset in football history!'"

Some people in Texas didn't appreciate my comments about Dallas, and perhaps I hadn't made myself clear. I was trying to say that there's a special relationship between Buffalo and its football team. Dallas, New York, Atlanta, Chicago—sure, they root for their teams, but in Buffalo it feels different. We are not a city of high finance, high fashion, or high rollers. There is a powerful, simple strength to Buffalo, and when the Bills win, it feels like an affirmation of our way of life. Often, when I'm walking through airports—even in Europe and South America—people will recognize me and, instead of calling my name or mentioning *Meet the Press*, they say, "Go Bills." And I love it when they do.

The fourth Super Bowl started well enough, and at the half, the Bills had a 13–6 lead. Unfortunately, there were two quarters left to play. As we were leaving the Georgia Dome, a blond woman in a rhinestone-laced denim jacket came up to me and said, "Hey, how 'bout them Cowboys?" I could feel my arms tighten. I would never strike a lady, but at that moment I wasn't sure whether a rhinestone-laced Cowboy fan qualified as a lady.

Back at the hotel, I was so upset that I actually snapped at Dad when he asked me what time our wake-up call would be. I apologized, and he quickly forgave me; he knew what I was going through.

There had been jokes after the third loss, but this time it was brutal. David Letterman devoted his Top Ten List to the things that Bills Coach Marv Levy might have told his team at half-time, such as—

"Boy, I'm sleepy. You guys sleepy?"

And, "Wait a minute. If we win, we have to go to Disneyland."

And, "Hey fellas, more fudge?"

Bills fans had a flicker of hope in early 2000, when Buffalo played the Tennessee Titans in a playoff game. The Bills had kicked a field goal with sixteen seconds left to give us a 16–15 lead with time remaining for only one play—the kickoff and the return. Tennessee running back Lorenzo Neal fielded the kick and lateraled the ball to tight end Frank Wycheck, who passed it across the field to wide receiver Kevin Dyson, who ran for a touchdown. But that didn't bother me, because Wycheck had thrown an illegal forward pass. To my shock, after a long review, the officials ruled that Wycheck's pass was legal.

During the final moments of that game, I was on the phone with my brother-in-law, who had called me to celebrate Buffalo's come-from-behind victory. "Hold on," I told him with the wisdom of a long-suffering Bills fan. "It's not over yet." As we watched the final play and the officials' response to it, both of us

were screaming and cursing at this blatant miscarriage of justice. Just then, my other line rang.

"Hello?"

"Chicken wings."

"Hello?"

"Chicken wings."

"Excuse me?"

"Chicken wings."

"What?"

"We had a bet."

"Who is this?"

"Al Gore." Then I remembered: the vice president and I
had bet on the game. If Buffalo won, he would pay off in
Nashville barbecue. If Tennessee won, I owed him some Buffalo
wings.

"You'll have your wings," I told him, "but we were robbed."

But a deal is a deal, so I got in my car, bought some chicken
wings, and drove them over to the vice president's house. At the
time, Sen. Bill Bradley was mounting a powerful challenge to
Gore for the Democratic nomination. A month earlier, their
debate on *Meet the Press* had been so contentious that when Gore
offered his hand, Bradley had refused to shake it. So, along with
the chicken wings, I included this note: "Dear Mr. Vice President:
They say you won the game. I owe you some Buffalo wings. Here
they are. I hope you enjoy watching Bill Bradley on *Meet the Press*
for the next three Sundays. —Tim Russert."

Three weeks later I was covering the State of the Union
address for NBC. As the official party came into Statuary Hall,

the vice president greeted me with his new catchphrase, "Chicken wings."

"Double or nothing," I replied. It wasn't really a double or nothing situation because I had already paid off my bet, but both of us knew what I meant. I was betting that the St. Louis Rams would beat the Tennessee Titans in the Super Bowl. As a fan of the AFC, I wanted the Titans to win, but I also wanted a free plate of ribs. (You gotta eat!) The Rams won, but the vice president was in no hurry to pay up.

When I interviewed him the following July, near the end of the show I said, "Mr. Vice President, on January 8 you witnessed a crime and never reported it. There was stealing in the state of Tennessee. Let me show you what happened." I then showed a clip of that final kickoff return with arrows indicating that the disputed pass was clearly illegal.

The vice president was ready for me. He took out what he claimed was a declassified spy satellite photo that supposedly showed that the pass was legal. He also held up a sign saying, "The pass was a lateral."

We argued about it a little longer, and just before the show ended, a big platter of ribs was brought in and set down on the table in front of us. It was a nice gesture...but it was still a forward pass.

The good people of Buffalo are still waiting, and still hoping. Maybe it will happen next year, maybe next century. As Big Russ likes to say, "Bills fans will live forever." If you ask him why, he'll say, "Because we won't die until we win the Super Bowl."

That's my dad. Big Russ. The most loyal and the most optimistic man I have ever known.

EPILOGUE

Dear Luke,

I wrote this book for your grandpa. As I finish it, I realize how much it is also for you.

Imagine. When Grandpa was just about your age, he left high school to help win World War II. When the war was over, he came home and took on another mission—raising a family and educating his kids. As you know, for most of his life he worked two jobs and never complained. I have never seen him bitter or cynical about anything, or anyone. To this day, Grandpa believes his glass is two-thirds full. Or, as he puts it, "I'm truly blessed." And so are you.

In the fall, you'll leave for college. You'll never have to struggle through loans or card games to pay your tuition. Your opportunities are unlimited, and with that comes a higher responsibility. As your namesake, St. Luke, tells us, "To whom much is given, much is expected."

Remember our Thanksgiving dinner a few years back when, because of a special Pentagon program that gave returning veterans academic credit for their military service, we presented Grandpa with his high school diploma—South Park High, class of 1942? I never saw him happier. He finally had it all—an honorable discharge and a high school diploma.

Whenever you think your studies are tough, think about Grandpa. The example he set and the lessons he taught—work, respect, discipline—are as important for you as they have been for me.

When I was around your age, I went off to the Woodstock Festival with some friends and didn't call home for five days. Mom and Dad were worried, and I didn't fully understand their pain, or Dad's anger, until the first time you went away with your friends and didn't check in the moment you arrived. So please, call home. I'll even settle for an e-mail.

Lukeman, along the way you'll hit some hurdles and experience some setbacks. I will always be there for you, as Grandpa was for me. But remember, while you are always, always loved, you are never, never entitled. As Grandpa likes to say, "The world doesn't owe you a favor."

You do, however, owe this world something. To live a good and decent and meaningful life would be the ultimate affirmation of Grandpa's lessons and values. The wisest commencement speech I ever heard was all of fifteen words: "The best exercise of the human heart is reaching down and picking someone else up."

Off you go. I am so very proud to be your father. Study hard. Have fun. Keep your honor. Pursue every one of your dreams. They really are reachable. As Big Russ would say, "What a country!"

Love,
Dad

ACKNOWLEDGMENTS

Bill Novak was my full partner in writing this book. For almost a year we shared words, stories, ideas, and plenty of laughs. I am forever appreciative of his extraordinary talent, professionalism, and friendship.

Bill Phillips offered valuable, thoughtful, and precise advice. He has a keen editor's eye.

Jeff Himmelman was a relentless and thorough researcher, all the while launching a successful music career.

Elaine Barone of the Buffalo and Erie County Library, and Mary Delmont, the College Archivist for Buffalo State College, were invaluable and ever cheerful in helping me re-create my old neighborhood.

The folks at Miramax Books—Harvey Weinstein, Jonathan Burnham, Kathy Schneider, Hilary Bass, Kristin Powers, and especially Susan Mercandetti—believed in this effort from the very beginning. Thank you for your confidence.

Tory Johnson suggested the title of this book five years ago. Inspired.

Bob Barnett was flawless in his legal, literary, and brotherly advice as he introduced me to the world of publishing. He is the very best.

NBC Washington deputy bureau chiefs Wendy Wilkinson and Brady Daniels, and the *Meet the Press* team—Betsy Fischer, Erin Fogarty, Michelle Jaconi, Courtney Kube, Chris Donovan, Ted Kresse, and Leigh Sutherland and her crew—were endlessly supportive. Senior producer Barbara Fant was unfailingly focused and creative in making my CNBC tapings of other authors enjoyable and instructive. Lisa Havlovitz organized my life and deftly deflected potential distractions, allowing me to do my job and write a book.

Hundreds of friends and neighbors from Buffalo and elsewhere provided a steady stream of memories, details, and encouragement. Thank you all. And, of course, Go Bills!

And my family. You were there. Always.

ACKNOWLEDGMENTS

by Luke Orth Russert

For my pure hearted mother—between her tireless philanthropic work in Colombia and extraordinary ability to put investigative journalism into the printed word, she is the true star of the family.

Thank you to the team at Weinstein Books and Bob Barnett for shepherding me through this process in such a professional and respectful manner. I am much obliged.

To my NBC family, thanks for all your kindness and help over the last five plus years, especially Shawna Thomas and Frank Thorp, I wouldn't have a "burgeoning career" without you. Lauren Skowronski, your counsel and friendship has meant the world.

All my buddies from St. Albans and Boston College thanks for keeping me grounded.

My extended family across the country, thanks for believing in me.

For my late Uncle Bill who I miss dearly at the start of every Bills season.

Lastly, Grandpa and Dad, I hope I make you guys proud trying to carry on these lessons, know I'm doing my best. Love you.

ABOUT THE AUTHOR

Courtesy of NBC News.

TIM RUSSERT was born in Buffalo, New York on May 7th, 1950. He graduated from John Carroll University and received his law degree from Cleveland-Marshall College of Law. Before joining NBC News, Russert was a counselor for the New York governor's office in Albany and a special counsel in the US Senate. From 1991 to 2008 Russert worked as moderator of *Meet the Press*, the longest-running program in the history of television. Russert was also a political analyst for *NBC Nightly News* and served as Washington, D.C., bureau chief of NBC News.

In 2008 *Time* magazine named him one of the hundred most influential people in the world. During his lifetime

Russert received forty-eight honorary doctorate degrees from American colleges and universities and lectured at the Kennedy, Johnson, Nixon, and Reagan presidential libraries. He is the author of *Big Russ & Me* and *Wisdom of Our Fathers*. Both books were *New York Times* bestsellers. Tim Russert passed away on Friday, June 13, 2008. He is survived by his wife, *Vanity Fair* writer Maureen Orth, and his son, Luke.

Courtesy of Frank Thorp V of NBC News.

LUKE RUSSERT, who graduated from Boston College with a double major in history and communications, joined NBC News in August 2008 as a correspondent based in Washington, D.C. He currently reports from Capitol Hill on the House of Representatives for *NBC Nightly News with Brian Williams*, *Today*, MSNBC, and NBCNews.com.

Since late 2011 Russert has served as a guest host on various MSNBC programs, including *Way Too Early*, *The Daily Rundown with Chuck Todd*, *Andrea Mitchell Reports*, *NOW with Alex Wagner*, and *The Cycle*. He lives in Washington, D.C., with his pug, Chamberlain.